D1299156

Praise for *Open Wide*

"Full of relevant insights and deeply personal anecdotes, *Open Wide* offers real tools and accessible advice that we can all put into action and practice. Thank you, Melissa—I'll be reading this several times and putting your work into practice for many moons to come."

–ELENA BROWER, AUTHOR OF *PRACTICE YOU* AND *ART OF ATTENTION*

"Full of loving guidance, deeply personal stories, and genuine 'aha' moments, *Open Wide* serves up real tools and relatable advice that you can put into action immediately for lasting results."

–CHRISTINE HASSLER, AUTHOR OF *EXPECTATION HANGOVER* AND HOST OF THE *OVER IT AND ON WITH IT* PODCAST

"Melissa Ambrosini is the down-to-earth best friend you've always longed for. In *Open Wide*, she shares her hard-won wisdom so you can rocket *all* your relationships to new levels of intimacy and fulfillment."

–ALEXI PANOS, AUTHOR OF *50 WAYS TO YAY!* AND *NOW OR NEVER*

"*Open Wide* is the real deal. This isn't your mother's relationship guide . . . Well, unless she wants a new one! In fact, every woman in your life—single or taken—needs a copy, pronto."

–PRESTON SMILES, AUTHOR OF *LOVE LOUDER*

"Want deeper, more soulful connections with the people you care about? Melissa Ambrosini's *Open Wide* provides powerful tools for enriching all the relationships in your life, including the most important one of all, the one with yourself."

–SELINA SOO, CREATOR OF IMPACTING MILLIONS

"So many relationship books feel a little stuffy and unrealistic. *Open Wide* is the antithesis of that! Instead of dishing out the same trite advice found in most self-help books, Melissa offers fresh, useful tools and techniques for upgrading and enriching all the relationships in your life—including the most important one of all, the one with yourself."

–EMMA ISAACS, FOUNDER AND GLOBAL CEO, BUSINESS CHICKS

"Melissa Ambrosini is someone that will help change your life. I'm blessed to call her a close friend and have witnessed her deep and soulful love in person! In *Open Wide*, she shares her hard-won wisdom and juicy insights so you can rock all your relationships to new levels of intimacy and fulfillment. A must-read."

**–RACHAEL FINCH, AUTHOR OF *HAPPY, HEALTHY, STRONG*
AND FOUNDER OF B.O.B FITNESS AND APPAREL**

"Melissa holds up a mirror to our deepest fears and desires, with an invitation to step in fully, so that we may be more love, to have more love. Her bold shares on living *Open Wide* have moved and inspired me to more explore myself, my marriage and my relationships with ruthless curiosity. With matter-of-fact strength and audacity, she takes on taboo, bringing self-pleasure, sacred sexual union and sex-positive family discussion out of the darkness and into the light—where they rightfully belong. Taking 'self-love' to a whole new level, this bible for her tribe will create ripples of change in the world, the results of which will be empowered women, liberated in their bodies and sexuality, tender-hearted to their loved ones, kinder to themselves."

–TARA BLISS, WOMEN'S MENTOR

"*Open Wide* is THE book we've all been waiting for. We've been fumbling our way through awkward and downright hurtful relationships without a guide for way too long. It's time we had a REAL life soul sister by your side guide that's packed full of useful tips and strategies that really work. This is exactly what Melissa delivers: a life-altering book that shows you how to create long-lasting and soulful relationships that are exploding with love and mind-blowing sex. If your sex life doesn't rock your world or if your relationships don't crack your heart wide open, then this book is for you. It's a truly comprehensive guide for both men and woman alike that will be passed down through generations."

–LEISA PORTEOUS-SEMPLE, HEALTH AND WELLNESS COACH

"This book is incredibly insightful. Melissa gives the most down-to-earth, fun relationship guide for REAL, modern women."

–MADDY SHAW, BESTSELLING AUTHOR AND NUTRITIONAL THERAPIST

OPEN WIDE

MELISSA AMBROSINI

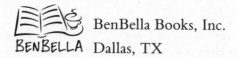 BenBella Books, Inc.
Dallas, TX

BenBella Books, Inc.
10440 N. Central Expressway, Suite 800
Dallas, TX 75231
www.benbellabooks.com
Send feedback to feedback@benbellabooks.com

Printed in the United States of America
10 9 8 7 6 5 4 3 2 1

Library of Congress Cataloging-in-Publication Data is available upon request.
ISBN: 9781946885074
e-ISBN: 9781946885166

Originally published by HarperCollins *Publishers*, Australia

Internal design by Hazel Lam, HarperCollins Design Studio
Proofreading and Americanization by Kimberly Broderick
Printed and bound by Lake Book Manufacturing

Distributed to the trade by Two Rivers Distribution, an Ingram brand
www.tworiversdistribution.com

Special discounts for bulk sales (minimum of 25 copies) are available. Please contact Aida Herrera at aida@benbellabooks.com.

This book is dedicated to YOU, my darling reader.
May you Open Wide *to your true magnificence and*
unlock your full potential.
Love, Melissa
xx

Contents

FOREWORD

I have been working with Melissa for some years, and I'm happy and incredibly grateful to say that we've been good friends ever since.

Aside from the fact that she has a contagious and unstoppable enthusiasm for life, the ability to light up a room with her smile, and is driven to create change, I genuinely believe that she is a thought-leader in her field and relentlessly committed to giving others real life tools to live their lives at 100 percent.

Anyone who's spent time with Melissa knows that she is a shining light and the "real deal" when it comes to enthusiasm for wellness and helping others. In 2016, I was so honored to award her the Active Living Award for all the incredible work she does to inspire and educate women.

Being with Melissa just makes you want to be a better human, and it's refreshing to find an openly generous and informative book about relationships, love, sex, and authenticity, written by someone who has the bravery to be so genuinely honest about her life, with the pure intention to help and support others.

I cannot imagine anyone who wouldn't benefit from the wisdom in these pages — and I'm excited for you to read it!

Open Wide is a gift to us all.

Lorna Jane x
Lorna Jane Clarkson, founder of Lorna Jane activewear company

Why a Book About Love, Soulful Sex, and Relationships?

It's taken me almost twelve long, grueling months to actually sit my bum down and start writing this book. With a looming deadline from my publishers I know I have to start, but I'm almost paralyzed by self-doubt, fear, and insecurity. You see, I have this presence called my inner Mean Girl. That's the name I've given to the annoying, fear-based voice we all have inside our minds. There are many different names for it — resistance, fear, your ego, your inner critic, your shadow self, your smaller self ... the list goes on. But I like "Mean Girl" (or "Bad Boy" for the dudes). Giving the voice a name really helps you separate yourself from its chatter and see that it's not *you*, or the Truth of who you are. (As you read this book, you will come to realize that the Truth of who you are is LOVE! But more on that later.)

We ALL have our own version of this little voice inside our head. Nobody is exempt — no matter whether you're a "Normal Nancy" or a monk meditating on a mountain. Heck, even the Dalai Lama himself has one (though I'm guessing he's mastered his like a boss). All of us are still growing and evolving in this classroom called life, so we've all got our own version of the voice. But the good news is, our Mean Girls (or Bad Boys) are here to teach us some incredibly powerful lessons and guide us home to our Truth.

Ever since my first book hit the shelves, I knew I had another one bubbling away inside me. But as always, when things are important to me, my Mean Girl reared her ugly head: *Who do you think you are writing a book about love, soulful sex, and relationships?! You don't have a PhD in this subject matter — you don't know enough, get over yourself! You won't be able to do it. People may have loved your first book … but who's to say that was anything more than a fluke?* And on and on she went. It's pretty handy that I wrote an entire book on *Mastering Your Mean Girl: The no-BS guide to silencing your inner critic and becoming wildly wealthy, fabulously healthy, and bursting with love*, because right now I need my own advice, fast.

To be honest, I'm scared to write this book and my Mean Girl is telling me I can't do it. But I have to practice what I preach. I have to master my own Mean Girl and share what's burning deep within, which I know — once understood and implemented — can profoundly shift the way you live your life, on all levels.

Before we dive deeper, let's get a few things straight. Outside of my own exploration, I'm not a sex, Tantra, or relationship expert. But I feel deeply compelled to share what I have learned about relationships, deep love, and soulful sex, because it's radically rocked my world and my hope is that it sparks you to Open Wide to depths of mind-blowing, heart-expanding love you may never have known existed.

It's also important to note that everything in this book is how I live my life. These are the tools I use to Open Wide every day in my own life.

So you might be thinking, why the heck did I write a book about relationships? Well, as you know, relationships are a huge part of life. They can be our greatest source of joy and happiness, or they can tear us down into quivering wrecks. They are the biggest "game" we play, yet we're not given a manual on how to play them! And no one ever teaches us! Imagine sitting down with a Sudoku grid for the first time and not being told what the rules are. You wouldn't get very far, would you? And yet most people are doing exactly that in their real-life relationships — thrust into the thick of things, flying blind, and hoping they can figure out what's going on before it's too late. And if you're anything like me, you fumble! You make poor (really poor) choices in men and friendships, wasting hours — scratch that, wasting days, months, and even *years* — holding grudges against people and agonizing, worrying, and stressing out over what he or she — or you! — once said or did.

If you've done any personal development work before, you probably know enough to look for the lesson in these moments. Because yes, there's always a lesson, and **everything is always unfolding exactly as it's supposed to.** These are important concepts to grasp. But (and this is a very big BUT), what if you knew the insider info that meant you didn't *have* to learn those lessons the hard way? What if you could play the game in a way that didn't end in pain? Think about all those times you've stressed, worried, expelled energy, and lost sleep over a particular situation or argument with someone … What else could you have done with that precious time? You could have learned another language, performed a random act of kindness, honed your photography skills, or become an epic pianist. (And I could have written a whole library of books!) But we didn't! Instead that precious time is lost and gone forever.

The truth is, we only have a certain amount of time here in this beautiful "earth suit" we've been given. Think about it mathematically for a moment: there are three hundred and sixty-five days in a year and the average life expectancy is seventy-eight years. That means we've got fewer than thirty thousand days on this planetary playground … and they'll go by in a flash. So don't you think we should figure out how to use our precious time wisely?

That's why I created this radically real relationship guide for *you:* so you can cultivate kick-ass connections with everyone you come into contact with, and experience deep love in ALL your relationships. I also want to light the way for you to experience soulful, heart-opening, expansive, mind-blowing sex with your lover too (or *lovers* — whatever floats your boat!). Does that all sound like your cup of herbal tea? If so, sister, buckle up, because you're in for one hell of a ride!

An Important Note Before We Go Any Further …

This is a book about deep love, soulful sex, and relationships. And as we all know, when it comes to romantic relationships, they come in all shapes and sizes — from male and female, to male and male, female and female, and any other combination you can think of.

For the sake of simplicity, throughout this book, I will mainly be speaking from my own perspective on intimate relationships, which is one male and one female. But make no mistake: I'm talking to *everyone* — even if I've happened to use one pronoun instead of another. These principles are universal, so no matter what your dream relationship looks like, please know that this info applies to you, you're so very welcome and loved here, and I can't wait to help you manifest your soul's deepest, heartfelt desire.

On that note, I should also say: I don't want to help you manifest deep love with *just* your honey-bun … I want to help you experience profound love in ALL your relationships — including your friends, your family, and anyone else who's important to you. The cool thing about this (which most people don't realize) is that in the vast majority of instances, **exactly the same principles apply to ALL your relationships** — whether they're romantic or platonic. So when you're reading this book, even if I happen to be talking about one particular kind of pairing, know that these tools and tips can apply to whichever relationship you'd most like to work on (or most like to call in). Yes, there are some topics we'll cover that are specific to your lover, like at the end of the book when we venture into the boudoir. But for everything else? These are universal laws we're talking about here, babe! So drink it all in with an open mind, and look for the cosmic truths that apply to you.

While we're talking housekeeping stuff, now is also a good time to mention that I've changed the names and identifying features of most of the people mentioned in this book to protect their privacy. And all stories are shared with love and permission.

With that out of the way, let's get straight to the juicy stuff!

My Story

Just to give you a little more background on me … I am in my thirties and I have had my fair share of relationships. I've experienced infidelity (and I too have been a wee bit unfaithful in my time), I've had my heart ripped out of my chest and stomped on (which you can read about in *Mastering Your Mean Girl*), I've dated some lovely men, and I've survived some not-so-lovely ones. I have begged (as in, on my knees pleading) men to love me (because I didn't love myself) and, although I don't regret anything, I've also done many things I'm not very proud of. But most importantly of all, I've learned a lot in the process. I am now married to my soulmate, Nick. He *is* the man of my dreams! I often pinch myself about getting to wake up next to this divine human being and share my life with him. My reality *is* wilder than my dreams. But before Nick, I didn't believe in soulmates, the concept of "the one," or even monogamy in general. I didn't want to get married, have kids, or subscribe to "till death do us part." I thought it was all a load of BS (and I had some deep wounds that needed healing and scar tissue that needed massaging). But truthfully, I probably doubted all of that stuff because I'd never before experienced the kind of deep love within myself or in a relationship that would make me believe in it, and the fact that it suited me. What unfolded when I finally Opened Wide was beyond anything I could have ever imagined, and I could not be more grateful.

But here's the thing, if you haven't yet experienced this kind of love within your own life yet, I urge you to stay Open Wide, because you *can* have spine-tingling sex and mind-blowing love that fills you up in ways you didn't know existed. It *is* possible! It *is* your birthright! You are worthy of all the love, joy, happiness, and inner peace you truly desire. Even if your Mean Girl tells you otherwise.

You are love! You deserve to experience love!

If you're rolling your eyes in disbelief and letting your Mean Girl say things like, *Yeah right, Melissa, this won't happen for me,* I invite you to Open Wide and suspend that disbelief as we go on this journey together. I didn't believe it either until I opened myself up to the possibility and entertained the idea just the slightest amount. That's the first step: openness. Stay open in your heart and mind and try not to close yourself off, my sweet friend! If you notice yourself closing off and shutting down, that's okay. But ask yourself why. Pull out your journal and write about what's coming up for you. I'm here to hold your hand and support you on your journey. I want *you* to experience deep levels of love, because *you* deserve it!

So let's get this journey started.

Think of me like one of your besties. I will guide you and show you how I manifested oceans of love in my own life — starting by falling in love with myself, something I never thought possible. Once I had the self-love sorted, I was then able to call in more love all around me — including manifesting my soul sisters and my soulmate. In this book, I'll show you how I did it all and how you can do it too. But please know, right here and now, that you already have everything you need inside of you. Everything! So don't think of me as a guru or an expert or a lecturer — I'm none of those things, and you don't need them anyway ... I'm simply the friendly travel guide holding the torch as you journey home to your Truth.

So are you ready to begin? Let's take it from the top, shall we?

For many years, I rented the penthouse in Struggle City, where I hosted destructive relationship after destructive relationship, not just with men, but with *all* my friends. I ran from men (and myself) because I was too scared to commit. When things got serious, I ran. When things got hard, I ran. When things were too easy, I ran. One of my ex-partners used to joke that I always had my running shoes at the front door, ready to sprint when things got too much. It's true! I was so scared to commit. I told myself I was missing out if I "settled down." What was really going on was that I was scared to truly see myself. As you will *remember* (yep, you already know everything; I'm just here to remind you), **relationships are our biggest mirror, our biggest teachers, and our biggest spiritual assignments**. Looking, and I mean *really* looking, at your relationships is the fastest way to grow and evolve. But back then, I wasn't ready, willing, or even the slightest bit open to looking at myself. And although it may have looked like I had it all together on the outside, I was falling apart on the inside, and dealing with depression, anxiety, panic attacks, and an eating disorder. I was so unhappy and uncomfortable in my own skin.

After running from myself for many years, burning the candle at both ends, and trashing my body, I ended up in hospital in 2010 with no more wick left to burn and nowhere else to run and hide. My "friends" didn't want to hang around me, and I had just come out of yet another destructive relationship where I found myself questioning why I didn't want to get married, have kids, or "settle down — yuck! I hated that term. The thought of 'settling down' with one person FOR THE REST OF MY LIFE made me want to puke!

So how did I go from an unwell relationship cynic to healthy and madly in love? Well first off, it's important to point out that this took time and backslides — and I didn't go from being in hospital to being entirely well, or from cynic to madly in love overnight. But the first step I took was to Open Wide! I mastered my Mean Girl and I entertained the possibility of there being another way. Because *there is*, my sweet friend. I'm not here to tell you to "settle down." Instead of settling down, we're going to rise together and open *you* up to the possibilities of there being another, more heart-centred way, so that you can experience deep love, connection, and soulful sex. And if you already experience deep love and soulful sex, get ready to take ALL your relationships to the next level.

After a spectacular encounter with rock bottom in 2010 (when my life and health collapsed around me), the Universe sent me a guardian angel, disguised as a man named Dom who then became my boyfriend. And although I was in the worst physical, mental, and emotional shape of my entire life, and maybe what I "should" have done was spend time on my own, learning to love myself, dialling up my worthy-o-meter and upping my self-care, I didn't. Because this was the journey I needed to go on with Dom. And to be honest I felt broken, and it felt so damn good to have someone scoop me up in his arms and care about me deeply.

We were together for about three years, and during that time we both experienced massive growth and were both so deeply committed to doing the inner work. I attended hundreds of personal development courses, workshops, and seminars. I read every spiritual book I could get my hands on, meditated daily, chanted out my demons, sage cleansed myself and everything I owned, and released the limiting beliefs and stories that were holding me back. I saw healers, coaches, counselors and shamans, had my cards read, and went to body-mind-and-soul workers and every kind of energy practitioner you can think of. I did past-life regressions, cleansed my aura, balanced my chakras, relived and recreated my birth, plus so much more. I was deeply committed to my growth, because deep down, I knew that the pain and suffering I was experiencing weren't my Truth. I knew that God, the Universe, source, love, the divine mother (whatever you want to call it), didn't put us here on earth only to suffer. I was open to there being another way. I didn't know what that looked like or how to get there, I just knew there had to be another way and I was open to it. To be honest, I was *done* with the suffering; it was exhausting and I was over it.

This was one of the hardest periods of my life and Dom held space for me so beautifully during that time of massive growth and supercharged healing, for which I will be forever grateful. But the more inner work I did on myself — and the more layers I peeled back — the closer I came to my Truth and to the deep knowing that our time together was coming to an end. I knew that we weren't going to get married, that we weren't meant to have children together, and that I didn't want to spend the rest of my life with him. This was so hard to admit because there was nothing "wrong" with that relationship. It had served such a divine purpose, but that chapter was coming to a close.

Still though, the fear was sky high and my Mean Girl told me that I couldn't be alone. But my growing self-awareness meant I was also experiencing deep inner pain and suffering from ignoring and denying my Truth. It ate away at me and caused my health to decline. I felt like I was hiding a big fat secret that was making me so unhappy and unwell. As I was realizing, there's only so much lying to yourself you can take before you start to implode, and all the self-deception was starting to send me toward an inevitable breaking point.

You see, we all have a built-in compass. This compass is often referred to as intuition, the higher self, the spirit, the soul, or the Truth. (For the sake of simplicity throughout this book, I will call it intuition.) And there is *always* a price to pay when you ignore your intuition. Sure, you can suppress and run from it for a few days, weeks and even years like I did. But eventually, its clarion call will be so loud that it pierces your soul with its cry. It can even manifest as a disease in the body. So let's just say, it's best to not ignore your intuition!

Although I had done a lot of work within myself, I still wasn't confident enough yet to walk away from the relationship. So I unconsciously manifested a man — let's call him Ab Man — into my life to give me the confidence and courage my Mean Girl needed to leave that relationship. This man was gorgeous, funny, successful, and (in case you hadn't guessed) had abs of steel. I was so swept up in his looks and the idea of us being together that I couldn't believe *he* was interested in *me* (the first telltale sign that my worthy-o-meter and self-love bucket were way too low). We flirted and my confidence grew. Although in hindsight I realize now it was fake confidence. This fake confidence led me to want to end my relationship with Dom. And because everything is energy, Dom picked up on this and he ended it with me first. The day I moved out, I felt like I didn't need to lie to myself any more. I felt like I could breathe deeply again.

From there I began to grow extremely fond — even obsessed — with the idea of a relationship with Ab Man. My fake confidence, courage, and worthiness continued to grow the more interest he showed in me. The chemistry was insane — I was SO physically attracted to this man. We flirted, and when he touched my hand or brushed past me, my whole being would shiver ... but we never made love or even kissed.

Before that could happen, he dropped me like a hot potato. He stopped returning my calls and decided he wanted to resume things with his own on-again, off-again girlfriend. I was devastated! I cried (actually, I wailed), grieved, and felt like I was spiralling back down into that deep dark abyss I was medicated for in 2010.

In hindsight, I can now see that the reason I was so devastated was because again, that "relationship" was built on fear not love. From day one, I was attracted to Ab Man because I wanted him to fill a void within me. My Mean Girl told me, *This is too good to be true, to have such a good-looking guy interested in you.* My worthy-o-meter and self-love levels were at an all-time low, and I desperately needed someone else to validate me. Not a good idea!

Any relationship built on fear has an expiration date. But relationships built on love go the distance.

So there I was again: single, incredibly unhappy, depressed, living at my sister's place, and with a very loud Mean Girl singing in my ears. Hey, rock bottom, we meet again! The great thing about rock bottom, however, is that the only way out is up … and up I got. I cracked open my journal, dusted off my crystals, whipped out my meditation pillow, went inward, and did the work. But this time? It was different.

I committed to being and sitting with myself in my own space, which felt very scary for someone who had spent decades avoiding herself at all costs. I dialed up my worthy-o-meter and worked on myself, not out of fear as I had done in the past, but from a place of love. None of it was because I felt like I was broken or needed fixing, but because I was finally open to the possibility of things being different, that there was or could be another way. I was so sick and tired of the way my life and relationships had been unfolding that I wanted to experience something deeper, more open, more expansive, and real. I wanted to experience love and unity on all levels. But was it possible? I had hope, but I wasn't sure.

I began shifting my self-work so that it had a distinctive focus on relationships. I studied the works of great relationship, sex, and Tantra teachers. I created space (physically and mentally) for the type of union I wanted to call in. And I journaled about my dream man and our relationship, including how I wanted to *feel* when I was in his presence, and about what we did and created in the world together. I had fun with it for months. And finally — for the first time in my life — I felt content within myself. I felt love for myself. I wasn't running after the next guy who walked into my life just to fill a void. I'd never experienced this type of internal alchemy — I hadn't even known it existed. Then, as the Universe so often does, it presented me with another opportunity for growth.

Enter another incredibly handsome, tall, tanned man. Let's call him Toned Tommy. Just like Dom, he was a divine being I loved to be around, but I knew deep down he wasn't "the one" … *Wait! Dear God, did she just say "the one"?!* Hang in there, sister! At this point in my journey, I was still not yet convinced of "the one" or "soulmates" either. Hell, I wouldn't have known soulful sex if it bent me over and spanked me.

But Toned Tommy was super sweet and super cute. We flirted, kissed, had fun, went on a few dates, and I could see myself being with him. In fact, in my head, I thought we could probably have had a very nice, simple life together — the white picket fence, the dog, the two kids. He was pretty damn fine … but was I okay with "fine"? Did I want "nice" and "simple"? To be honest, I couldn't fault him. But deep down, my intuition was adamant that we weren't meant to be together, and I didn't want to ignore it ever again. My Mean Girl also piped up with some valid-sounding arguments: *You won't get any better than this, Melissa. He's a nice guy, so stop being so picky. You're verging on thirty and all your friends are getting married and having kids. You need to hurry up and find a husband, and here's a perfectly good man sitting right in front of you!* Old Melissa might have been taken in by these perfectly aimed barbs. But I decided to master my Mean Girl and not let her win. I had to rise up, be brave, and eventually Toned Tommy and I ended it, even though there was nothing "wrong" with him or the relationship. I just knew in my heart that he wasn't "the one" for me, and I had to honor that. At the end of the day there is no "right" or "wrong": your labeling depends on your perception of the matter, and you have to respect that.

There was another good reason I had to end it too. You see, **when you entertain a relationship out of fear, it takes up space — space for a potential relationship bursting with love to enter.** And let's face it, the Universe is *not* going to throw a dream lover your way if both your hands are busy gripping onto your safety net … How would you catch him?

Newly single (again), I started questioning things (again). I questioned monogamy itself, and wondered how, as naturally promiscuous beings, we could "settle down" with one person forever. It sounded crazy to me. I found myself asking questions … Like, why don't I want to get married and have children? Why can't I "settle down"? Why am I not excited about the same things my friends are? I felt that marriage had lost its true meaning and was no longer all it was cracked up to be. Most of us will have either witnessed in person or in the movies the weddings where the bride and groom act like puppets as they repeat vows they haven't really thought about, sing songs they don't care about, all in an environment their parents have chosen. And with the divorce rate unfortunately rising, to me, it didn't take a genius to see that the modern model of marriage and monogamy was quite possibly doing far more harm than good. Yes, I knew some people had long-lasting marriages and long-term relationships. But that seemed to be the only way people measured a "successful" relationship — by whether or not the couple were still together. Huh? That's not good enough in my book! What about spiritual, physical, and emotional growth? What about quality over quantity? From my perspective, it seemed like a doomed proposition from the start. Half of all marriages straight-up end in divorce. And with the other half, as a society, we seem to care about little except length, with only glancing regard given to the health or happiness of the respective parties. Why would I voluntarily sign up for that?!

It was in this moment that I decided: *I am done! I am over it! I am not getting married or having kids. I am better off alone. Who needs a man?* I thought. *I can do this all on my own.*

Then another test from the Universe.

… Enter Nick!

Nick and I had known each other for about three years before this moment. But the funny thing was that we never really looked at each other. We never gave each other the time of day. We were polite (of course) but it was like there was a brick wall between us with a "Do Not Enter" sign plastered over it. I mean, I think Nick is seriously freaking hot! He is super successful and sexy in every way — from his intensely beautiful brown eyes that reflect his health, to his insanely chiselled face, his golden glittery skin that is totally flawless, and his body that you could grate activated cashew nut cheese on. He is also the successful music artist BROADHURST, and his voice, on its own, will make you want to Open (extremely) Wide, if you know what I mean! Not to mention the soft, yet masculine, loving, open energy that he exudes from his soul. Why the heck did I not jump him back then?

The Universe had a different plan for us all along ...

All of a sudden, we kept finding ourselves at the same parties and events. I was so curious and instantly drawn to him, but (unusually for me) it wasn't out of fear, or of wanting him to fill something within me: it was deeper than that. It was like magnets joining together. It was undeniable! I was fascinated by him and his story and wanted to get to know him on a deeper level.

One of our first proper conversations was on the beach, where we sat and talked openly for hours. We spoke about monogamy, not wanting to have children (Nick already had a beautiful son, Leo), having open relationships, Tantra ... everything! We were so open, real, and honest, something I had never experienced before. There were no barriers and no holding back, because we had no expectations and nothing to lose. Our eyes were locked in a transfixed state. We were both deeply present and connected and didn't realize that three and a half hours had flown by until we were interrupted by my phone alarm going off telling me my parking had expired. This was the first time I experienced how fast time flies when we are fully present with each other. It was a total time warp. For the first time ever there was no agenda or expectation, just pure openness. It felt safe and oddly familiar. After hours of soulful conversation, we reluctantly parted.

Until our next date, which again was hours of deep, open, and soulful conversation on the beach. This was the first time we started speaking about sex in explicit detail and about some of Nick's experiences with Tantra (a 5,000-year-old Hindu mind-body practice of slow sex for intimacy — and mind-blowing orgasms) and Taoism (an ancient Chinese religious and philosophical tradition). There had been a shift in our dynamic. Our openness went to a new level and I was starting to really explore the possibilities of my sexuality for the first time. Again, we were both incredibly open because we had no expectations. Let me say that again, in case it didn't sink in the first time ... *no expectations*.

In the past, when I was beginning a new relationship, I always put on my best front. I would only expose the shiny me, the "best" version of myself, so that I came across as someone the other person would want to be with. Not this time. With Nick I was my full, open, and authentic self, warts and all.

At this stage, we still hadn't even kissed. In fact, we were exploring the idea of having an open relationship and seeing other people. Nick read me a text message he'd sent to another girl he was going on a date with that night. I was blown away by what he'd written — it was so deep, honest, and poetic. I was inspired by his words and not jealous at all. In the past I would have been triggered at the mere mention of him going on a date with someone else, but I was so confident and so sure of who I was that it didn't bother me.

We both knew something between us was about to ignite. We didn't know what or when or how, we just knew. Our time together flew by again. I was so inspired by this man, which was something I hadn't experienced before. I didn't know you could be inspired by your partner.

I *thought* I wanted him, but I wasn't sure or attached in any way (the freedom of no expectations!). I was simply in the moment and totally open to anything. He was open too, with no baggage, expectations, or agenda. We didn't speak about our past or the future. We were fully present and simply wanted to share and be totally open with each other without fear.

When two people come together without expectations, agendas, or baggage, and allow themselves to Open Wide, the result is flow and *unity*. Very quickly, we fell madly, deeply, and passionately in love. Still with no expectations, just pure openness. Being with him felt like home. Like I had been with him in many lifetimes before. It was effortless and I truly felt like I could be my full self and I wasn't being judged. It was so easy! (*Wait, was it too easy? Shouldn't it be hard?* Shhhh, Mean Girl.)

Two weeks later, he proposed to me, and less than six months after that we were married. That was April 2014, and as I write this we are still bursting with love today. Of course, we're in the early years of our marriage. I don't have a crystal ball, and no one knows what the future holds. But right now, in this very moment, this is my Truth, what I believe in my heart and what's resonating deep within.

I tell you the story of our relationship not to brag, but to inspire you that it truly is possible to ditch your baggage, expectations, agendas, fears, and limiting beliefs, and open yourself up to a deeper kind of love that makes your heart sing. If I can do it, so can you, because I'm no more special than you. When we were being created, God didn't give me a bigger spoonful of specialness than he gave you. Sure, there are certain privileges I have, such as being born and raised in Australia, with parents who love me, and a healthy body. But if I can ditch my limiting baggage and Open Wide to deep love then so can you.

How to Use This Book

I've designed this book to be a beautiful journey, with each section building on the one that came before it. We start, in Part One, by looking within. This is where you'll learn how to unleash the divine energy that lives inside you (a.k.a. your Goddessence). In Part Two, we zoom out and look around us. This is where you'll discover the secret to rocking relationships (including how to call in your soulmate, and experience the most divine, fulfilling love EVER!). Then, in Part Three, we'll dive headfirst into the bedroom, where I'll be sharing the keys to spine-tingling, mind-blowing, soul-filled sex (yum!).

But can't I just skip straight to the sexy stuff? The temptation is strong, I know! But the truth is, the kind of sex I'll be teaching you about is grounded in connection, authenticity, vulnerability, truthfulness, honesty, self-love, and getting radically real with your lover … Which means you need to have mastered the other building blocks first — the stuff in Parts One and Two — *before* you can put them into practice in the boudoir.

So though it might be tempting to jump ahead to the sexy stuff, I want to encourage you to stick with me while we lay the all-important groundwork. (After all, you wouldn't skip straight to dessert before eating your veggies, would you?!) Besides, if you're open to it, **every single stage** of this journey is filled with excitement, insight, and the thrill of discovery … not just the nudie bits. So to continue the food analogy, it's not like you're going to have to struggle your way through a bowl of soggy, overcooked Brussels sprouts. (Gross.) Instead, I'll be dishing you up a gorgeous helping of the tastiest, crispiest, most nutrient-dense kale chips you've ever tasted. (Mmm, yes please!)

Why Open Wide?

When it came to naming this book, right from the start, there was one name that sailed into my soul, dropped its anchor, and wouldn't let go: *Open Wide*.

If I had to sum up everything I've learned about loving myself and others, living as my best self, uniting with another soul, and experiencing life-changing sex, it would be with these two simple words.

"Open Wide" has become my mantra, my philosophy, and my guiding light. When I feel my Mean Girl start to whisper her fear-based nonsense to me, I say it to myself ... *Open Wide, Melissa*. When expectations barge into my head and block me from the present moment ... *Open Wide*. When shame or fear cause me to contract and shrink ... *Open Wide*. When I'm stuck in my egoic energy and start barking orders at my stepson ... *Open Wide*. When I'm hiding my Truth from Nick, demanding that he somehow read my mind ... *Open Wide*. And when I'm lying in bed in the arms of my man, and all I can think about is my to-do list ... *Open Wide*.

These two little words have become a powerful catalyst to springboard me back to love, softness, warmth, and openness. They soften my edges. They reconnect me with my Goddessence. They melt me into the present moment. They raise me to be the best version of myself. And they bring me home to my Truth.

My wish is that these two words become a powerful anchor for you too — a potent, ease-filled tool you can use whenever you catch yourself out of alignment and are desiring a return to Love.

Throughout this book, I'm going to be using this phrase as an invitation to you — to soften your body, mind, heart, and soul, to gently let go, to sink deeper within, to surrender further, and to peel back another layer. Whenever you see these two words — Open Wide — I encourage you to stop for a second, place your hands over your heart, take a deep breath, soften, tune in to your inner wisdom, and allow the energy of the present moment to flow through you.

Whenever I accept this invitation in my own life and allow myself to Open Wide, the insight and energy that follow never fail to instantly change my state, to uplift and inspire me to new levels. I *still* find myself astonished how such a simple action — consciously opening yourself up to what is — can have such powerful, profound results.

So, beautiful — are you ready to accept this loving invitation for yourself?

Are you ready to take your life, relationships, and lovemaking to new heights?

Are you ready to Open Wide?

Great! Let's dive in.

UNLEASHING YOUR DIVINE GODDESSENCE

CHAPTER ONE

Understanding the Masculine and Feminine and Firm and Fluid

Why does your heart beat?

Have you ever stopped to ask yourself that question?

If you're scientifically minded, you might have an answer at the ready: *Duh, Melissa! Your heart beats because of an electrical impulse that originates in the right atrium, causing the atrial walls to contract and the cardiac muscle to pulsate. This forces blood into the ventricles.*

Okay. But tell me, what causes that electrical impulse? And what causes the impulse before that, and the one before that, and the one before that? How far back can we go?

This kind of deep, spiraling thought experiment has occupied great thinkers from all fields for millennia — from scientists to philosophers, religious mystics, artists, and poets.

There's only one answer that's ever rung true for me, and it's this: **ultimately, underneath everything, there is a divine life-force that runs through every living thing**. It's the innate intelligence that beats our heart, sprouts a seed, and blooms a bud. It's the magical force that turns a caterpillar into a butterfly, an acorn into an oak tree, and that grows a baby inside a woman's belly.

This life-force is in all of us. It's what makes us alive and conscious and curious. It's what gives us our is-ness; it *is* life.

So when we question the meaning of life (as all of us humans have done, from the earliest cave people to the angstiest of modern teenagers), we could just as easily question the meaning of this life-force itself. Why is it here? What is its purpose? What makes it tick?

It took me a long time to find an answer to these questions, especially one that made sense to me on an intellectual level *and* a heart and soul level. But when I did, so many things I'd been wondering about clicked into place. In fact life, as a whole, made a lot more sense.

So what's the answer? What's the great, ultimate, driving desire of this mystical life-force? Well, **this life-force longs to know itself**. It longs to dance, tickle, delight, dive, swim, immerse, converse, collide, and play with itself. It longs to be in communion with itself — to know itself inside out, upside down, from one farthest edge to another.

And because it is inside all of us — inside every living thing — one of the best ways this life-force can know itself better is by communing with other living things. That's what it is seeking, above all else: **to better know itself by being 'in relationship' with others**.

You can see this divine truth play out in nature — oak trees commune with each other underground, sending messages in ways we're only just beginning to understand. Ants have complex social structures and relationships with each other. Even marine plankton live in communities, "talking" to each other and "helping" each other. And of course, no pet owner could deny the sacred, heartfelt bond between themselves and their beloved pet.

Then, of course, there are human relationships — the ultimate playground for this divine life-force, and the underlying theme of this whole book.

As humans, our natural state is to be "in relationship" with others. (Our innate life-force gets off on it!) Relationships are our divine right and sacred classroom, and, *boy*, do they give this divine life-force a chance to play, dance, and delight at the highest level.

Of course, at times, relationships can also feel really challenging. We popped out into this world without a manual, and have been forced to navigate our way in what feels like total darkness. Without an alternative, we learned by watching those around us, or soaking up the throwaway comments our elders themselves had picked up from the generation before. Someone we loved and looked up to, like our parents or school teachers, may have said, "Here are the rules. This is what you should and shouldn't do and say. This is how you should move through life. This is what you should do for work. This is what you should believe. This is right and this is wrong. This is truth and this is not truth. We only hang out with these people here, but we don't talk to those people over there, and we definitely don't like *those* types of people at all."

It's safe to say that from childhood you get conditioned. And unless you wake up, Open Wide, and do something about it, you will play out those beliefs (that weren't even yours to begin with) all your life. And that is not why we are here on this planet. **We are here to learn, grow, evolve our human consciousness, and unlock our FULL potential**. And if we don't, not only can life feel like a hard slog, but, depending on your beliefs, you may have to come back time and time again until you learn your lessons.

You might have felt the exciting rise in consciousness that's taking place right now. It's got everything to do with relationships, life-force energy, and the magical union of the divine masculine and feminine energies — everything this book is about! So it's important to understand where it all started ...

According to a study published in the journal *Science*, until a few thousand years BC, women and men were seen and treated as equals. With the advent of agriculture and the ability to accumulate resources, men set about creating a patriarchal society — a male-dominated culture that repressed the feminine and looked down on its way of being. What had previously been a divine dynamic tango between men and women — with each respecting and cherishing the other, and each made better by the other's presence — suddenly became totally out of whack. Men ruled all, and qualities prized as "masculine" (like assertiveness, ambition, and physical strength) were prioritised over "feminine" qualities (like care-giving, softness, and listening). We'll go into this in more detail later, but to give you the outcome in an activated nutshell, things did *not* go well for women.

Luckily for us in the West, we now experience more choice, freedom, balance, and equality than possibly any of our female ancestors. Of course, there's still a long way to go. (And it's worth noting that there are still far too many parts of the world that have yet to experience this awakening, and where women are still fighting to be treated as equal humans.) For us, though, this shifting and rebalancing of men's and women's roles is fundamental, necessary, and oh so welcome! In fact, we are in a time some thinkers call "the feminine rising" — a unifying natural global process that brings the world together for the inclusivity of all living things, justice for all, and a new model of global identity that transcends national boundaries. It is taking place right now and is happening from the inside out. It will change the way you think, how you perceive, and what you believe. It will alter your perception of the world around you and, more importantly, it *will* change your relationship to absolutely everything that you know. It is very exciting and very expansive.

But first ...

There's a question we need to answer: how did we get here? How did everything get so out of whack?

I believe it stems from a fundamental misunderstanding of the nature of "masculine" and "feminine" energies. For a truckload of reasons — including millennia of social conditioning, a lack of cultural education and awareness, and way too much time caught up in our heads (rather than our Truth) — it's become incredibly difficult for the average person to grasp the true essence and beauty of both types of energy. This, in turn, exacerbates the problem, the cycle is perpetuated, and it gets even harder to see the truth that's right in front of us: **that both energies are sacred, divine, and totally necessary**.

Defining the Indefinable

Before we go any further, we need to talk about *how* we talk about the concepts of masculine and feminine energy. Sometimes these two words — "masculine" and "feminine" — can limit or even block our understanding of this divine concept, because they carry gendered connotations. For that reason, it's totally fine to exchange them for words you feel more drawn to. Perhaps you resonate with the language of "yin and yang," or "Shiva and Shakti," both of which are often used in Eastern traditions. Maybe you like word pairings like "firm and fluid" or "strength and flexibility" — these are great too. Or perhaps you prefer imagery, and would rather conceptualize it through symbols like "the rock and the river," or "the sun and the star." Whichever you prefer, it's all perfect, and I encourage you to use the language or symbols that resonate most with you. I love and resonate with ALL of these, but in my personal life, I most often use "masculine and feminine" and "firm and fluid," so I'll be swapping between these pairings throughout this book.

Despite the traditional allocation of masculine energy (i.e. the firm, yang, Shiva side of the equation) to men, and feminine energy (i.e. the fluid, yin, Shakti side) to women, we ALL possess both types of energy — regardless of our gender. And every relationship possesses both energies too — this is nothing to do with your gender or sexuality: within a same-sex partnership there are firm and fluid energies, and they're present in platonic relationships as well as romantic ones.

Understanding how to dance between these two types of opposing but synchronous energies will transform so many different parts of your life — from how you show up in your work to how you feel in the bedroom, how you live out your relationships, and everything in between. When you truly "get it," on a deep level, it feels like you've got the keys to the Universe in your hands. *Really? Life can actually be this simple? And this fulfilling? Who knew?!* So if having this kind of insight and ability sounds like your cup of tea, you are definitely in the right place.

Understanding Polarity

POLARITY
/pə(ʊ)ˈlarɪti/

noun, the state of having two opposite tendencies or aspects

Think of firm energy like a flagpole: strong, sturdy, stable, unshakable and, despite the sometimes turbulent and wild winds, able to hold up its flag and stand strong. Think of the fluid energy as the flag. Floaty and flexible, it dances, twirls, and swirls in the wind. It wants to be and feel free, to flow, to create, and express itself in expansive ways.

The part that most people miss? In their purest form, these different types of energy don't cancel each other out, or seek "supremacy." Instead, they complement and enhance the other in a dance of divine polarity.

This divine polarity plays out on every level of our lives — from the global political stage (which is desperately in need of some fluid Goddess love-energy right now!) to companies and corporations, communities, interpersonal relationships, and all the way down to us as individuals … Heck, even on a micro level, our cells are constantly reaching for harmony, balance, and collaboration!

Fluid energy is diverse and flexible, and can do many things at once while it twirls around. Imagine an artist in their studio with four brushes in one hand, paint palette in the other. He swirls between tins of paint at his feet, while humming a tune and gripping a brush between his teeth. That's true fluid energy right there. Sure, it can get frenetic at times — the dance of the whirling dervish, if you will. But it can also be the world's most elegant, graceful ballet — a true symphony that thrives on its many moving parts.

Firm energy is the polar opposite. It is focused and destination driven. It too is beautiful in its way. If we looked at it in terms of geometry, it would be made up of straight lines and angles, while fluid energy would be made up of swirls and curves.

The thing is, when one type of energy tries to overpower the other, the different energies can't connect and they get out of balance very quickly. Friction occurs, tensions rise, and, if this is occurring between two individuals, you start to butt heads. Instead of slotting into each other nicely — click! — you repel each other like two magnets facing the wrong way. Spending too much time in this state is exhausting, not to mention can lead straight to "D Land" (Divorce Land). And it's even more exhausting when the imbalance is happening inside just *one* person!

Understanding the fundamental principle of polarity — that one energy cannot exist without the other, and that neither is "better" than the other — is imperative, because together these two halves make a sacred whole.

The ancient yin-yang symbol is a perfect representation of this — both halves intertwined, harmonious, and absolutely necessary. And if you look closely at the yin-yang symbol, you'll see that each half contains the potentiality of the other. For so long, one half of our material dynamic — the male — has dominated human behavior and relationships, and this is reflected in the imbalance in global energies. But just as men cannot exist without women, firm energy truly could not exist without the fluid, and both are stronger through the presence of the other. Without their complement, they'd be one-sided and weak. United — when they literally embrace their opposite — they form a divinely perfect whole.

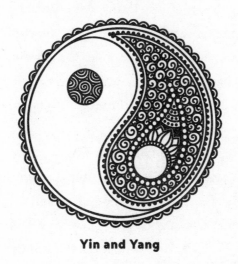

Yin and Yang

Creating Harmony between These Two Polarities

Of course, while the yin-yang symbol shows a geometrically perfect split between the two, real life is rarely so clean cut. Each of us embodies these energies in our own way at different times — some of us naturally lean toward one end of the spectrum, some the other, while some are squarely in the middle. These differences are part of what makes each of us unique ... and awesome!

But all of us contain *both* energies — no matter our gender. And *all of us* can sometimes let our energies get out of balance. It's important to note, though, that when we talk about "balanced" or "imbalanced" energies, we're not aiming for a precise fifty–fifty split. We're aiming to achieve divine harmony inside ourselves — whatever that might look like for you, taking into account your natural tendencies.

To understand how imbalance plays out, it can be helpful to see it in action. When firmness lacks fluidity, it becomes so driven as to be destructive. Think of a Wall Street CEO who has all the money, power, and possessions she could want, but no time to breathe and no family to love. Or a friend who's pushing themselves hard and is close to burnout, but can't give themselves permission to rest ... both of those are signs that the person is lacking fluidity within.

On the flipside, when fluidity lacks firmness, the structure of the energy is very scattered and unpredictable. (Imagine pouring water onto the surface of a table — it's bound to spill everywhere, as it's not contained, focused, or directed. There is no structure — that is, no firm container — in place to hold the fluid energy.) An example? Think of that friend who always has a million ideas, but nothing to show for them. Or that feeling when you really want to achieve your goals, but can't seem to stop watching Netflix ... That's when you know you may need to turn up that firm directional energy.

So we know what imbalance looks like ... but what about divine harmony?

Divine balance might look like someone who is absolutely kicking butt on their business goals ... while also enjoying a robust and fulfilling social life. Or someone who is creating their soul's work ... while also looking after themselves and their body. Or someone who lovingly fills their own cup ... while also devotedly looking after their kids and family.

Once you understand the fundamental qualities of both energies — including the natural strengths of each — you'll be better able to find your own perfect balance and create more powerfully from that fullness. Then, when you step into a relationship, you'll continue to hold the belief that you count. There will be no push or shove, no competition or invalidation. Neither will there be a winner and a loser, a better or worse, a right or a wrong. There is simply balance *between* the two of you and *within* yourself. And once balanced, you will recognize yourself and move forward, joyfully painting outside the lines with others who celebrate with you.

The Sacred Dance of Energies

Consciously and intentionally incorporating both energies into your life is a sacred dance that we can embody with either elegance or resistance. It's a conscious choice. *Your* choice!

There are times in my life when I need to call more on my firm energy. For example, when I'm in the middle of a business launch, changing a car tire, packing for a vacation, getting my stepson Leo organized for school, running team meetings, looking at profit-and-loss statements, about to walk out on stage, or listening to my husband chat about index funds and compound interest. This doesn't mean I can't still bring fluidity to those tasks. In fact, that's the goal! It simply means that for me personally, those activities require me to be more firm, so I call in more of that energy.

Then there are times when I need to soften and embrace my fluid energy. For example, when Leo comes to me crying after hurting himself, when my bestie breaks up with her boyfriend, when I'm holding a baby, when I'm with my parents, when I'm in the kitchen cooking, in yoga or dance class, while I'm meditating, painting, drawing, journaling, writing a love letter or thank-you card, when I'm taking a bath, or when I'm responding to an email that needs extra love and attention. I know deep in my bones that these times are the moments when calling on that divine fluid energy is very much needed.

The moral, of course, is that *both* energies are necessary and serve a purpose, and the best thing you can do is know when *you* need to call on one more than the other, and recognize when they are out of balance and act accordingly. This knowledge is as unique as the individual and there is no right or wrong. It requires you to tune inward and not compare yourself to anyone else because we are all so different. And let it be said, it's an incredibly valuable skill to master.

So, let's learn how to do that right now ...

INSPO-ACTION

- When do you notice you are more in your firm energy? For example, maybe at work or in boxing class?
- When do you notice you might need more of that firm energy? Maybe you need to be more assertive at work or with your boss?
- When do you notice you are most fluid? Maybe it's when you are tucking your kids into bed at night, when you're making love, or baking a cake?
- When do you notice you might need more fluidity and softness? Maybe you need to soften when your kids come to you with their homework, when your partner walks in the door, or when you're learning or trying something new?

- How are you orchestrating both of these energies to create the beautiful symphony that is your life? Are there any times when you require both of them in equal balance?

_____

_____

_____

_____

_____

_____

_____

_____

_____

_____

_____

_____

Dancing between the sacred energies is a skill that gets strengthened with use. Like the tango, the more you practice the smoother the transitions. Embrace both, embody both, play with both energies, and, most importantly? Have fun with it, because this plays out in ALL your relationships.

PSSST! WANT TO SEE FIRMNESS AND FLUIDITY IN ACTION?

It's one thing to read about these life-changing principles in a book ... It's another thing entirely to see them in action in a real-life relationship! That's why my husband and I have teamed up to create the **Open Wide Video Masterclass**: a free online workshop to help you to take these potent concepts *off* the page and bring them to life in your home, your relationship, and yes — even your bedroom.

Head to www.melissambrosini.com/openwide to watch now.

KEY TAKEAWAYS FROM CHAPTER ONE

- **THERE IS A DIVINE LIFE-FORCE THAT RUNS THROUGH EVERY LIVING THING.**

  It's the innate intelligence that beats our heart, sprouts a seed, and blooms a bud. And it's seeking communion, above all else. It wants to *know* itself. And because it's in everything — in all of us — it means that we too are seeking communion. Our natural state, as humans, is to be "in relationship" with others.

- **AN AWAKENING IS HAPPENING!**

  In the West, we are witnessing an energetic renaissance as people "remember" (because deep down, they've always known) the divine interplay between the masculine and the feminine. Change is possible, and it starts with us!

- **EVERY PERSON HAS FIRM AND FLUID ENERGY WITHIN THEM, REGARDLESS OF WHETHER THEY'RE MALE OR FEMALE.**

  Every relationship has both energies too, regardless of whether they're heterosexual or same-sex.

- **WHEN BOTH ENERGIES UNITE IN A DIVINE DANCE, CREATIVE MAGIC IS THE RESULT!**

  Remember the yin-yang symbol — each half honors the other, holds space for them to flourish, and will help unlock their full potential.

CHAPTER TWO

Unleashing Your Goddessence

When we speak of the divine feminine energy, which I call your "Goddessence," by no means is this something that applies only to women. As I mentioned in Chapter One, we *all* possess both masculine and feminine energy within us, regardless of gender or sexuality. Its presence is innate — it's part of you, it's always been there, and you couldn't get rid of it if you tried, sister (or brother)!

Goddessence is part of us all — men and women, boys and girls.

Your dad, grandfather, uncle, boyfriend, the guy you sat next to in high school English — ALL of them have feminine energy inside them, just as all the women in your life have masculine energy too. In Eastern traditions, the left side of the body is believed to correlate to the feminine and the right side the masculine. In yoga these energies are known as yin and yang or Shiva and Shakti.

This is of course not a new concept. It is, however, experiencing a re-emergence, an exciting rebirth back into the collective consciousness. Why? Because we need her! We need to tap into and reconnect with our Goddessence energy now more than ever! The world is craving her softness, grace, love, warmth, openness, intuition, light, strength, and leadership more than ever before.

To make sure we're on the same page here, let's talk definitions. Divine feminine or your Goddessence stems from a place of receiving, softness, being, allowing, listening, absorbing, and nurturing. She embodies full acceptance of all, which means no longer trying to fix, change, or improve others or oneself. She is relaxed yet resilient, sensitive yet strong, gentle yet firm, loving, and compassionate, and knows how to hold her boundaries. By contrast, she is *not* the energy of aggression, doing, fighting, or forcing.

For the millennia since the birth of the patriarchy, true Goddessence energy has been downplayed, demeaned, and removed from her place of honor and reverence ... which has caused a serious imbalance.

This is why, for most of us — male or female — our relationship with our innate Goddessence is ... well, kind of screwy. Right from birth, we've been programmed in a myriad of ways — some subtle, some overt — to believe that feminine energy and qualities are "less than," that we should embody as many of the masculine qualities as possible, and do our best to hide and diminish everything else. I distinctly remember crying as a young girl and my father demanding I pull my socks up and get on with it. "Big girls don't cry," he would say. That may be why many of us have some healing to do on our relationship with our divine feminine.

Before we go any further, let's get one thing straight: this isn't about dissing men, or promoting the idea that women are superior, better than, stronger, or taking over … Not at all! **This is about rebalancing the divine feminine and the divine masculine and reconnecting with your Goddessence so that we can consciously create TOGETHER as individuals, and collectively as a whole in this modern world.**

Goddessence lives in each of us already, but due to the repression she has been experiencing for so long, it takes healing at an individual level for a woman to reignite this power inside herself.

So are you ready to come on the journey? Are you ready for some deep soul nourishment to unleash your divine feminine and balance your divine masculine? It's time to ignite the powerhouse goddess inside you that has been waiting for the chance to shine.

Let's do it, beautiful!

One of the most powerful ways to reconnect with your Goddessence is by consciously embodying one of her archetypes.

What's an archetype? Essentially, it's an idea, theme, or motif that is so deeply embedded in our collective psyche that we all relate to it without even thinking. These universal themes are so powerful, they transcend time, culture, gender, everything. If you've ever read a fairy tale and encountered a "gallant knight" or a "wicked witch" or a "damsel in distress," then you've experienced the power of an archetype before — instinctively, we know the essence of those characters, without even being told. (Though it must be said, many of the feminine archetypes in fairy tales aren't exactly empowering!)

Thankfully, there are plenty of archetypes that *are* empowering. By figuratively "stepping into the shoes" of these different figures, you can start experiencing and strengthening different aspects of your feminine self and observing how the different character traits *feel* in your body. Though there are many archetypes present in the psyche, the following six are my favorites.

The Six Archetypes

THE WARRIORESS

Due to the dominant patriarchal culture, the Warrioress has been the least understood and represented archetype. Think Wonder Woman, Pocahontas, Joan of Arc, and Buffy the Vampire Slayer. She is strong yet remains warm and will stand up for what she truly believes in. She is clear, selfless, humble, directional, courageous, and decisive — particularly with respect to her role in serving others.

I call on this archetype when I'm about to walk out on stage and want to feel grounded and confident. I also channel her when I want to feel collaborative, compassionate, and not competitive. The Warrioress treats all with love and respect, and makes you feel safe and calm in her presence.

You may like to call on her when you're about to give a presentation at work or need to address someone about a challenging situation.

THE LOVER

The Lover archetype is a blend of sex and spirit. Think Aphrodite, Mary Magdalene, Shakespeare's Juliet, and Belle from *Beauty and the Beast*. She is passionate, creative, ecstatic, and exquisitely engaged in life. She desires all forms of sensory contact and basks in the beauty and joy of life.

I call on her not only when I want to feel sensual and sexy, but when I need to play and want to express myself freely.

You might like to call on her when you're wrapped in the arms of your honey. Or when you want to play or come back to the present moment via some form of creative expression.

THE GODDESS

She is the domain of spirituality, mystical experience, and intuition. Think Athena (Greek goddess of strength and clear thinking), Diana (Roman goddess of nature and hunting), Branwen (Celtic goddess of love and beauty), Freya (Norse goddess of love, sex, beauty, and fertility), Tara (Tibetan goddess of compassion), Kali (Hindu goddess of time, creation, destruction, and power), and Turan (Etruscan goddess of love, health, and fertility). She is the Creatrix, intrinsically desiring newness, and actively seeking out fresh experiences, possibilities, and connections out of stagnation.

She is my favorite archetype to embody. I call on her daily because she is bursting with energy, wisdom, and creativity. When you are in the presence of someone fully expressing their Goddess archetype you feel it, and can't help but want to soak up some of their inspired energy, groundedness, love, drive, and wisdom — it's contagious.

You might like to call on her when you want to feel energetic or express yourself creatively.

THE QUEEN/MOTHER

The Mother is the strongest of the archetypes. Think Mary, Cleopatra, and Euripides's Medea, or if we look to contemporary culture, Daenerys Targaryen in *Game of Thrones* and Miranda Bailey in *Grey's Anatomy*. Perhaps the best known embodiment, however, is Mother Nature — maternal creator and nurturer of earth and all its inhabitants. And although she is the giver of life and the Queen of the castle, she is also the one who can at times get the most overwhelmed with her role, which is as the authority and stewardess of the home and family.

I not only call on her when I'm nurturing and mothering Leo, my friends' children, and the elderly, but also when I want to birth ideas or products into the world. Because just as the Goddess archetype is the Creatrix (inspiring vision and imagination), the Queen is the one who gives birth to the creation then actively looks to its growth and prospering.

You might like to call on her when you're caring for your loved ones or when you're about to send a new project out into the world.

THE WISE WOMAN

This much-misunderstood archetype is often labelled a "witch" by the patriarchy and is feared for her abilities. The Wise Man is very common (think Dumbledore, Gandalf, Obi-Wan Kenobi), but the Wise Woman trope is frequently distorted to only show her shadow side (like the Evil Queen in *Snow White*, Maleficent in *Sleeping Beauty*, and Ursula in *The Little Mermaid*).

But rather than being a tool for evil, her wisdom is actually a powerful force for transformation, healing, and growth.

She advocates "right action" (also known as dharma in the yogi world) and is notorious for observing without judgment. I call on her in heated moments when I need to be the observer in a situation. It can feel challenging at times to not react, so it takes awareness and consciousness to sit as the Wise Women and just observe. This is often when new possibilities are revealed to us, possibilities we may not have noticed had we not been the observer.

THE PRIESTESS

The Priestess is the domain of intuitive awareness and insight. Think Pythia (priestess of Apollo's temple at Delphi, known for her prophecies) and Ishkhara (priestess of Ishtar and Babylonian goddess of love). She is intentional and reflective, having great depth to her presence and intellect. She is the connector between the material and spiritual words, and knows how to dance elegantly between the two. She understands that the inner and outer worlds are reflections of each other, and she doesn't let them rock her from her grounded presence, because she knows there is something bigger at play. She knows deep down everything is unfolding exactly the way it's meant to, so I personally call on her when I need to remember that, and I aim to bring grace to those times, just as she would. You can call on her when you feel your boat is a little rocked and you need to channel some ease and grace.

INSPO-ACTION

- Is there a particular archetype that resonates with you right now?
- Which of her qualities do you feel most attracted to?
- How could you embody more of her essence in your life?
- Is there a particular area of your life where you especially need to call on her?

_____

_____

_____

_____

_____

_____

_____

_____

_____

_____

_____

_____

_____

_____

_____

_____

At different times you may connect with one goddess in particular, or perhaps a blend of two or three. Look closely at the qualities you want to cultivate more of, then see how you can call on and embody the corresponding archetypes for different periods in your daily life.

One of my favorite ways to embody a particular archetype is to choose a personal talisman that represents her. For example, I have many long flowy skirts that, to me, have always symbolized the Goddess. If I want to draw on that power and essence, I'll wear one of those skirts.

I also have a big, heavy wooden necklace that immediately makes me feel like Cleopatra, or some sort of tribal queen! When I want to feel especially Queen-like, I'll pop this necklace on and I'm instantly reminded of my sovereign power.

Of course, there are plenty of other ways to spark up your divine Goddessence …

How to Unlock, Embrace, and Nurture Your Goddessence

There are many ways to unlock, embrace, and nurture your Goddessence, but here are some of my favorites ...

MASTER YOUR MEAN GIRL

As I mentioned at the start of the book, your Mean Girl is that little voice inside your head that lives in a constant state of fear. Some people call it your ego, your shadow self, your smaller self, your dark side, your inner critic, maybe even a name like Frank, Bob, or Mary. I call that voice my inner Mean Girl (and for the sake of simplicity throughout this book, I will refer to it as my Mean Girl). What do you call yours? The actual name you give this voice isn't important, but the act of giving it a name is! This is because it reminds you that that voice is NOT the Truth of who you are. **You are pure LOVE!** And when you give it a name, it helps you remember that you are not that limiting voice.

The thing is, we all have that fear-based voice inside our head: no one is exempt from this. But we are ALL also love. And although you may think some people don't or aren't love and only have a dark side, this is not the case. We all have both, and your inner Goddessence knows that and embraces both the light and dark.

There is a front and a back, light and dark, to everything.

Just in case you're not clear, your fear-based Mean Girl voice says things like ...

You're not good enough.

You're not pretty enough.

You're not smart enough.

That won't happen to you.

You'll never get out of debt.

You won't find your soulmate.

You're going to be alone forever.

You'll never heal.

Get over yourself.

Financial freedom doesn't happen for people like you.

Give up before you humiliate yourself.

Who do you think you are?

You're not worthy of XYZ.

She's prettier, skinnier, and more worthy of XYZ than you.

Sound familiar? Don't worry. Mine used to say a lot worse than this …

Where most people fall short is they think that they ARE those thoughts and they believe them to be true. But this is not the case. You are NOT those thoughts and they are not who you are.

This doesn't mean we suppress any feelings and emotions when they arise, oh no! The divine feminine knows how to use them to her advantage to support her growth and evolution … even if they seem totally "negative." When she is triggered by something or someone (resulting in one of those fear-based Mean Girl statements popping up) she masters her by following my three-step mastering your Mean Girl process.

Step one: Practice awareness

Become aware when your Mean Girl pops up and tells you, *You're not good enough, pretty enough, thin enough, smart enough, earning enough, sexy enough, whatever enough.* For most people, these sorts of fear-based beliefs pop up the nanosecond they are in their Truth. Yet we're usually so unconscious and not present that we're not even aware of this internal dialogue, so we can't do anything about it. That's why bringing your awareness to her and what she is saying is the first step.

Step two: Gently close the door on her

Once you're aware that she has popped up, you can now choose to gently close the door on her. It's not about fighting her, or waging an inner battle — that'll just cause more pain and suffering. Instead, it's a gentle, grateful act that comes from a place of love. Think of her like an annoying salesperson who comes knocking on your door. You don't invite them in for a cup of tea and let them give you their forty-five-minute spiel about a product you don't want. You would simply say, "Thank you, but no thank you — I'm not interested." Simple!

Step three: Choose love instead

Once you have gently closed the door on her, choose to come back to your heart and choose love instead of fear. It's so much more fulfilling when you do. Do this every time your Mean Girl pops up and you will be well on your way to mastering her. It's important to note that like everything, the more you practice the easier it gets. Deepak Chopra says women have roughly between sixty and eighty thousand thoughts per day, so that's potentially eighty thousand times you can practice mastering your Mean Girl in one day. Do it every time and you'll soon become an expert.

Light and dark. Love and fear. That polarity must exist, and the divine feminine can see when she is heading toward the dark and knows how to return to the light as quickly as possible. She does that through coming back to the present moment, the only moment we have.

INSPO-ACTION

Write down absolutely everything your Mean Girl is currently saying to you. Then I want you to turn each of those statements into light. For example, if your Mean Girl is saying, *Financial freedom doesn't happen for people like me*, you can turn that into, *I am abundant, generous, and financially free; money is a source of happiness for me.* Or if your Mean Girl is saying, *You're not pretty and skinny enough to call in your soulmate*, you can transform it into, *I am whole, complete, beautiful, and love myself unconditionally; I feel this deep in my heart and so will my soulmate.* Or if she is saying, *You will never heal*, you could turn it around to, *I am healthy and strong and glow from the inside out.*

We're going to go into a whole lot more detail on how to master your Mean Girl in the next chapter, but for now, this soul-fuelled flip from dark to light will help you steer yourself toward love (your true nature) and put your Mean Girl in her place.

_____

_____

_____

_____

_____

_____

CREATE SACRED PRACTICES/RITUALS

Since I embarked on my quest for truth, I've read a lot of books, studied the great leaders, and attended more personal development workshops than you can poke an organic cinnamon stick at. I became fascinated with spiritual teachers such as Eckhart Tolle, Gandhi, Oprah, Louise Hay, Marianne Williamson, Buddha, Tony Robbins, Nelson Mandela, Deepak Chopra, and many more. And what I discovered was that all these "successful" people had daily rituals and practices they performed that allowed them to connect to their Truth. Eckhart Tolle, for example, meditates every day. Tony Robbins has an elaborate morning ritual that includes breathwork, bouncing on a rebounder, and cold therapy. Deepak Chopra uses affirmations and mantras every single day.

Seeing how many successful people used rituals in their life, I thought I would be my own human guinea pig and give some of them a go. So as the over-achiever I am, I meditated, chanted, journaled, did morning pages, sang, saluted the sun, downward dogged, sun gazed, oil pulled, scraped my tongue, did coffee enemas, did water, garlic, oregano, and probiotic retention enemas, pulled angel cards, danced nude, took cleansing baths, read spiritual texts, saged myself, cleansed my aura, did breathwork, prayed, wrote out my fears then burnt them, sat at my altar and prayed, rebounded, dry body brushed ... and all before nine a.m.! And you know what? It's all great and it felt freaking awesome. BUT ... I am not saying you have do all that, absolutely not. You don't even need to do nine-tenths of it. And let's face it, I work from home and don't have four kids so time allowed me to do all those things, but not everyone has as much time.

As a starting point, you could simply close your eyes, breathe deeply, and sit for one minute. That's it! To be honest, it doesn't matter what you do, as long as it brings you a deep level of connection with your true higher self, love, consciousness, spirit, your heart, your soul (whatever you want to call it), and allows you to honor that we are all a part of something far greater than ourselves.

SACRED PRACTICE MENU

- Create an epic playlist and dance to it while nude and alone in your bedroom or in your sexiest lingerie.
- Sing like nobody's listening.
- Meditate.
- Be still.
- Walk barefoot in nature — preferably without your phone.
- Write poetry.
- Sip herbal tea in the sunshine.
- Play with your Jade Egg (more on that later).
- File your nails.
- Give yourself an organic homemade face scrub or mask.
- Paint, draw, create "art" (whatever that means for you).
- Play with angel cards.
- Pray.
- Take breaks throughout your day to just sit and be.
- Slow down with everything you do.
- Set an intention for the day or before you to go sleep at night.
- Journal or do morning pages.

- Diffuse some organic essential oils and spend quiet time alone.
- Dry body brush your entire body, while repeating "thank you" or "I love you" out loud.
- Take a goddess bath with Epsom salts, essential oils, and rose petals.
- Make your own essential oils self-care products such as oil perfume blends, rollers, and massage balls.
- Light a beeswax candle and give yourself a goddess massage using organic coconut oil.
- Move your body by stretching or doing yoga.
- Create your own sacred altar with candles, flowers, crystals, affirmations, your vision board, meaningful symbols, and angel cards. Kneel before it each morning and set an intention for the day.
- Do pranayama or any other cleansing breathwork.
- Invoke goddess archetypes.
- Go for an aura cleanse bath (a.k.a. a dive in the ocean!).
- Connect with Mother Earth by hugging a tree, staring at the sky, or feeling your feet on the grass or sand.

Sacred practices work best when you consciously carve out time in your day to slow down and replenish yourself. So if you can add little pockets throughout your day, please do. And just as with everything else, remember that what's right for someone else may not be right for you. Your friend might LOVE coffee enemas, whereas you'd rather let nothing near your bum except toilet paper! That's totally okay: you do you. As long as you choose something that awakens your femininity, fuels your heart and soul, and feels divine to you, you're on the right track.

UNDERSTAND CYCLES

Women are cyclical beings and when you tune in to the natural cycles of life — and especially your own menstrual cycle — not only will you get a deeper understanding of yourself (and your body) but you will strengthen your connection to your divine Goddessence.

I'm the living, breathing proof of this. It wasn't until I stopped hating my body (and my period) and deeply connected to my own internal rhythm that I was able to unlock a neglected part of my creativity, strengthen my intuition, flex my self-love muscle, and experience true wellness, self-awareness, and soulful sex.

Unfortunately, my "period story" is not that unusual. From eighteen to twenty-four, I was on the pill, which completely numbed any connection I felt to my body or my cycle. I went on the pill at eighteen because I didn't want to become pregnant, and to clear up my skin. I skipped periods too many times, because I thought that bleeding during a holiday, a party, or an audition was totally not okay. I also thought that experiencing PMS, cramps, vomiting, diarrhea and fainting were "normal." I responded to these symptoms with the strongest painkillers I could find, numbing myself at every opportunity. I thought pads were gross, so I would shove toxic tampons full of bleach and chemical-laden cotton (which is what ninety-nine percent of tampons are made of) up my vagina and leave them in all day, and even sleep with them in overnight... All because I had so much shame over one of the most natural and beautiful things our bodies do.

When I finally discovered the repercussions of being on the pill and what it was doing to me, I decided to stop taking it, assuming everything would instantly right itself. Um, no! I didn't get my period again for almost two years. According to my friend Dr. Nat Kringoudis (a natural fertility expert), "The pill takes your hormones offline. It can numb you, making you feel detached from your own body." Once I heard this information, I made it my mission to get my absent period back naturally, and to chart my cycle, and I made a promise to myself to honor my body as the temple and incredible giver of life that it is. This didn't happen overnight. It was a journey, and one that I'm still on. But holy Shakti has it been a worthwhile ride! Connecting with my internal cycle has been life changing and has allowed me to fully embrace who I am and what it means to be a woman. It has been truly profound. If only this taboo topic was talked about in schools!

Before I understood the magic of menstruation, I thought we ladies were linear. Like, you were either bleeding or not, and that was it — on or off, like a light switch. I didn't understand that our cycles are complex, and that our body, mood, metabolism, and hormones fluctuate throughout the month.

There is a ton of science-y information out there about how our hormones go up and down like a rollercoaster through the menstrual cycle, but for me, it was reading so many great books that talk about the different phases we go through as "seasons" that finally made everything click.

What do I mean by "seasons"? Well, just as the natural world has seasons (summer, autumn, winter, and spring), so does our body go through similar phases each month.

We kick off with menstruation (when you're actually bleeding), which falls on approximately days one to six of your cycle. This is known as your "winter." It's a fluid phase, and, just like the winter in nature, this is your time to go inward and "hibernate" if you can. You may feel very low in energy as your body undertakes the mammoth task of releasing the previous cycle through your blood. This is essentially a "dying" phase, as we shed what is no longer serving us before we are reborn again. Unlike "summer," this phase is about your relationship with yourself and is a great time for self-reflection, to slow down, switch off social media, to say "No, thank you" to invites, turn off your phone and emails, and to rest and recharge as much as possible. Your hormones are at rock bottom here, so this is the time to really up the self-love and self-care. Journal, rest, don't set an alarm, and let your body wake when it wants to if you can, connect with Mother Nature by lying belly to belly on the earth, eat hearty slow-cooked warming foods, sip raspberry leaf tea, curl up with a good book, use heat packs, and up your magnesium — especially in the first two days. If you work for yourself, give yourself permission to take your first day (or two) days off if you can. If you work for someone else, why not Open Wide and lovingly express to your boss how you feel on your first day and ask if you can work from home that day? It may not be possible but at least you asked. The UK social community group Coexist created a "period policy" that allows women to take time off during their cycles. Japan has offered menstrual leave policies for decades, and recently Italy was the first European country to introduce this policy too. This is very exciting.

You can also tell your partner, friends, and kids you are in your winter so they know to give you a little more space and to be a little gentler with you. Maybe your partner or roommate can cook for you, or they could go out so you can relish your alone time.

I used to hate bleeding and considered it a massive inconvenience to my social calendar because I couldn't go full steam ahead — bleeding got in my way of doing and achieving, or so I told myself. I now *love* the winter phase. I allow myself to stay in bed on my first day. I go inward, grab my heat pack, and journal. I mostly use reusable organic cotton Red Moon pads or a JuJu cup. These products are great, especially if you work from home. I know some women who wear reusable organic moon pads to their office on their lighter days, but when I'm out and about I prefer my JuJu cup or organic tampons. To be honest I rarely use tampons, as most are full of toxic chemicals. I will also always aim to use my pads over my JuJu cup as I feel it can limit my natural flow and connection with my cycle, and I believe we are meant to be letting the blood flow out, not keeping it in. I also put my legs up the wall, rest, watch *Sex and the City,* and sip herbal tea. I practice Crystal Clear Communication (CCC) with Nick and Leo, letting them know that I need some space, and politely and with love ask them to honor that. I give myself permission to just be. Your winter is about introspection, which is why it's important to have some time to yourself. You become an open source of wisdom as you shed, so it can be an especially powerful time to ask yourself questions like, *What needs to be let go of? What needs to be released and purged? And what needs shedding?*

CRYSTAL CLEAR COMMUNICATION OVERVIEW

CCC is the best relationship tool for your tool kit. CCC is about speaking from your heart (not your head), being fully present with the person in front of you, and listening with both ears. It's about Opening Wide and speaking your Truth honestly and crystal clearly.

After you have fully allowed yourself to rest and you're feeling a little more energy return, you can start to set your intention for the coming month. This is a great time to get clear on what you want to create in the weeks ahead. But don't go gung-ho just yet! All you're doing is getting clear and setting intentions for what you want to manifest. The energy and space you hold in your winter will set the intention you carry forth, so make it count. But winter is *not* a time for doing and go, go, go; it's a time to *be*, rest and restore.

Of course you may have to work and/or be responsible for family duties, and you may not be able to take the whole first day of your winter as a rest day. BUT … all it takes is a few minutes. Get up before everyone else and simply sit and breathe. Ask your partner or a friend to take the kids outside after school so you can do ten minutes of yin yoga, or get everyone into bed earlier so you can take a bath. Think creatively here about how you can make it happen, communicate it with your family, and then take action. The weeks we have Leo, I move things around in my calendar so I make sure self-care is still at the top of my to-do list. If it's not and I let it slip, I'm not a very nice human to be around … and no one deserves that.

Our "spring" phase is approximately days six to thirteen in our cycle, and it's when we are pre-ovulatory (or possibly ovulating, if you're an early ovulator). This is a very yang phase and you may feel a surge of firm energy. This is the time to take massive action on your dreams and goals. Working out logical problems can feel like a breeze as you re-emerge into the world after your winter feeling renewed, refreshed, and with a spring in your step. Your energy is up and you may even feel trim, lean, and light. This is the time to get back into exercise, start new projects, launch a program, try something new or spring clean your house. But remember, this isn't summer yet — so still be gentle with yourself and don't go full steam ahead all at once, or you run the risk of driving yourself into the ground.

Our "summer" (approximately days fourteen to twenty-one) is when ovulation and post-ovulation take place, and you may feel more energized and ready to tackle big tasks and goals. This too is a very yang phase and a time we may feel more playful, social, and extroverted. The summer phase is all about relationships with others, so this is a great time to host dinner parties, give that presentation at work, go on vacation, catch up with your besties, do your workshop, and be around others. You may also find you have more energy to exercise, lift heavier weights at the gym, and go the extra mile (literally and figuratively!). You may also be more tolerant and patient, which is great if you have kids.

The next phase is your "autumn" (approximately days twenty-two to twenty-eight), when you are post-ovulation and premenstrual. Just as the leaves drop off the trees, your hormones drop too. Unlike summer — when we feel social and extroverted and ready to launch big projects into the world — autumn is more about taking stock of what did and didn't work that month and in our life. It's about telling the truth, getting real, and letting go of anything that is no longer serving you. You are preparing for your monthly release, so anything you've been hiding from can show up. There is a very "keep or destroy" energy in the premenstrual phase, and you can feel less tolerant than in your summer. You may want to say "No, thank you" to things that require you to be more extroverted, like a presentation at work, dinner parties, events, or birthdays.

Of course, sometimes this may not be possible and you don't have the option to decline. And for women with irregular cycles (which is many of us!) trying to organize future events around your moon can be tricky. The best thing you can do if you find yourself in your winter and having to engage in tasks that you don't feel like doing is to make sure you give yourself loads of extra self-love. Up your self-care and be kind and gentle with yourself. This always helps me.

Connecting with your own body's natural rhythm is one of the most precious gifts you can give yourself and teach your daughter/s. Your true self embraces all of the phases of her cycle and is in awe of the capability of her temple.

CYCLE RECAP
- Winter (menstruation, yin) — Time to reflect on the past month, let go, and Open Wide to receiving clarity. Also a great time to start planning, setting goals and intentions for the spring.
- Spring (pre-ovulation, yang) — This season is all about implementation and taking inspired action.
- Summer (ovulation, yang) — Time to take serious action and bring your dreams to fruition.
- Autumn (post-ovulation/premenstrual, yin) — Time for introspection, to edit, and refine. Ask yourself what worked and what is no longer serving you.

GOING DEEPER ... CONNECTING YOUR CYCLE WITH THE MOON PHASES

Did you know that the word "menstruation" is derived from the Latin word for "month," which itself also means "moon"? And it's no mistake that the lunar cycle and our menstrual cycles are both on average 28 days long. Of course, this varies from woman to woman — and even in the one individual might not be the same from month to month — so please don't beat yourself up if your cycle is longer or shorter than this, or if you vary widely each cycle. My average cycle is thirty days, but can be anywhere from twenty-seven to thirty-seven days. Your cycle is affected by your environment; things like stress, sleep, your diet, alcohol, medication, travel, hormone disorders like PCOS, illness, and even exercise will all have an impact. But once you know yourself intimately and understand your body on a deeper level, you'll be able to embrace and flow *with* your cycle — no matter what it is — and pivot accordingly.

INSPO-ACTION

The best way to become more connected to your cycle — and ultimately, your divine feminine — is by charting your cycle. You can do this manually in your diary, or by using an app like I do. Some great apps are Period Tracker, Clue, Natural Cycles, The Daisy, Kindara, and M Cycles. I'm sure there are plenty of other great ones too, so have a little search and pick the one you like best. I personally love and use Period Tracker, and really find joy in connecting with my body and charting my cycle. You can make notes about anything — the foods you're craving, any relationship conflict, what's working, what's not working, and soon you will start to see patterns (or cycles) more clearly. You will see when you feel more sensual, when you're more intuitive, and when you're most likely to be a bit short or even snappy. Once you've chosen your preferred method of charting, get started today and enjoy becoming deeply in tune with yourself.

What's the moon got to do with this?

When you know where you are in your cycle and what the moon is doing at the same time, you're more deeply attuned with yourself, which is only going to benefit you and those around you.

Some women like to consciously sync their own cycle with specific phases of the moon, to enhance their monthly experience and connect deeper with the cycles of nature. If you'd like to experiment with this, try to stay away from artificial light and bask in as much moonlight as possible (ideally, bathing in the moon's glow while you sleep). But do keep in mind that women can ovulate at all different phases and all are okay! There is no right or wrong, and I want this information to empower you ... not give your Mean Girl extra ammunition. Take this information, but please don't be hard on yourself if you don't bleed on the new moon! It's okay, my sweet friend, and no — you are not broken! I'm simply giving you this information because knowledge is key. **Knowledge is power.** The more equipped you are, the better you understand yourself and others.

WAXING MOON PHASE

This phase of the moon represents newness — new beginnings, new growth, new sparks of insight. Ideas are being planted, cogs are turning, and exciting experiences are within reach.

As far as your menstrual cycle goes, the waxing moon is a time to go inward, nourish yourself, and spend time thinking, learning, reading, journaling, setting intentions, and making new plans.

FULL MOON PHASE

This phase represents power. This is the time to own your strength, make decisions, and bring something into being. For your menstrual cycle, this means it's a great time to focus outward. Put your extra energy to use by celebrating, feasting, and gathering with your tribe. If ever you're going to dance the night away, or make crazy-fast progress on a project, this is the phase to do it. (Full moon party, anyone?!)

THE WANING PHASE

The waning of the moon represents maturity and harvest. It's a time for buckling down and doing the work. If you want those seeds you've sown to bloom into life, this is the phase where your efforts can make that a reality. Your menstrual phase is (again) outwardly focused. The harvest is within your reach. Do practice patience and persistence until it's ready to be reaped.

INSPO-ACTION

According to the lunar cycle, where do you currently menstruate? Start to add this information to your charting diary or app and become aware of how you feel at different phases of the moon cycle and your own cycle. And remember, knowledge is key. Resist the urge to compare or judge yourself. All you are doing is empowering yourself with ample information to understand your sexy self better!

THE NEW MOON PHASE

The new moon represents darkness. Just as the moon disappears from sight, so must the things that are not serving you disappear from your life, to be replaced by that which you actually desire. With its strong theme of shedding, releasing, and renewal, many women consider this the ideal time to bleed. You may feel sensitive, so going inward is imperative. Any emotional detritus that surfaces should be dealt with and let go.

CONNECT WITH NATURE

Mother Earth — the goddess of all goddesses, the mother of all mothers — is the greatest healer of all time and mother to us all. She sparks creativity, soothes our nervous system, reconnects us to our soul, brings us back to the present moment, and can even freshen our perspective.

Have you ever had headaches, felt agitated, had a low attention span, or a restless night after spending too much time indoors in front of your devices? Maybe you just brushed it off, but it's the lack of negative ions. Professor of anatomy Marian Diamond from UC Berkeley has found that levels of negative ions are inversely related to levels of serotonin in the brain. Negative ions suppress serotonin levels in much the same way that natural sunlight suppresses melatonin. Hence the invigorating effect of fresh air and sunshine and the correspondingly depressed feelings associated with being in a closed in and dark space for too long.

What are ions? Ions are charged particles, and they can be charged negatively or positively. One type of negative ions — which are the type found abundantly in nature — is oxygen ions with two extra electrons attached, and is commonly produced from water molecules. There are approximately thirty to one hundred thousand negative ions per cubic centimeter in the air near a waterfall. Compare that to a stuffy, locked-up car, home, or office which, at best, can contain zero to a few hundred negative ions per cubic centimeter. Quite the difference, right? This lack of negative ions can in some people lead to skin conditions such as eczema, psoriasis, rashes, and itchy eyes, and can also leave you feeling parched.

My client Gabby came to me with what she thought was postnatal depression, and with eczema all over her hands and face. She had recently given birth to her second child and was desperate to feel like herself again. She told me that most days, she kept herself and her bub cooped up inside the house — windows closed, air conditioning on, and blinds shut, so as to stop anyone seeing in. No wonder she was feeling a little crazy: she had created a prison for herself! So I gave her the simple task of letting in fresh air and sunlight daily and making sure she got outside for a walk with her bub twice a day. After two weeks of doing this, she couldn't believe how much happier and more alive she felt — not to mention her eczema had started to heal as well … a pretty sweet outcome from such a simple solution!

Some scientists say negative ions increase the serotonin levels in the brain without any of the crazy side effects that can accompany prescription anti-depressants. So remember when your grandma used to tell you to get outside for some fresh air? Turns out she was right on the money. (Go, Grandma!)

WAYS TO CONNECT WITH MOTHER
NATURE OUTDOORS

- Get outside as much as possible. Eat your meals outside in your backyard with your feet on the grass, or on your balcony, if you can.
- Take your shoes off and walk on the grass or beach.
- Dive in the ocean, or swim in a lake, river, or waterfall. There are so many beneficial reasons to get your booty in the ocean: it boosts your immune system, provides relief from skin conditions (such as eczema, acne, psoriasis, and rashes), is awesome for your circulatory and respiratory systems, can ease aches and pains, serves you up a hefty dose of minerals (like magnesium, sodium, potassium, and calcium – all of which can be absorbed through your skin), helps eliminate toxins ... and it makes you feel fan-fricking-tastic! You can even experience some of these benefits just by breathing in the ocean air!
- Hike in the bush.
- Hug a tree.
- Get out of the gym and work out outside in the fresh air by the beach or in a park.
- Have a walking meeting instead of sitting down in a stuffy boardroom with no windows.
- Catch up with your besties for a walk or a swim at the beach instead of sitting in a cafe and drinking lattes you don't really need.
- Stop driving or taking public transportation and walk or ride your bike to work if you can. Not only will you reap the benefits, but you'll save loads of cashola too.

- Go camping. Instead of booking a hotel for your next weekend trip, head to a campsite. Not only will you have a ball, but it's much cheaper too.
- Walk your dog. Don't have one? Walk someone else's! So many animals are cooped up inside all day, which can cause depression in doggies. (Yes, this is a thing!) So do your pooch and yourself a favor by getting outdoors together.
- Take your kids to the park daily.
- Instead of "wining and dining" business associates, take them on a fun adventure, like stand-up paddle boarding or kayaking.
- Work on your laptop in the park.
- Meditate outside in your backyard or on your balcony.

WAYS TO BRING MOTHER NATURE INTO YOUR HOME AND OFFICE

- Open your windows daily to let out toxins and let in fresh air.
- Let in the sunshine! It will help regulate and balance your hormones and your body's natural melatonin response.
- Go outside and feel the sunshine on your skin for two minutes first thing in the morning to regulate your circadian rhythm and tell your body (and hormones) it's time to wake up.
- Let in the moonlight. If you don't have street lights right outside your window, you can sleep with your curtains open and get that beautiful healing moonlight on your skin. (As an added bonus, this can help sync your menstrual cycle with the moon cycle.)

- Turn off your bright blue lights and use Himalayan salt lamps. These babies release negative ions, and give off a beautiful soft glow to boot.
- Get yourself an air ionizer to clean the air you breathe.
- Get some indoor plants. A NASA study found that peace lilies, gerberas, and bamboo palms are the best plants for removing air toxins and generating negative ions.
- Change your lights to amber-toned bulbs, not fluorescent blue ones. Blue artificial light (which is very high in positive ions) stimulates cortisol and tells your body it's time to wake up ... which is not what you want when you're trying to wind down in the evening! Also, scientist Dr John Ott – a specialist in attention deficit disorder – found that fluorescent blue lighting is linked with poor behavior in school children.
- Turn off your wifi at night and whenever you're not using it. Better yet, quit using wifi altogether if you can and plug into the wall via ethernet.
- Ditch all the toxic cleaning and beauty products in your home. These can be full of nasty chemicals and toxins that wreak havoc on your health and are just another thing you have to detox out of the air and your system. Save yourself the hassle and don't touch them in the first place.

You can see that too much time spent indoors in front of your devices is physically not good for your body and mind. But it's also not good for your soul. When we deny ourselves connection to Mother Nature, we deny an inherent part of our true nature.

INSPO-ACTION

Start with the two previous lists, add some of your own ideas, then write (or type) out your very own "Nature Menus." Stick them on your fridge and commit to doing one thing from each list per day. You can also get your family involved by letting your kids pick what they want to do, then work out when you are going to do it — maybe first thing in the morning or right after lunch or the school pick-up. Find a time that works for you and add "Nature Time" to your calendar. If you don't do it now, it won't happen ... so go ahead and add it to your calendar right NOW.

INTEGRATE REST

As women, we play many archetypal roles and wear many hats — wife, mother, partner, boss, business owner, stepmother, team member, sister, daughter, bestie, friend, aunt, godmother, carer ... just to name a few. And the thing is, we want to be good — scratch that, we want to be great — at all of them. But at times, it can feel like we are being pulled and pushed in many different directions, which can disconnect us from our true Goddessence.

With so many hats, roles, and responsibilities, it can make us feel like we are always "on." Don't get me wrong ... all that striving, achieving, and doing is imperative for getting stuff done. But it can make you more firm and less fluid, and you need rest, rejuvenation, and to recharge daily (not just on #selfcaresunday), otherwise you will burn out.

If you suspect you might not be doing the best job of switching off, don't worry — you're so not alone, sister! When I first officially became a stepmama, I wanted to do a really great job. In fact, I wanted to be the best damn stepmama I could be. But that feeling of always being "on" exhausted the heck out of me and burnt out my adrenal glands. "No rest for the wicked" was my motto, along with "go go go." We have Leo fifty per cent of the time — one week on, one week off — so of course, for the "Leo weeks" I wanted him to have the best, happiest, most amazing, fun time with us … but holy Zeus, did all that "trying" and orchestrating wear me down! I was so tired with all the adventures, so overwhelmed with getting him from one play date to the next, and so stressed worrying that he wasn't having "The Best Time Ever" that I wasn't MY best self. I was the cranky, shitty, tired, stressed-out version of me, which resulted in me having a very short fuse with Leo, Nick, and myself. So all my hard work to create a beautiful time for Leo was being undone. I soon realized that in order for me to show up fully for my family, I needed to rest, rejuvenate, and recharge daily — not just on the weeks we don't have Leo, but daily! Once I started incorporating some rest into the days when we had him, everything shifted and I was a much nicer person to be around. (Just ask the boys!)

In our modern-day society, there is a strong emphasis on the DOing instead of the BEing, but that's not how we humans are wired and it's not how we've evolved. Back when we were hunter-gatherers, there would have been a lot more time for rest, rejuvenation, and recharging (which I call "RRR"). Just think — there would have been songs and dancing around the campfire, days spent lazing in the shade of a tree, even entire weeks spent hunkering down in a cave, riding out the wet season. These "off" times are part of our nature, yet in our modern, always connected, fast-paced world, we disregard that side of ourselves completely and push super hard in the opposite direction all year long. We manage one vacation per year (if that) and either side of that we push, push, push. But our soul needs and craves regular RRR.

RRR looks different for everyone. It doesn't mean you have to take two hours out in the afternoon to have a nap (or spend a week in a cave!), but if you wish to, and can, please go for it. You could simply take three minutes to do some deep belly breaths, have a cup of tea outside, or even just sit in the sun and — wait for it — *do nothing*. (How's that for a novel idea?!) You could meditate, take a nap, rest on your bed, look out the window, have a bath, lie on the grass, look up at the clouds, or do some mindful coloring or painting. Whatever makes you feel rested, rejuvenated, and recharged, do that! There is no right or wrong here, as long as you do what feels good for *you*.

INSPO-ACTION

How are you going to add more RRR into your day? And when are you going to do it? Is RRR something you want to schedule into your calendar or is it something you will intuitively tap into throughout the day? I do both. I schedule in time every afternoon for RRR and I also check how I'm feeling throughout the day. If I'm feeling like I need to get up from my computer and do some RRR, I will — without any guilt or Mean Girl chatter. Letting go of the guilt is super important. Social conditioning to DO DO DO has created this sense of guilt — like we are letting down our team, family, or community by taking the fifteen-minute nap we so desperately desire. It makes us worry that we're being lazy, not contributing enough, not productive enough ... But deep down we know that we're more productive when we create space and prioritize time for RRR.

UNLEASH YOUR CREATIVITY

I am not a creative person.
I don't have a single creative bone in my entire body.
I can't do that: I'm not the "creative type."
Sound familiar?

I hear this often and used to let my Mean Girl tell me the same. I thought that because I wasn't a singer, a potter, or a painter — meaning, because I wasn't good at traditional "arty" stuff — I couldn't call myself "creative." But the truth is, creativity comes in many different forms, and I simply express myself creatively in other ways — through my writing, the way I move my body in yoga class, how I dance around the kitchen while preparing a delicious meal, and how I tend to my plants. These are all ways I express my creativity.

Creativity is an always present trait that needs to be expressed.

When we deny this truth and suppress our creativity, it festers away inside us, causing dis-ease in the mind and body. The good news is, you don't have to be a musician, a sculptor, or a prima ballerina to be "creative."

Creativity is whatever it means to you!

Creativity is that thing that makes you feel "in flow" and present, and when you do it, hours can fly past without you even noticing. It might even be that thing you did as a child that lit you up from your core. I *know* you know what I'm talking about!

Not only will this allow you to connect to your Goddessence but it also helps you access a different part of your brain, which can spark brilliant ideas and even help you get perspective and solve any big problems that have been swirling around in your head.

There have been many times where I have felt stuck with a particular issue then I put on some music and danced around my office, or I went outside and did some yoga on the beach and let out a bit of creative energy, then when I returned to my work … BOOM! The answers came flooding in.

CONNECTING TO YOUR DIVINE GODDESSENCE THROUGH CREATIVE EXPRESSION CAN ALSO HELP YOU:

- release stress by elevating you into a "flow" state
- increase your self-awareness. When you get your creativity on, you access your deep desires and Truth, which ultimately (when done on a regular basis) makes us more connected and in tune with ourselves and others.
- experience tremendous joy
- improve your health. A study published in 2004 in the *Journal of Psychosomatic Medicine* used writing as an adjunct treatment for HIV patients, and found that this simple act of creative expression resulted in "improvements of CD4+ lymphocyte counts." In lay speak, this means that the act of writing improved their immune systems and actually *altered* the cells inside their bodies. (After all, everything is energy.) So

creating doesn't just make you feel good; it might well benefit the cells inside you.

- feel purposeful. Creativity can make you feel like you're giving back and contributing to those around you or the world at large.

- switch (the heck) off! These days, information is constantly bombarding us. (Fact: we now receive *five times* as much information every day as we did back in 1986.) So with stimulation and temptation constantly at our fingertips, we need to consciously make sure we turn "off." A great way to do that is through creativity – particularly if you can lose yourself in flow.

There are so many great benefits to creative expression, but for me, the biggest one is that it simply makes me feel good. And I'm all about doing more of what makes me feel good and less of what doesn't.

INSPO-ACTION

PART ONE

So that you can express yourself creatively each day, we are going to create your very own "Creativity Menu." Here you will come up with ten things that make you feel creative – and remember, creativity is whatever it means to *you*.

Here are some ideas to get you started:

- Writing or journaling. Open up a blank document on your computer or whip out your journal and pen, and simply start writing. You can pick a word or a theme and go from there. For example, let's say you choose the theme of love. You simply start writing with that as your guide. There are no rules here, just start writing.

- Move your body. You can do this in private in your bedroom with some epic tunes blasting, or take yourself to a dance class. Whatever feels right for you.
- Try something new like painting, drawing, creating a sculpture, or woodwork.
- Sing without judgment. I LOVE singing (although Leo and Nick probably wish I didn't!). When I do it, I feel alive and free. My favorite place is in the car, windows up and volume loud.
- Make something using your hands – pottery, a vision board, or a scrapbook, or sew, knit, or crochet a garment.
- Get in the kitchen and cook. I love being in the kitchen alone. I get into a flow state and let the magic unfold.
- Do an acting class.
- Get in the garden.
- Paint.
- Knit a scarf.
- Write sweet love notes.
- Make your own essential oil bath blends and products.
- And don't underestimate the power of sitting in stillness to get your creative juices flowing.

There is no right or wrong when it comes to creativity. What's important is that you do what makes you feel creative and do it often – the more the better!

PART TWO

Now it's time to whip out your calendar and lock in some "Creativity Play Time." You can do anywhere from fifteen minutes to two hours, whatever works best for you. I personally feel the most benefits when I express myself creatively daily. Regardless of the frequency, make sure you schedule it in your calendar now, otherwise it won't happen. Saying "I'll do it later" isn't okay because it won't happen. Do it now!

TAP INTO YOUR INTUITION

Your intuition is also known as …

Your gut feeling or gut instinct

Your spirit

Your soul's voice

Your heart's knowing

Your heart's voice

Your Truth

Your inner wisdom

Your higher self

Your true self

Your internal GPS

Your internal compass

Your inner voice

Your innate wisdom.

It doesn't really matter what you call it, all that matters is that you're deeply connected to it. Your intuition is that feeling that often can't be explained through words. It sometimes may not make rational sense to your logical mind, but to you (your higher self) it does. It's an all-knowing force that you must honor. **I believe our intuition and our rational mind are BOTH powerful. In fact, I believe they're most powerful when dancing together …**

Back in 2010 when I hit rock bottom and ended up in the hospital, if you had asked me what my "intuition" was, I would have raised my eyebrows in bewilderment. Back then, I was so unconscious and disconnected from myself that most days I didn't know whether I was Arthur or Martha. But reflecting back, when I was lying in that hospital bed, there was a little voice inside me that said, *Sort yourself out, get your health and life in order, and you will live an epic life.* I didn't know it at the time, but that was my intuition speaking to me. It's always been there and so has yours. Most of us have simply shut ourselves off from it and allowed our Mean Girls to take center stage.

These days, my whole life and business are built on intuition. For every business decision I make, I tune in and make sure it's a whole-body *HELL YEAH* from my intuition, otherwise it doesn't get the green light. For every personal decision too — whether it's accepting a dinner invitation, booking a trip away with friends, or simply deciding whether I'd rather move my body that day or rest — I tune in and wait for a yes or no from my intuition. Everything — and I mean *everything* — comes from my intuition.

There have been times when I've ignored my intuition. For example, I hired someone for my team because my rational mind told me she was "good on paper," even though my intuition was bellowing *Noooo!* You can probably guess how things turned out ... She didn't fit into our team and caused a whole lot of stress and anxiety in the process. Not to mention almost $10,000 in legal fees (or "Dumb Tax," as Nick and I call it). At least I learned my lesson.

Then there was that time my intuition said, *Don't eat that sugar-and gluten-filled chocolate brownie,* and my rational mind said, *One bite won't hurt!* Then I was crouched over in agony all night, with stomach cramps and fiery eruptions that sent me dashing to the bathroom.

And then there was the time my intuition told me to jump on the next available plane when I could sense my best friend Jess was almost ready to don her angel wings, so that I could spend her last days with her. But my rational brain kept saying, *No, the doctors are saying she'll be fine, not to worry, and that she will be out of the hospital in a few days ...* A few days later, when we were finally on our way to the airport to see her, she left her physical body, and although I know everything is perfect there are still times I wished I'd listened to my intuition.

None of this means you should ignore your rational mind; please, *always* consider it. But remember to tune in to your intuition too, and give it equal weight and attention. It's waiting for you to turn to it and ask for its guidance. And remember: there's always a price to pay when you don't listen to it. Ignore your intuition at your peril. I've tried to trick this sacred system many times by convincing myself otherwise, but the Universe always gives me a big fat lesson when I ignore my Truth.

The beautiful thing about your intuition is that it's like any muscle in your body: the more you use it the stronger it gets. So if you practice listening to your intuition and living from that space, it will become so prevalent and "loud" (so to speak) that in times when you need to make a fast or important decision, you'll "hear" it loud and clear. *But what if I don't know the difference between my intuition and fear?* I'm glad you asked … what has worked best for me and how I differentiate the two is that my intuition I can feel in my body, mostly in my gut, whereas fear usually comes from my head. So if you're unsure which is which, tune in to your body. It holds the answers you're seeking.

HOW TO STRENGTHEN YOUR INTUITION

- Be still. One of the best ways to strengthen your intuition is through stillness. When we get still we're able to "hear" that inner voice. But so often we're surrounded with so much noise from the outside world – not to mention our Mean Girl – that it's too loud to hear. Make sure you take time out each day to get still. Quiet down your Mean Girl and connect inward. Make sure you show up with no agenda or expectations. Just sit and BE and allow whatever's there to rise to the surface.

- Tune in. Ask yourself, *How do I feel right now as I talk to this person? How do I feel right now as I do the dishes? How do I feel right now as I work on this project?*

- Meditate. A daily meditation practice allows you to connect with your intuition by helping drown out some of the Mean Girl chatter you may have going on in your mind. There is a common misconception that you must stop *all* thoughts during meditation, and that if you don't or can't you're not meditating properly. This is not the case. Thoughts are part of meditation. Just as clouds pass across the sky, thoughts are the same. When they pop up, we let them pass on by – we don't swear at them or get angry they are there. We simply let them keep floating on their way. When I first started meditating my thoughts were popping up every few seconds. It would have looked like this: cloud, cloud, cloud ... cloud ... cloud, cloud, cloud. Now, after years of practicing, my meditation might look more like this: cloud... cloud............ ....cloud.. ....cloud. The space between your thoughts broadens, and in that space is an opportunity for your intuition to speak up. But if we fill that space there's no room for our intuition to shine. This is why a regular meditation practice to strengthen your intuition is imperative. And if you already have a meditation practice, you can take it to the next level by writing down any intuitive feelings, insights, or callings you had during your meditation. Then honor them by writing down ways you can embrace and put them into action.

- Free write. First thing in the morning, when you're still moving from the unconscious to the conscious realm, whip out your journal and write. Don't let your mind jump in. Express yourself freely and uncensored. This is a great way to tap into your intuition.
- Slow down. When we're busy racing from one task to another, frantically ticking things off our to-do list, we can't "hear" our intuition. Being slow and intentional with your movements and pace throughout the day allows your intuition to jump in whenever needed.

INSPO-ACTION

Close your eyes, place your hands over your heart, let go of any Mean Girl thoughts, and fully allow yourself to be here. Once you feel present, tap into your intuition. What's it saying to you right now? If nothing comes up, that's okay — sit with it a bit longer. Once something pops up, you can gently open your eyes and free write. This is often the time when big ideas or perspectives come flooding in.

_____

_____

_____

_____

_____

_____

VALUE VULNERABILITY

Often we shy away from vulnerability out of fear of others' judgments. We're so scared of people seeing who we truly are that we keep them at arm's length and insist on wearing "masks" to hide our so-called "flaws." But I'm about to drop a massive truth bomb on you … **vulnerability connects us and makes people lean in**. It is the most transformative, life-altering aspect that connects us to our Goddessence.

I have experienced excruciating, gut-wrenching, makes-me-want-to-vomit, wailing-like-a-baby, heartbreaking, rip-my-heart-out-of-my-chest-and-reverse-over-it-a-million-times-with-a-semitrailer pain twice in my life. Once was when my best friend Jess left her body in 2015, and the other was after my first heartbreak at age twenty-three. That first time, I thought my life was over. The pain was so intense, and I'd never experienced anything like it. So I did what I thought was the smartest option, and that was to close off my heart, lock it up, and throw away the key. That way (I thought) it could never get broken like that again.

As a result, the years that followed were shallow — shallow relationships and shallow friendships — because I never allowed anyone to get too close. But your Truth yearns for deep love and connection, the kind you only experience when you Open Wide and get real and vulnerable.

Of course, don't get me wrong, it can feel totally scary to do this, and your Mean Girl will tell you to stay closed up like a vault … but don't listen. Unlock your heart and let people in. Being Open Wide is where the real magic happens.

INSPO-ACTION

Answer these questions in the space provided below:

- Are you being fully vulnerable, open, and honest with yourself? If not, what are you not wanting to see? What are you hiding from?
- Are you being fully vulnerable, open, and honest with others? If not, why not? What are you scared of? What do you see in them that you refuse to see in yourself?
- Where can you be more vulnerable?
- Who can you be more vulnerable with?

_____

_____

_____

_____

_____

_____

_____

_____

_____

_____

_____

_____

I know speaking your Truth and being vulnerable can feel terrifying, but it's the best way to connect with yourself and others, which means it's going to help you have richer, more fulfilling relationships — not to mention body-quivering, soul-stirring sex. (And remember, that's the point of ALL these tools, tips, and exercises: **by dialling up your divine Goddessence you can rock the bejesus out of your relationships and experience soulful sex**. But it all starts with this uber-important groundwork.)

LOVE YOUR TEMPLE

True Goddessence energy loves the temple she has been given for this lifetime. She knows there's a whole lot more to her than just this physical form, but she looks after, honors and cherishes her vehicle. She befriends and loves her body. She accepts what is, and lets go of the past — including how she used to look. She doesn't compare her body to others' or to hers when she was eighteen years old. She accepts that women need more body fat than men for balanced hormones and to bear children. She also knows that the more she loves herself and her temple and truly sees her own beauty, the more beautiful she becomes.

INSPO-ACTION

Place your hands over your womb (the inner sanctum of your most sacred temple) and repeat, *I love you, I love you, I love you, I love you, I love you*. Do this every morning before you open your eyes and jump out of bed.

COLLABORATE/CONNECT

For years, women have gathered together to share, support, and bless each other. There were goddess groups, blessing circles, red tents and more, all created as venues where women could hold space for each other.

That's exactly why I first created my own "Goddess Group," as a way for myself and my soul sisters to unleash our divine Goddessence. The idea was simple — a monthly gathering in my lounge room, on the full moon, with a bunch of my besties. Though it started off as just a casual thing, it quickly became one of our favorite events on the calendar, one that none of us wanted to miss, even though we all had "full" lives (if you've read *Mastering Your Mean Girl*, you'll know I don't use the word "busy"!). We all had loads of things going on, people to catch up with, loved ones who needed feeding, and to-do lists as long as the Mississippi … but for us, that wasn't a good enough excuse to not make it each month, because we *knew* our own inner Goddessence was craving that oh-so-important sister-to-sister connection.

The truth is, ALL we humans are hardwired for soul-to-soul connection. This is not something to be ashamed of: it's something to celebrate!

SO HERE'S EVERYTHING YOU NEED TO KNOW TO HOST A DIVINE GODDESS GROUP WITH YOUR OWN SOUL SISTERS

---

1. PICK THE HOST
Pick a host and the date (preferably on the full moon if you can; that way you can soak up all the full moon energy together).

2. GIVE PLENTY OF NOTICE

The host sends out an email or digital calendar invite confirming the details. Mine looked something like this:

> *Beautiful Goddesses,*
>
> *Please join together for the next Goddess Circle on [insert next full moon date] at my place*. Please arrive at 6 p.m. and bring an organic dish to share.*
>
> *Looking forward to seeing you then.*
>
> *P.S. Please R.S.V.P. A.S.A.P.*
>
> *Love, Melissa*
>
> **134 Love Street, Heart Town*

It's important to send out this email a month in advance, especially if your friends have kids – they need extra time to make arrangements for a babysitter.

3. PLAN THE FEAST

The host usually cooks one main dish, with guests bringing along a share plate as well. I'd often make an organic vegetable curry, which was cost effective, easy to make enough for everyone, suited all dietary requirements, and a huge hit. In my circle, we try to ensure that all of the food is organic, and gluten, dairy and sugar free. We also make sure there are a few vegan options for those who choose not to eat animal products.

Stuck for ideas on what to make?

Check out some of the delicious recipes in my ebook *The Glow Kitchen*. Get creative! Think colorful salads, roasted veggies in coconut oil, cultured foods, warm soups, coconut curry, kelp noodle pad thai, vegetable frittata, and hearty casseroles.

4. SET THE MOOD AND FEEL

As the host, the atmosphere you create for your sisters is so important. I like to light beeswax candles, burn sage before they arrive, put on some beautiful heart-opening music, dim the lights, diffuse some essential oils, and make the space as warm and comfortable as possible.

5. WELCOME THE GUESTS

As the host, you can pop a cute jewel or flower crown on their head as they enter for an extra dose of goddess-ness, or give everyone a cleansing sage "bath" as they enter.

As a guest, always be conscious of the energy you bring into the space. Also, try not to be late – the energy of rushing and hurrying isn't an ideal way to start your evening of sacred sisterhood. If you're running late, send the host a text and let them know. (And always leave enough time to find parking so you don't stress yourself out.)

6. BLESSING

Once everyone has arrived, we all sit. The host gives thanks for the food and for each other, and then says a little prayer. We then eat and talk, eat and talk ... then eat and talk some more.

7. SACRED CEREMONY AND TALKING STICK

After dinner we all sit on the floor in a circle. You can have your herbal tea and raw cacao goodies to the side, but this is the more intimate part of the night. This is also a great time for the host to mention that whoever has the "talking stick" (or "talking crystal") is the only person allowed to talk. We go around in the circle and, if someone bursts into tears, you don't rush over to them or say anything. Allow that person to fully express themselves and feel heard. The rest simply sit and hold space for that goddess to Open Wide and speak freely without judgment.

8. RELEASING RITUAL

There are so many ways this can unfold. I like to hand out some pens and sticky notes and get everyone to write down one thing they want to dissolve or let go of currently in their life. Once everyone has something written down, you start with the host and go around the group, reading them out to each other, then scrunching 'em up and throwing them in a bowl in the middle. (Some people like to burn the papers, but I prefer the less risky – and less smoky! – practice of scrunching and releasing.) There is also something really powerful about publicly declaring what you want to let go of. It helps hold you accountable.

9. GRATITUDE

After releasing comes gratitude! We all write down one thing we're deeply grateful for and one thing we want to call into our life. Again, we all go around the group and share what we've written, and that piece of paper we take home with us as a reminder.

10. WRAP UP

The night wraps up whenever you feel like it. For us, it's usually with plenty of hugs and loads of divine, grounded energy thrumming in our hearts.

HELPFUL TIPS

- As above, be on time!
- It's important everyone knows that what happens in the circle stays in the circle. The circle is a safe space for

everyone to express their Truth, feel held, and show up authentically. Honor that sacred sisterhood pact.

- Throughout the night, we like to recommend books, recipes, cafes, healers, films, albums, and documentaries to help support each other, so bring a notepad.
- In summer, it's great to hold the goddess circle outdoors, so you can soak in the divine energy of the full moon. There is something so incredibly powerful about tuning in to the potent energy of the moon while with other women, especially at "that time of the month."
- Employ the "no phone" rule. We have a "no phone after food" rule. Sure, take photos of the epic feast and each other, but then put your phone on silent or on airplane mode. It's very distracting when someone's phone keeps dinging every two seconds! Respect your sisters and be present.

INSPO-ACTION

Now it's your turn to plan your own goddess circle.

1: Write down the names of some women you would like to invite.

2: Get on Google and check when the next full moon is.

3: Send out the email invite.

4: Get planning, sister!

_____

_____

_____

_____

KEY TAKEAWAYS FROM CHAPTER TWO

- **DRAW ON THE ARCHETYPES WHENEVER YOU WANT TO UNLOCK YOUR SACRED POWER.**

  The Warrioress, the Lover, the Goddess, the Queen, the Priestess, and the Wise Woman are all there to help you unleash your true Goddessence.

- **MASTER YOUR MEAN GIRL DAILY.**

  That fear-based voice inside your head doesn't have to be your reality. Master her whenever she pops up.

- **CREATE SACRED PRACTICES AND RITUALS.**

  Design your own, then show up daily. Any practices that slide you into a state of mindfulness are particularly powerful for unlocking your divine Goddessence.

- **REMEMBER THAT MOTHER NATURE IS YOUR BESTIE!**

  Nothing switches off your stress response (or gets your inner goddess glowing) faster or more effectively than getting out into nature. Whether you're a beach babe, a mountain maven, or even just a backyard beauty, get outdoors as much as you can.

- **UNDERSTAND YOUR MENSTRUAL CYCLE.**

  Women are cyclical beings, and when you tune in to your own internal menstrual cycle, not only will you get a deeper understanding of yourself and your body, but you'll strengthen your connection to your divine Goddessence.

- **CONNECT WITH YOUR SOUL SISTERS AND BROTHERS.**

  Collaboration is the name of the game! Gather your nearest and dearest friends, and host your own goddess circle.

CULTIVATING ROCKING RELATIONSHIPS

CHAPTER THREE

It's Not Woo-Woo, It's You You! Love Yourself First!

You yourself, as much as anybody in the entire Universe, deserve your love and affection.

BUDDHA

Some of the things mentioned in this section I touched on in my book, Mastering Your Mean Girl. But I really want to encourage you not to skip over it, because it's a great reminder. One of the most ignorant things we can say is, "I know this." Yes, you may have heard something before (and let's face it: there's really no such thing as "new information" when it comes to spirituality and personal growth — everything has already been said before by someone over the last few thousand years). BUT, the real question is, are you living it every single day of your life? Are you the walking, talking example of these principles? For most of us, a timely reminder is always a good thing! So even if your Mean Girl "thinks" you know this, I encourage you to dive in with an open heart and beginner's eyes, because you can never hear this information too much. More is always better!

To cultivate rocking relationships, it starts with *you*! It's all about self-love, self-compassion, and softness toward yourself. And you, my friend, are about to become an expert on the topic. To experience deep love and soulful sex, the first step is becoming bursting and overflowing with love within yourself.

Loving yourself first and foremost is paramount if you want to experience deep love.

Radical Self-Love = Rocking Relationships

Self-love is not selfish, and just like the quote says, you — as much as anybody else in the entire Universe — deserve your love and affection.

So, let's dive in, shall we?

Self-Love Lesson One: Quit People Pleasing

The first lesson toward deep self-love is quitting people pleasing. All my life I watched my mom, and all the women around me, people please. I grew up in a very Catholic Italian environment with a huge focus on family and loads of "shoulds". You "should" do this for your brother because he is your brother. You "should" act a certain way when we're at church. You "should," "should," "should!" These words were drummed into me for as long as I can remember. So naturally, because this is what I saw, this is what I copied.

From as young as seven, I remember people pleasing. Case in point: a girl at school wanted my new doll, and because I didn't want to upset her, I gave it to her, even though I really didn't want to.

Then at fifteen I remember downing a bottle of vodka because the group of "friends" I was hanging out with were peer pressuring me. In that moment I wanted to say no, but I ignored my intuition and did it to please them, and to be liked and accepted.

I've also got into bed with men when I really wanted to say no. Said yes to dinner invites when I really meant no. And driven three hours to drop something to a friend when I had loads of work to do, was exhausted, had a child to tend to, and I really wanted to just say, "I can't right now." But I did it because I was too scared to stand in my Truth and do what was right for me in that moment.

It's super important to note that saying no doesn't mean you have to be forceful or rude. It can totally be done with love. One of the most powerful sentences you can say is, "No, thank you." Or, "Thank you so much for the offer but I'm going to have to pass this time." You don't need to give an explanation if you don't want to and you don't need to justify your Truth. You do, however, need to *honor* your Truth! If you don't, the Universe will give you a swift kick in the bum.

There is always a price to pay when you ignore your Truth.

Every single time I have said "okay," "sure," or "yes" when I really truly deeply wanted to say "no thank you," there has always been a consequence. Like the time I agreed to run an errand for a friend, got pulled over by the police, and got not one but two fines for speeding and crossing double white lines. Then there was the time I let a friend move in when I knew it wasn't a good idea and it ended in tears. She almost tore my then-partner and me apart, and caused a lot of stress … not to mention didn't pay her rent.

It took hitting rock bottom in 2010 for me to realize people pleasing was a stinky habit I had learned, and that it was something I wanted to *unlearn*, because frankly I was over it. People pleasing had burned me out, given me fatigue, and scorched my adrenal glands. But when you've had twenty-four years of practicing something, you tend to get pretty good at it! So unlearning how to people please was a mighty task. But I did it and so can you! It's important to note that no, I'm not "perfect," and there are still times when I catch myself wanting to people please, but I'm aware of it now and I can stop it in its tracks.

Are you willing to quit people pleasing, once and for all?

Because I was surrounded by people pleasers growing up, I didn't have many examples of how to model the opposite kind of behavior. That is, until I manifested an amazing example in my father-in-law Grazie. A few years back, my parents and mother-in-law flew into town to celebrate Leo's birthday, but Grazie didn't come. When everyone arrived my father asked where he was. I said, "He doesn't like flying and didn't want to come." The look on my father's face was like I'd just told him Jesus wasn't the Son of God! Yet I felt totally neutral about Grazie not being there and so did everyone else. My father flew off the handle and responded with, "That's ridiculous, he should be here!" To which I replied, "Actually, Dad, it wasn't his Truth, he doesn't like flying, and if he came out of obligation he would probably be a total grump and spoil the fun for everyone else. Much better that he honored his Truth." This took my father by surprise. After the redness left his cheeks, he responded with, "I guess you're right, love."

What happens when we people please is we're actually stopping ourselves and the people around us from having a true, authentic experience. It's fake because your Truth is saying and desiring something different. Which is okay, my sweet friend! You can't do and be *everything* for *everyone* all the time in every moment. You'll burn yourself out like I did.

This doesn't mean you can't do nice things for other people. Please keep doing them. I'm constantly doing nice things for others, but I do them because I want to and from a place of love, not because I think I "should" … there's a big difference. There may be times when you have to drop your grandma's laundry off, but all you want to do is hang on the couch. If you've been living in alignment to your Truth you'll find you actually have accumulated such a generosity boost it'll be easy to put your grandma's needs ahead of yours. It'll be easier to say yes when it's important, because you've given yourself permission to say no when self-care is what you really need.

INSPO-ACTION

Think of a time when you've done something for someone because you thought you should. How did you feel?

Now think of a time when you've done something for someone just because you wanted to? How did that make you feel?

_____

_____

_____

_____

_____

_____

_____

_____

_____

_____

Reflecting on what you wrote, can you feel the difference? It's a very different energy when you do something because you think you *should* versus doing it because you simply *want to* out of love and kindness. It's so much more impactful and meaningful. Same applies when someone does something for you — if they genuinely want to do it, YOU can feel the difference too. When my mom does something for me and I know she wants to, it feels very different from when she does it out of obligation and thinks she should because I'm her daughter.

Think about a time when someone has done something for you when you know they didn't really want to. How did you feel?

Think of a time when someone did something for you and you knew they really meant it. How did that make you feel?

_____

_____

_____

_____

_____

_____

_____

_____

_____

_____

There is a definite difference; can you feel it?

But that still leaves us with a big question: how do we stop people pleasing?

Answer: Through awareness.

Awareness is key for growth!

To ignite any sort of transformation, awareness is your best friend. Once you know something, you can't un-know it. (I guess that's why they say "ignorance is bliss," because you don't know what you don't know.) So simply acknowledging that people pleasing might be an issue for you is an important and powerful first step.

The second step is deciding that you no longer *want* to people please. For some, people pleasing can give their lives short-term satisfaction, purpose, and meaning. It also can keep their stories alive. But this "benefit" is short lived. I used to be addicted to that temporary gratification like a drug addict looking for her next hit, but it doesn't last and it's not real. So I had to decide with my whole being that I no longer wanted to participate in the destructive practice of people pleasing.

Awareness combined with a wholehearted decision to stop *will* help you quit people pleasing once and for all.

Be aware that your Mean Girl will pop up and want you to keep people pleasing. She will tell you, *You need to do XYZ for that person, you should also do ABC, and you may as well just do the rest of the alphabet while you're at it.* When that happens, master her, come back to love, and remember this is one of her biggest games — but awareness will stop her in her tracks.

SURRENDERING YOUR PREFERENCE

I now don't do anything unless I'm bursting out of my skin to do it and it's an absolute full-body *HELL YEAH!* But, there *are* times when I surrender my preference. Like when Leo wants me to come watch his five-hour-long cricket game. No, I don't love cricket, and sitting down for half a day watching kids (or even professionals, for that matter!) batting a ball around a pitch is not my idea of fun. But I love him and I know how much it means to him, so in that moment I surrender my preference (whatever that might be) and I find the love in it.

Finding the love in everything you do is critical for internal peace and happiness.

Instead of being dragged along by Nick and forced to reluctantly watch the game, I decide to wholeheartedly go and be fully there because I love Leo, it means the world to him, and to do what I need to do to find the love and joy in it — otherwise I will be bitter the entire time, and that isn't fun for anyone.

Another time I found myself getting annoyed when Nick left all the dishes after dinner for me to do. The kitchen looked like a bomb had gone off and I was exhausted. But he was in the middle of a recording period for his next song and I knew how important it was for him to get back into the studio after dinner. So instead of cursing him under my breath, I surrendered my preference (which was to *not* do the dishes alone) and decided to be grateful for: (1) the fact that I had a loving and lovely husband, (2) that I had a husband who was following his dreams and on his mission, (3) that I could afford the food that made the dishes dirty, (4) that I had dishes to eat off in the first place, and (5) that I had the abundance to do the dishes in a kitchen with fresh hot water, soap, and a cloth. Once I shifted my perspective, doing the dishes was no longer a chore but something I was honored to do for a man I deeply love.

I also found myself surrendering my preference when Nick asked me to be in his music video "Just Us," which is about us and our love. I had already been in another music video called "The One" and I didn't realize I was going to be in more. I honestly thought I had hung up my performing shoes. But being in the video wasn't the issue; it was more the fact that he wanted to do a scene where I was naked in bed — a bit how you doing, if you know what I mean. My immediate reaction was HELL NO! My Mean Girl started screaming: *What are people going to think? It's too much! You can't do this, Melissa — it's too risky.* But I realized how much it meant to him. I had to surrender and get to a place of excitement within myself, otherwise it wasn't going to work. And I did! Of course we made sure it was tasteful, so in the end I saw it as art and a creative expression. I then felt grateful that this beautiful man wanted me to be in his video. What an honor! I felt so proud that he was living his Truth and pursuing his dreams. And you know what? It wasn't that bad after all, and my generosity and service cups were overflowing. Once I wholeheartedly decided I was going to surrender my preference I could fully show up, which as a result created a beautiful music video.

INSPO-ACTION

Where have you surrendered your preference, dropped your expectations, and chosen instead to do something out of love for someone else?

Can you remember a time when someone has surrendered their preference to do something for you? How did that feel for you?

_____

_____

_____

_____

_____

_____

_____

_____

_____

_____

_____

_____

_____

_____

Make sure that when you surrender your preference, you do it with love. There's no point surrendering your preference and still being bitter about it — everyone will feel it. Don't do it unless you can do it with love.

Self-Love Lesson Two: Judge No More

Whether we're aware of it or not, from the moment we wake up to the moment we put our head on our pillow at night, we're judging — both ourselves and others. Some of my internal judgments used to sound like this: *That was a crap night's sleep. You look so tired. Your dark circles are gross. Your thighs are too big. That dress makes your hips look wide. You shouldn't eat that.*

The judgments weren't limited to myself, though — they also extended to others: *That is such an ugly dress. Those two will never last. Why would you post that on social media? I can't believe she said that! I wouldn't do that. I wouldn't say that. What an idiot! Who does she think she is?!* … and on and on it went, my Mean Girl having an absolute field day in the process.

Can you relate to any of this?

If so, I'm about to drop a truth bomb on you:

Everything is a reflection of us, and what you judge in others, you are ultimately judging and not fully owning within yourself.

INSPO-ACTION

Take a moment now to think about a time when you judged someone else. What did that trigger within you? What are you not owning or looking at within yourself? What are you projecting onto others?

Those three questions are very powerful. These days, when I catch myself judging someone, I go through these questions and I'm often astonished by the answers that swirl up from the depths. So ask, and the answers will come ... and you just might find out something enlightening about yourself.

Much like people pleasing, the two major steps in quitting judging are awareness and wholeheartedly deciding that you want to live a judgment-free life.

Let's make that pledge to our beautiful selves right now by signing the Judge No More sacred contract:

I, _____, commit to living a judgment-free life. I promise to do my best not to judge myself or others, and when I catch my Mean Girl getting judgy (whether about myself or someone else), I will return to my Truth–Love–as quickly as I can ... without any judgment!

This I promise.

[Sign name]

Self-Love Lesson Three: Let Go of Comparisons

If you want to explode with self-love so you can experience rocking relationships, you've got to quit comparing yourself to others. **Comparison is the thief of joy and will rob you of deep inner happiness.**

From a very young age I compared myself to others, and then at fifteen years old I entered a profession where comparison was par for the course. As an actress and dancer, I compared the way I looked, the way I talked, how smart I was, how cute my boyfriend was, how big my bum was, how spiritual I was, how much money I had, how big my house was, how trendy my clothes were, how fancy my car was … even how happy I was. It seems ludicrous when I type it out, but if I'm totally honest with you, I used to compare everything about myself to other people's qualities because I was so unhappy in my own skin.

Comparison is one of the sneaky games your Mean Girl likes to play, and if you don't stop her she will take control and keep you in the downward comparison cycle.

Are you someone who compares yourself to others, whether it's someone you know or a complete stranger on social media? If so, I'm going to teach you how to let go of comparison once and for all.

INSPO-ACTION

Knowing your triggers is vital to combat comparison. What are the things that trigger you to compare yourself? Is it social media, glossy magazines, a particular girl at work, going to the gym, or watching TV? Write down all the things that trigger you to compare yourself to others. Now, I want you to ask yourself, why is this triggering me? What is it about X that's making me want to compare myself?

_____

_____

_____

_____

_____

Often, comparison creeps in when we're not overflowing with self-love. I know that, for me, it's always when I'm feeling crappy within myself that I start to compare myself to others. On the other hand, when I'm feeling confident, content, grounded, centered, and worthy, comparison doesn't even enter my consciousness. (Yet another reason to jump aboard the self-love train!)

Knowing your triggers is really important, for two reasons. First of all, so that when you feel crappy you can remove them. Get off social media and get your nose out of the magazines and sit with yourself instead. That's not to say you can never go social media scrolling again, it's just that when you're feeling "at risk" of "comparisonitis" — when your resolve isn't as strong and your heart's not as overflowing as it could be — it's better to remove yourself.

The second reason is that your triggers can reveal a lot about you. I want you to put your detective's cap on and investigate why those particular things are triggering you, because there *will be* nuggets of wisdom in there for you. So next time you catch your Mean Girl comparing you to someone else, do two things: remove yourself from the trigger, then ask "What is this triggering within me and why?" Then let it go and come back to love.

STAY IN YOUR OWN LANE

At times we can get very swept up in the fake-ness and unrealistic "perfection" that is portrayed in the media. It can make you worry you're moving too slow or too fast or in the wrong direction altogether. The key is to remember to *stay in your own lane*, and keep your gaze on your own lane. Trust me, when you're on your own mission, in your own lane, and you're paying attention to what feels right for you ... you won't give a damn about what Fiona is doing in the lane next to you.

No one can *be* you or *do* you better than you! Stay true to that and know with all your heart that you can live without comparison. The more you embrace your truest and most authentic self, the more you will attract all that you desire into your life, including love-filled, authentic, nurturing relationships that will bring out the absolute best in you. It's time to let go of comparisons and stay in your own lane.

Self-Love Lesson Four: Eradicate Expectations

You must look like a Victoria's Secret model all the time.

You must earn a certain amount.

You must drive X type of car.

You must be with a man who earns X amount, looks like Brad Pitt, can ravish you, and give you multiple orgasms into all hours of the morning.

You must look like you "have it together" all the time.

You must not have a hair out of place when you pick Leo up from school.

You must be able to backbend and headstand like Tara Stiles in yoga class.

You must have glowing skin.

These are just some of the expectations I have placed on myself in the past. Exhausting, huh?!

Expectations are another sneaky Mean Girl game that you don't need to play. She tells you things like I just mentioned to keep you stuck in fear, but **you can live expectation free. It's a choice, and the choice is always yours!**

INSPO-ACTION

As you now know, awareness is key for inner transformation and growth. So let's get clear on what expectations you're placing on yourself.

Before we get into it, in case you're wondering, let me clear something up: eradicating your expectations does not mean you won't have the drive or oomph to kick goals and achieve great things in life. You surely will! It just means you'll be able to hit those benchmarks with a lot more ease and grace and a lot less pain and suffering. (By far the more preferable route, right?!)

Expectations are the fastest way to ruin relationships.

Expectations will not only ruin your relationship with yourself, but your relationships with those around you. You can bet your bottom dollar that if you place a truckload of expectations on yourself, you will most likely have placed a load of them on others too.

Who are the five most prominent people in your life? This might be your partner, mom, brother, colleague and/or best friend — whoever it is for you, write down their names. Now, next to each name, write down all the expectations you have of each of those people. Don't be shy here. Let it rip!

_____

_____

_____

_____

_____

_____

_____

_____

Now, ask yourself what happens when one of those people doesn't fulfil one of *your* expectations that *you* have placed on them? Shit hits the fan, right? You're disappointed, pissed off, and angry. Same goes with the expectations we place on ourselves.

I'm going to give you an example from my own journal here, so you can see how this might look in action:

Person who is prominent in my life: My bestie Gabby
Expectation I place on her: Sometimes I make plans for us to do something special and I expect her to act in a certain way — e.g. to be enthusiastic, happy, and grateful. When she doesn't show up the way I desire, I end up feeling disappointed, resentful, or angry — and then NEITHER of us ends up having a good time ... all because I've placed a ton of expectations on her.

Disappointment only occurs when one of your expectations has not been fulfilled.

So whose fault is it?

Most likely the other person is completely oblivious to the expectations you've placed on them, so the only person who needs to take responsibility here is you! It's a tough pill to swallow, I know. But when you wholeheartedly commit to eradicating your expectations of yourself and others you will experience a much deeper love in all your relationships.

Instead of placing expectations on your partner to do the dishes and take out the trash, simply practice "Crystal Clear Communication" (a.k.a. "CCC," which we'll dive into in more detail later) with him.

Instead of wanting your kids, family, or friends to act and show up a certain way, or do things the way *you* desire, eradicate your expectations, and simply allow them to show up as their true authentic selves.

Instead of expecting yourself to look a certain way, simply take the action steps daily to nourish your body, mind, and spirit. Show up every day from a place of love, and let go of your fear-based expectations.

Life is a lot more enjoyable when you've got no expectations, so let's commit to eradicating them once and for all. Sign the contract below to do that right now.

I, _____, commit to no longer placing expectations on myself and others.

Instead I will simply allow others to show up as their true selves and I will do the same. I will be the example of what it means to live expectation-free, for myself and for those around me.

This I promise.

[Sign name]

Self-Love Lesson Five:
Let Go of Your Past, Get Out of
the Future, and Be Fully Present!

When I was five years old, my appendix burst and I almost died. I was rushed to hospital to have emergency surgery to remove my appendix and seven cups of pus. (Charming!) When this happened, I naturally got a lot of attention from the people around me — especially my parents, family members, and friends. My mom was about to give birth to my brother and, subconsciously, I think I was craving her love and attention. I knew things were about to change dramatically and I was no longer going to be her baby girl.

Things did change — of course — when my brother was born and I became the middle child. I had to help out and be more independent, and the special alone-time I got with my mama all but ended. (Naturally, of course — she now had three kidlets to attend to, one of them a newborn baby!)

Still, five-year-old me couldn't make much sense of this. But I did learn something quite quickly: when I was sick, I got loads of attention and love from my mom. This quickly became my "story." I'd get sick — asthma, eczema, tummy aches — and the attention and love from Mom would go back to how it used to be. I didn't really understand it, but this link somehow got cemented in my brain: sick = love. So for most of my life this story played out: I'd get sick, and Mom would shower me with love. Sick, love, sick, love — it was as reliable an equation as $2 + 2 = 4$. As it went on, it became the primary way we bonded, connected, and spent time together. After all, she was a busy mom of three, working full time as a night-shift nurse, so her time was limited. But I craved more, and it felt like I'd finally cracked the code for getting it.

I remember the days when she would pick me up early from school to take me to the dermatologist for my eczema. It was our "special" time together — no brother, sister, or husband to distract her: it was just us. I loved it! She was my hero and I craved her deep love and affection. This story continued to play out until I woke up to what was really going on. At the grand old age of twenty-four — while lying in hospital and suffering from more sickness than I ever had in my life — I finally saw what was happening and decided I no longer needed to hold on to this story or experience illness to get love and attention.

Of course, **you don't know what you don't know**. And that pattern stayed hidden from me for a long time. But then one day, I knew! It was like the lights came on for the first time. I realized what was panning out and how much it was holding me (and her, and our relationship) back, not to mention causing me physical pain in the process. It was also a super-expensive pattern to have fallen into too. (Medical bills and antibiotics are *not* cheap!)

I knew that if I wanted to experience deep love with myself and others, I needed to let go of this limiting belief that was not serving me, my growth, or my evolution. But it wasn't as easy as clicking my fingers and being done with it for good. No sir! I mean, I had completely wrapped my identity around this story. I was "the girl with eczema and asthma." I was the girl with "health and skin problems." I got "special" treatment at school, dancing, and sleepover parties. So who the heck was I without this story and the identity I'd created around it? I was scared to let it go, but I knew it was time. So, as with all of the self-love lessons in this chapter, I had to decide that I wholeheartedly wanted to let this belief go. Once I did that, it became *my* responsibility (not my mom's or therapists') to become aware of it every time it was about to play out, and to catch my thoughts and remind myself that this was no longer the story I wanted to live by. Like anything, it took time and awareness, but the more I practiced catching it, the easier it got.

Another limiting Mean Girl story I used to tell myself was that you have to compromise in your relationships. Of course there is a healthy level of compromise in relationships: for example, I want Indian and he wants pizza and maybe he compromises (or, as I like to call it, surrenders his preference) in that moment. But when you have to compromise on your core values and beliefs (which you will learn about in Chapter Four) this to me is not okay. Before I realized this, I compromised with every man I was with. Don't get me wrong: there was unity and alignment in many areas, but there were also many where there was not. And because my Mean Girl kept telling me, *You have to compromise in your relationship*, that is what I created. Until, that is, just before Nick. As part of my manifesting practice, I was journaling about the lover I desired and I wrote down that I didn't want to compromise on my core values and beliefs any more. I no longer wanted to subscribe to that paradigm, and I held the vision of unity in all areas with my love. And guess what? Unity is what I got. We are aligned and unified on all significant levels, from health to money to parenting. I didn't know it was possible, but it is! This doesn't mean that we agree on everything or that we don't disagree — we absolutely do. However, our underlying core values are aligned, which makes communication easier.

I truly believe that when you let go of old stories and decide you no longer want them to be part of your current reality, you can create whatever your heart desires. The blank canvas is yours and you can paint whatever you want on it.

INSPO-ACTION

Do you have any stories from your past that you keep telling yourself? Maybe it's something to do with your health? Maybe you have a money story that you picked up from your parents? Or maybe it's about your parents' divorce? Write down all the stories you're still letting play out in your life right now.

_____

_____

_____

_____

_____

_____

_____

_____

_____

_____

_____

_____

_____

_____

_____

I know it can feel challenging to let go of the stories we've built our identities around, but you already know in your heart that they're no longer serving you. And in order for you to experience deep love with yourself and others, you have to Open Wide and let them go — that creates space for new stories and new truths.

Our stories aren't only from the past ...

It's not just childhood stuff that leads to limiting stories. We also tell ourselves stories about the future:

When I have X amount of money in the bank, then I will be happy.
When I meet my dream man, then I will be happy.
When I fix my gut issues or heal from X, then I will be happy.
When I get out of debt, then I will be happy.
When I have a bigger home and a nicer car, then I will be happy.
When I move out of this shared house, then I will be happy.
When my home is clean, the emails are replied to, and the to-do list is ticked off, then I will be happy.

"Future tripping" in this way is a sure route to unhappiness. In order for you to overflow with self-love, you've got to quit it. You are creating your life moment by moment — if you want your reality to be wilder than your dreams, get out of the future (and your own way) and get back into the present moment as fast as you can.

Be ALL here.

If you do want to create an affirmation or belief about your future, make sure you frame it in a way that feels good in your body NOW, for example: *I am bursting with love and happiness, and everything I desire is magnetized toward me.*

Self-Love Lesson Six:
Dial Up Your Worthy-O-Meter

How worthy you feel is reflected in all areas of your life. Many years ago, my worthy-o-meter was at an all-time low: I dated men who treated me like a doormat, I trashed my body with junk "food," I escaped myself with drugs and alcohol, I took uninspiring jobs that I loathed just to make money, and I surrounded myself with unhealthy relationships. I mean, I was such a loser, why would I deserve any better? At least, that's what my Mean Girl told me.

Today I feel like a ten out of ten on the worthy-o-meter scale. I feel deeply worthy of all the love, joy, and happiness I'm experiencing within. I *know* I'm worthy of what is unfolding in front of me and I *know* I'm worthy of whatever my heart desires. But these shifts only took place after I got conscious about my self-worth, and got serious about dialing up my worthy-o-meter. Here's how you can do the same — fast!

Worthiness is a choice — your choice!

Unless you're bursting with worthiness, I wouldn't even think about calling in your lover. Otherwise — like me with some of my past relationships — you will fill a void in them and they will fill a void in you, and that whole setup is rocky territory. You want to be exploding with worthiness within yourself first, because then you will attract someone else who is also exploding with worthiness. And when two people who are already full of self-love and overflowing with worthiness come together, fireworks are sure to follow.

This applies to all your relationships. If you feel worthy of supportive soul sisters, that is what you will attract. **Your vibe attracts your tribe.** But if you treat yourself like crap and don't feel worthy of divine friendships, then that's what you will create.

Like the other self-love lessons, the best way to dial up your worthy-o-meter is by awareness and by deciding that you are and want to feel worthy. This doesn't mean you won't sometimes feel less than a ten on the worthy-o-meter scale — there may be days or moments when you do. But because you now have awareness, every time you slip down you can dial it back up again, pronto.

There are still times when I catch myself slipping down the scale. For example, a few years ago we decided we wanted to move back to the beach, and because the Universe works so beautifully, a real estate listing for the most stunning home landed in my inbox once we'd wholeheartedly made the decision that we wanted to move. Nick immediately said, "This is perfect, baby, we have to go see it!" He made some phone calls while I tried to rein in my shock at the price. After I picked my jaw up off the floor, we went and saw the place. Nick knew it was a goodie and had the deposit ready to go, but I on the other hand was internally battling it out with my Mean Girl ...

You can't afford this place; it's way too expensive.

This is very lavish, Melissa — are you sure you want to be spending this much a week? Maybe you should stick within your means.

Get over yourself, you're not going to be able to afford this.

People like you don't live in places like this.

You're such a show-off.

And on and on she went.

Until I realized what was happening: I didn't feel *worthy* of living in such a beautiful home by the beach, even though I felt like it was my Truth to live there. My Mean Girl was telling me that I wasn't worthy and didn't belong in the home, while the rest of my body was saying a full-blown *Hell yeah!*

I realized that in order to master my Mean Girl, I was going to have to face the fear, dial up my worthy-o-meter, and do it anyway. Saying yes to this move was scary because the fear was so loud, but I did it, and you know what? I was supported by the Universe every step of the way.

You are always supported for what is true for you. The Universe rewards the brave.

When you master your Mean Girl, face the fear, and do it anyway, you get rewarded. That situation was incredibly uncomfortable for me. But because I had the awareness, I was able to see what was really going on, then wholeheartedly decide to move forward despite my fear.

Feeling ten on the worthy-o-meter is your birthright. You don't have to do anything to earn it. Just being born you are a ten. How cool is that?!

INSPO-ACTION

How worthy do you feel right now? Are you a four, or are you a ten on the worthy-o-meter scale?

No matter where you are, know that you can decide to dial it back up right now. It's a choice — *your* choice, my sweet friend — and you deserve to feel bursting with worthiness in every moment ... even if your Mean Girl tells you otherwise.

Self-Love Lesson Seven: Go Inward

Back in 2010 when I embarked on my spiritual journey, I was very outwardly focused. I placed all my attention on finding healers, teachers, mentors, body workers, and practitioners to "fix," change, and improve me. I so desperately wanted them to save me, help me heal, and make me happy again. And yes, they absolutely helped ... but only to a degree. I swiftly realized that if I wasn't willing to go inward within myself, I would never be happy.

You are your own best guru!

No one knows you better than you. No one knows how you're feeling deep within or what's really going on with you. You can try to articulate it as best you can, but no one will *really* understand what it's like to be in your skin. Which means *you are your own best guru*. Not a healer, not a doctor, not a robe-wearing, aura-seeing, sermon-giving swami ... *YOU!* Now this might sound scary, but it shouldn't — it's exciting! It means you hold all the power. (It's a much cheaper scenario too!)

Of course, this doesn't mean you can't seek support from others —
I'm all for support, sister. And I highly encourage you to reach out
and get it whenever you feel the desire. You don't have to do life
alone. But often, simply sitting with yourself and your journal will
help dissolve the "issue," and you may even come to your resolution
on your own. That's happened to me many times. I was once sitting
in my holistic healer's office and as the words were spilling out of my
mouth, I realized I already knew exactly what had to be done. So
never underestimate the power of openly and honestly expressing and
trusting that you already have the answers within.

**To find your own answers and be your own guru, you
have to venture inward ...**

When you make the decision to go inward, connect with your
Truth, and really get to know yourself, you will uncover the
answers to all your questions. There is no other way.

That said, if you're anything like me, you're often too full to
stop and connect and go inward, right? Well, tell me this: are you
too full to be happy? Going inward and connecting with your true
self doesn't have to take hours. All it takes is a few minutes of
presence. Close your eyes and go inward, connect with how you're
feeling and what's coming up for you. Once you're done, you can
journal about your experience if you like. That's it! Easy peasy.

Meditation is the quickest, easiest, and cheapest way to go
inward. When you start your day with a few minutes to connect
with yourself, your day will unfold very differently. When you do
this you're basically saying to the Universe, "I honor myself, I truly
love myself and I matter." And trust me, **the Universe has ears
and it's always *listening*!**

Another note on the "I don't have time" front: if you don't honor
yourself enough to make the time for reflection — i.e. if you don't

act as if you *deserve* at least a few minutes of your day for soul work —
then the rest of the world will behave as if you don't deserve it either.
After all, we teach people how we want to be treated. So if *you* don't
treat yourself with love, why would other people treat you with
love? Make the decision now to give yourself that small (or large)
amount of time and space each day. You are so worth it.

Self-Love Lesson Eight: Date Yourself

I used to be that person who had every second of my weekend
booked: Friday night was drinks with the girls. Saturday morning
was usually a walk (or a BodyPump class), then brunch with my
besties. Saturday lunch was with a friend, followed by shopping for
a new outfit (that I didn't need) and errands like grocery shopping.
Saturday night was dinner, drinks, partying, and dancing till the
wee hours of the morning. Sunday brunch was a greasy recovery
meal to cure my hideous hangover. And from Sunday lunch
onward, we would head to the local for more greasy food and more
drinks. (Hair of the dog, right?!)

My weekends were jam packed and booked up months in
advance. Why? Because I was so scared to be alone. I didn't want
to spend a single second on my own. I had a very loud Mean Girl,
and the thought of going inward (as in Self-love Lesson Seven)
sent shivers down my spine. So in order to avoid myself, I packed
my schedule as tight as a tin of (wild-caught) sardines. Until I
hit rock bottom, that is, and realized that **you have to become
your own best friend. You can't expect anyone else to love
you if you don't love yourself.** This was hard for me to grasp,
as I'd spent years becoming an expert in self-loathing, battling

depression, an eating disorder, anxiety, and panic attacks, and I didn't think I could ever get to that place of overflowing self-love. But the beautiful thing about hitting rock bottom is... the only way out is up! And to be honest, I was so sick and tired of being extremely unhappy and unwell that I was willing to try anything. So, reluctantly, I thought I would give this self-love stuff a go. Couldn't hurt, right? Each day I made a conscious decision to love myself wholeheartedly. I made this more concrete by deciding to date myself. I thought that if I wanted to call in my lover, I first needed to love myself so much that *I* would want to date myself.

INSPO-ACTION

Try any of the following ways to date your beautiful self:

- Have a bath with Epsom salts, coconut oil, and a few drops of lavender essential oil. Dim the lights, maybe have some soft meditation music playing in the background, and tell everyone you live with "do not disturb!"
- Lie on the beach with a good book (or not) and feel the sun on your skin.
- Take your favorite blanket to the park, along with a book, podcast, or your journal. Or you could simply stare up at the sky and ponder!
- Get dressed up and take yourself out to lunch or dinner alone and BE fully there, not on your phone.
- Pop an herbal tea in a to-go cup and take yourself to see a hilarious rom-com at the movies.
- Go to the beach or park to watch the sunrise or sunset (sans phone).

- Have a shower then give yourself a full-body coconut oil massage. Make sure you touch every part of your body with love, while feeling deeply grateful for your arms, legs, toes, hands, etc. Then get into bed and try some self-pleasuring with your Jade Egg (more on that later!).
- Cook your favorite dish for yourself.
- Take yourself on a solo hike (keep your phone on airplane mode — use it for emergencies only!).
- Go to your favorite yoga class, then out for an herbal tea at the local cafe, and simply revel in your own company.

Using this list as inspiration, write down ten things you love doing alone. Be as specific as possible. Once you have your list, stick it somewhere you can see it and each week put a reminder on your to-do list or phone to book a date with yourself. Then when the reminder pops up, pick something from your list and schedule it in your calendar. Don't just say, "I'll do it later," because most likely your self-love date won't happen. If you want to be bursting with love, taking yourself on love dates is key, because if you want someone else to love you, you have to love yourself first!

Self-Love Lesson Nine: Master Your Mean Girl

This lesson is last for a reason ... it's the most important (which is why I wrote a whole book on it!). You have already learned how to master your Mean Girl in Chapter Two, so head back there if you need a refresher. Learning to master your Mean Girl is imperative because she will stop you from truly bursting with love within yourself and from learning any of the other self-love lessons mentioned. She will tell you you don't have enough time, that it's too hard, that it's too expensive, that you should be doing something else, that other people will judge you, that you're a dreadful mom/sister/friend/whatever for taking time out for yourself ... Whatever your deepest, darkest fears are about yourself, she'll try to use them against you. But don't let her! Take the time to learn how to master her, or she'll be the bane of your existence and you won't be able to move forward on any of this oh-so-important self-love stuff.

Mastering your Mean Girl isn't just important so you are overflowing with love within *yourself*, it's also imperative if you want to experience deep love in all your relationships. Think about the stuff she says when you're about to get intimate with your love: *You look fat, quickly dim the lights! Don't let him see your cellulite! Make sure you're on top so he can't see how flabby your belly is when you're on the bottom!* She is also the voice that will say, *He's too good to be true! It won't last — you're not good enough for him! Did you really think he would like you? Get over yourself!* And if you don't learn to master her, she will ruin your life and your relationships. So make the commitment now by signing the sacred contact to master your Mean Girl once and for all.

I, _____, commit to mastering my Mean Girl every time she pops up. I will take myself through the three-step process and return to love with as much ease and grace as possible. This I promise.

[Sign name]

There you have it! Nine Self-Love Lessons you can master! Have fun with them, don't take it too seriously, and — most importantly of all — remember that you're not broken and you are worthy of feeling infinite love within yourself. It IS your birthright because you are LOVE!

KEY TAKEAWAYS FROM CHAPTER THREE

- **FOR ROCKING RELATIONSHIPS, EMBRACE THESE NINE ESSENTIAL SELF-LOVE LESSONS:**
  1. Quit people pleasing.
  2. Judge no more.
  3. Let go of comparisons.
  4. Eradicate expectations.
  5. Let go of your past, get out of the future, and be present!
  6. Dial up your worthy-o-meter.
  7. Go inward.
  8. Date yourself.
  9. Master your Mean Girl.

CHAPTER FOUR

Dive into Your Ocean

Imagine standing on the deck of a boat, looking down into the sea, and spotting a fish darting through the water. You, as an observer, can see the fish and its environment as a whole. You know that it's swimming through molecules of salty water, which form part of a greater body of water called the ocean. But the fish? It is completely immersed in its surroundings, and has never known anything different. So our sweet little angelfish has no idea that it's in water. It has no idea it's part of an ocean. And it has no idea there's a whole other world out there …

When you're deeply immersed in something, it can be incredibly difficult to see the reality that's all around you. Just like the fish that doesn't realize it's swimming in an ocean full of water, **often we don't realize we're living our lives by a set of values, beliefs, and principles**. They're so obvious to us, and so ubiquitous, that we often don't even see that they're there. But even if we're not aware of them, they still govern how we think, feel, and navigate through life ... which means they also have a huge impact on how we show up in our relationships.

Knowing what part of the "ocean" you're swimming in, then, is an important step along the path to creating rocking relationships. Of course, just like the fish, if we want to see what's right in front of us, we've got to look carefully and closely ... otherwise we might miss it. So this chapter is going to guide you through the process of uncovering the depths of your own personal ocean — that is, the values, qualities, and interests that make you intrinsically *you*.

Let's dive deep into each one in turn ...

Values

Values are the beliefs you have about the most important, fundamental aspects of life. Values are so innate, they're like a lens through which we view the world — a pair of glasses we don't even realize we're wearing. For this reason, we can be less conscious of them than any other aspect of our ocean. And because they relate to such significant areas of life, we have a tendency to hold on to them dearly and tightly. In fact, they can feel like they're a part of us — that they're the thread from which our hearts are woven.

You can have values relating to any number of topics, but below I've identified twelve key areas where most people have strong foundational beliefs. You'll notice many of these areas can be "hot-button topics" — the kinds of things that can start an argument at the dinner table when two people hold opposing views (I've seen it happen). This shows just how important they are to us, and how divisive they can be when people aren't aligned!

KEY VALUES

- Love/relationships
- Money
- Health
- Sex
- Work/career
- Life purpose
- Religion/spirituality
- Politics
- Equality (whether gender, racial, sexual, etc.)
- Parenting
- Education/learning
- Philanthropy

Did you have any strong reactions as you read through this list? Maybe straight away you thought, "Heck, yes, I know what I think about THAT!" Or for other topics, were you maybe a bit surprised to think people have strong enough beliefs in that area that they'd call them a core value? *(Really? People care about that?!)*

Whichever end of the spectrum you happen to fall on, for whatever topic, it's all perfect. And though it might not seem this way at first, you're actually revealing depths of your ocean by discovering things you don't care that much about, as well as the things you do.

To help you dive deep into your values, I've compiled a list of questions for each area. Before you plunge in, though, a divine disclaimer: some people will get super excited and inspired by all the questions and exercises in this chapter, and will get extreme satisfaction from writing an essay-length answer to each. But others, by contrast, will want to stay with the flow of the book and keep on reading, maybe only answering a couple of questions, or perhaps none at all. Before your Mean Girl pipes up and tells you one way is better than the other, or that you "should" answer every single question, I want to liberate you from your own expectations. Please don't put any pressure on yourself; choose whichever path resonates most with you. Want to answer every question with prose that would make your high school English teacher proud? Awesome. Want to scrawl a few points here and there? Great. Want to keep on reading the rest of the book, and just mentally mull over anything that resonates? Fan-fricking-tastic. Beautiful, I'm just so proud of you for being here and exploring these concepts. However you choose to process this stuff, it's all good.

With that out of the way, let's start the deep-dive into your values …

LOVE/RELATIONSHIPS

What does self-love mean to you?
    How do you believe others should be treated?
    Do you believe relationships are our greatest gifts/teachers?
    What are your beliefs about "the one" and soulmates?
    What are your views on fidelity?

MONEY

What are your beliefs about money?
    What are your beliefs about saving, spending, credit, and debt?
    What are the top five things you spend your money on?
    Do you believe we vote with our dollar?
    Do you believe in abundance?

HEALTH

What does "health" mean to you?

How important is your health to you and why?

What are your beliefs about food and exercise?

What level of influence do you perceive you have over your health — both now and in the future?

What are your health goals?

SEX

Do you believe that sex is a healthy and natural part of life?

When do you believe it's okay to have sex, and when is it not?

What is acceptable for you in the bedroom, and what is not?

What is your idea of healthy sexual expression?

What prerequisites need to be met for you to feel safe during sex?

WORK/CAREER

Why do you engage in your work?

What do you most want to contribute through your work?

What do you believe is the work you were put on this planet to do?

Do you feel you have the power to influence your destiny?

At the end of your career, what do you want to have achieved through your body of work?

LIFE PURPOSE

Why are you here, on planet earth?

Do you believe there's a purpose to your life? What is it?

Do you believe that everyone else has a life purpose too? How does it relate to your own?

What happens if you don't fulfil your purpose (if you have one)?

What legacy do you want to leave?

RELIGION/SPIRITUALITY

Do you have religious or spiritual beliefs?

DO YOU BELIEVE IN SOME SORT OF GREATER POWER/S?

What are your beliefs about the cosmos, the world, the Universe?

What are your beliefs about death and dying?

What are your beliefs about "right and "wrong" — Are there consequences for our actions? Is there only one version of "right" and "wrong"? What are your beliefs regarding people who disagree with you, or who have different spiritual or religious convictions?

POLITICS

Do you have political beliefs that are important to you? What are they?

Do you feel an affinity with a particular political party or ideology?

What are your beliefs about the role of government?

What does it mean to you to be a "citizen" in society?

Do you believe that you, as an individual, have the power to effect change in your community?

EQUALITY

How do you see yourself in relation to other people?

Do you believe in equality? Are you worth more than, less than, or the same as other people?

How do you respond or react when you encounter beliefs that are different from your own?

How do you respond if you are affected by inequality?

How do you respond if you witness others being affected by inequality?

PARENTING

How do you perceive the role of parent?

How do you want to parent?

What three qualities would you most like to instil in your children/future children?

What are your views on disciplining children?

When your children are sixty, and reflecting back on their life, and they say, "My mom taught me XYZ," what do you want that XYZ to be?

EDUCATION/LEARNING

What does education mean to you?

How important is formal education to you?

How important is ongoing learning to you?

How do you keep educating and learning yourself?

How important is growth to you?

PHILANTHROPY

Do you believe in "giving back" to others and/or your community?

Do you practice philanthropy in your life? If so, how?

Do you feel a responsibility to other humans on the planet?

What are your beliefs about service work?

What are your beliefs about charity?

This list is, by necessity, incomplete and imperfect. Think of it as a starting point. As you're going through it, feel free to flesh out your answers and add questions for yourself that dig deeper into your own personal values.

If you're feeling stuck, here are some of the answers I jotted in my own journal...

WHAT ARE YOUR BELIEFS ABOUT DEATH AND DYING? I am not scared of dying because I believe we are not this body. I believe our soul (or spirit, or whatever you want to call it) goes on, even when our heart is no longer beating and we've left this mortal plane.

HOW IMPORTANT IS ONGOING LEARNING TO YOU? I am a committed student for life. I never want to stop learning, growing, and evolving in all areas of my life. I am Open Wide to being the best version of myself and it's very important that I am with someone who also values education and personal evolution.

DO YOU BELIEVE IN "GIVING BACK" TO OTHERS OR YOUR COMMUNITY? I believe our role here on earth is to give back and serve others and our community as much as we can.

Unearthing your values can be a surprising exercise. Sometimes it takes deliberate digging to realize what your values about a specific area actually are.

IT'S ALSO IMPORTANT TO NOTE THAT YOUR VALUES CAN CHANGE AND EVOLVE – THEY'RE NOT SET IN STONE FOREVER. Going through your answers, you might be surprised to find that a value you once held dear has dropped off your radar, or vice versa — that something you never used to care about has suddenly shot to the top of the list. Major life events or self-discoveries can trigger shifts too. (For example, as a kid, you might not place a huge value on education. But as soon as you become a parent, it might become a helluva lot more important to you!) This means the way you answer these questions today might not be the same way you would answer them in a year or a decade's time. Heck, you might even answer them differently *tomorrow*! And that's okay. The most important thing is being honest with yourself so you can understand your own belief system on a deep and truthful level.

Qualities

What **qualities** do you aspire to, as a person? What qualities are really important to you to embody and live by? Who do you want to BE and what do you want to represent?

Below is a list — again, by no means exhaustive. It contains a whole range of qualities that may or may not resonate with you. As you read it, take note — which of these are most important to you? Or are there some missing that you'd like to add (this is totally fine — in fact, creativity is encouraged!).

IT'S MOST IMPORTANT FOR ME TO BE …

- Adventurous
- Affectionate
- Authentic
- Aware
- Bold
- Brave
- Charismatic
- Compassionate
- Courageous
- Creative
- Curious
- Daring
- Decisive
- Dedicated
- Disciplined
- Disruptive
- Empathetic
- Ethical

- Faithful
- Firm
- Flexible
- Forthright
- Full of integrity
- Generous
- Happy
- Hard-working
- Honest
- Honorable
- Imaginative
- Independent
- Innovative
- Insightful
- Inspiring
- Intelligent
- Joyful
- Kind
- A Leader
- Loving

- Loyal
- Mindful
- Moral
- Nurturing
- Non-judgmental
- Open-minded
- Persistent
- Playful
- Respectful
- Responsible
- Funny
- Sincere
- Soulful
- Spiritual
- Strong
- Thoughtful
- Trustworthy
- Virtuous
- Wild
- Zen

INSPO-ACTION

Which five qualities (whether from the above list, or ones you've come up with yourself) are most important to you as a person? Whip out your journal and if five don't immediately come to you, write down all the ones that resonate, then halve it, then halve it again and again until you've got a solid five that feel true to you. This exercise may take some time to distill — it certainly did for me! So be patient.

In my journal, I wrote that it's most important for me to be honest (both with myself and others), generous (with my time, energy, and resources), loving (to others and to myself), kind (again, to others as well as myself), and curious.

Keep in mind that the qualities you want to embody might change. In fact, they may change quite frequently (mine do!). That's why I like to make a habit of revisiting this list at least once a year, to make sure I'm always tuned in to the kind of person I want to be, and living my life in a way that's truly aligned.

Now, go through the list again: what qualities are most important to you in a **partner**? You might want all of them, but try to choose the five that are absolutely MOST important to you.

For me, right now, the most important qualities in a partner are that they are loving, honest, open, adventurous, and intelligent.

The qualities you desire in a partner are also subject to change. What's important to me these days is very different from what was high on my list in my teens and twenties. For example, back then, honesty wasn't something I actively thought about. It wasn't until the guy I was dating when I was twenty-two cheated on me that it skyrocketed to the top of my list.

Interests

Another important depth of your ocean is your **interests** — the things that inspire, delight, and fascinate you. This could include your hobbies, your passions, and any other areas of interest you care about.

Usually, your interests aren't as deep-seated as your values and qualities — they're the next layer up. There's usually more fluidity here, often dictated by age and stage of life — so the things that interest you in your twenties may not be the same things that interest you in your thirties, and the things that light you up when you're a school student are likely not the same as the ones that fascinate you when you're a mother or a CEO.

Take a moment to think about your interests ... Grab your journal and answer the following questions.

What is your favorite way to spend a weekend? What are you doing? Who are you with?

What books do you naturally gravitate to?

What sort of podcasts do you listen to most? (*The Melissa Ambrosini Show*, I hope.)

What topic could you talk about for hours?

What topics do you naturally know a lot about, and enjoy diving into?

If you find yourself deep in an internet rabbit hole, what is the topic you're most likely reading about?

Do you have any hobbies?

What are you naturally skilled/talented/gifted at?

What do you spend most of your money on, that other people might not?

Do you do any classes or workshops outside of your career? On what topics? (And if not, if you *were* to enroll in a class or workshop, what sort would excite you?)

What are you passionate about?

What have you said you have always wanted to do? E.g. a photography course, study fashion design, travel to Mexico, etc.

If you're feeling stuck, here's a list of interests I came up with, after canvassing some friends. In no way is this list exhaustive, but if you're struggling to identify and home in on your interests, it might help get your creative cogs cranking ...

- Astrology
- Astronomy
- Business
- Candle making
- Collecting things
- Cooking
- Craft
- Dancing
- Drawing
- Entrepreneurship
- Essential oils
- Fashion
- Fitness
- Gardening
- Health/wellness
- Herbal medicine
- Hiking
- Horse riding
- Interior design
- Kinesiology
- Learning a second language
- Mindful/conscious parenting
- Music
- Painting
- Pets
- Photography
- Pottery
- Reading
- Renovating
- Singing
- Spirituality
- Sports
- Surfing
- Travel
- Writing
- Yoga

When it comes to your interests, you can get as specific and granular as you like. Some people might say that they're interested in "music" in general, whereas for others, it's a particular type. For example, I have a friend who is absolutely crazy about a kind of music called "Gypsy Jazz" — which I'd never heard of before I met her. But she can list loads of facts about it, and listens to it every day.

It's also totally okay if you DON'T have super-strong interests. For example, you might enjoy your yoga class once a week, yet have no desire to get any more involved, and would hesitate to actually call yourself a "yogini." This is totally fine — lots of people engage more generally in several activities, rather than getting intensely into just one.

Take a moment now to look over your answers … Are you surprised by any of them? Or did you know straight away what your interests are?

My personal list of interests is extensive, and includes things like health and wellness, essential oils, yoga, meditation, conscious parenting, cooking, hiking, camping, being in nature, living a toxin-free life, dancing and moving my body, gardening, conscious business, and entrepreneurship.

Your Unique Depths

We've now dug deep into your values, interests, and qualities … Your answers to all of the previous questions make up the unique, wonderful person who is YOU. And hopefully, they've helped you see the water you're swimming in — particularly those aspects you might not have been aware of.

Because you're so immersed in your own ocean of beliefs, it's easy to assume that other people share exactly the same philosophy and worldview as you do — particularly when it comes to your core values and the qualities you aspire to. They're so ingrained and "normal" to us that we assume they apply to everyone. On top of that, most of us also end up living in a sort of "bubble" too — an echo chamber where most of the people we associate with share similar viewpoints, and our own perspectives are mirrored back to us on a regular basis. It can be funny when you remember there's a whole world of different beliefs out there. Heck, even within your own social circle there'll be a rainbow of perspectives… And that's part of what makes life so fascinating.

If you have a partner, I highly recommend inviting them to

answer these questions with you. Remember, everything is an invitation and they may be open to it or they may not. All you can do is present the invitation with love, and know that whatever happens is fine.

When Nick and I were first courting each other, this stuff was all we spoke about. Intuitively, I asked him questions that revealed who he was at his core: *What inspires you? What do you love to read and learn about? What books are on your bedside table? What do you dream about?* At the time I didn't really understand the importance of knowing your own ocean or that of your partner, it was just something I started exploring because it felt right and because I wanted to dive deeper in this relationship.

YOUR OCEAN CAN CHANGE

Water, by definition, is fluid. So your "water" might change — and that's okay. As mentioned earlier, even the staunchest believer can find themselves undergoing a personal watershed of change and evolution. It's all good, it's all perfect ... you do you.

Personally, I like to check in on all three of these elements — my values, the qualities that are important to me, and my interests — at least once a year. New Year's seems to be a great time to do it, so you can ride that wave of fresh January energy and possibility. Nick, Leo, and I have incorporated these questions into our start-of-the-year family ritual. Along with mapping out our goals and intentions for the year ahead of us, we each dive into our own ocean to make sure we're living our lives in a state of alignment and truth.

For Nick and me, this kind of personal development deep-dive is fun (we get excited by this stuff!). **But it's been particularly beautiful to see how much value and joy Leo gets out of**

the exercise too. So parents, don't be scared to invite your kids to join you on this journey inward. You may just discover unexpected things about your little ones!

FIRMNESS AND FLUIDITY IN YOUR OCEAN

At first glance, it might seem that you and your partner need to have exactly the same answers to all of these questions in order to be compatible. But that's not the case at all. **Each of us is as unique as a snowflake**, and just as you won't find anyone else on the planet with exactly the same fingerprints as you, neither will you find someone with exactly the same matrix of values, qualities, and interests. (And to go in search of this would be a fool's errand!)

This means that when you come together with another person in a relationship, though they may share a lot of the same answers as you, there will most likely be points of difference too. Your job is to figure out in which parts of your ocean you're willing to accept difference (that is, in which areas you're willing to embrace fluidity) and in which parts you require alignment (that is, the areas where you are firm).

There are no right and wrong answers here. And no one can make this determination other than you. It's deeply personal, and figuring it out requires you to Open Wide, get incredibly honest with yourself (and your partner, if you have one), and be accepting of whatever comes up.

As a general rule, **values** are likely to require significant alignment, especially any that you have a particularly strong belief system about. For example, for some people, religious values are an area of firmness. Their beliefs on this subject are so fundamental and important to them that they require complete alignment before a relationship is possible. For other people, religion might still be very important, but they do *not* require their partner to share the same values; that is, they are fluid, and do not require alignment. For others still, religion may not be an important value at all: these people are likely to be fluid on this point too — not minding what their partner believes.

The **qualities** you desire in a relationship are also likely to require some alignment. For example, if you care massively about having a partner who's trustworthy, honest, loyal, generous, and committed, while your date is looking for a partner who's fun, playful, adventurous, creative, and novel, you might find yourselves butting heads because you desire such different things.

Your **interests** are likely to be the most fluid out of the three elements. There might be a particular interest you'd prefer to be able to share with your partner, but only you can decide if you're willing to be firm or fluid on this; only you can decide if it's a dealbreaker.

For example, I have a friend who really needs to share the same interest and taste in music with any partner. She recently broke up with a guy because he didn't share her love of classical music. She is so passionate about music and it's such a big part of her life that she couldn't get past it, so she chose to be firm. On the other hand, I'm not so fussed. Obviously, the fact that my hubby is a musician means he has a massive interest in it. I like music (especially his), and I respect his love of music, and we happen to share a similar taste ... but it wasn't a dealbreaker for either of us, like it is for some. Remember, of course, **this isn't about right or wrong, or comparing yourself to others**: it's simply about recognizing where you're going to be firm or fluid.

It's also important to remember that, **in a relationship, it's possible to develop entirely new interests together** — ones you've never cared about before. This can be immensely gratifying, and can be the grounds for a really strong, fulfilling, and enjoyable bond. For example, our shared interest in gardening, hiking, camping, interior design, and service work only really took off when Nick and I got together. These are interests we have created and bonded over as a couple. Before that, neither of us was really interested in those things, and it's been beautiful to share these passions and watch them grow. Similarly, one of my friends never realized she was interested in painting until she started dating this guy who was an epic graffiti artist, while another friend didn't know how to boil an egg until she started dating a chef, igniting her passion for cooking.

Take a moment now to look back over your answers to the questions above. Which values, qualities, and interests do you require complete alignment on? And in which areas are you open to fluidity?

I'm firm in my values on health, money, and parenting in particular. It's very important to me that my partner is aligned with me on these topics (and our alignment there was one of the things that drew me to Nick in the first place). On the flipside, I'm much more fluid in my beliefs about religion and spirituality. Though I have beliefs and values in these areas, I don't require as much alignment and am willing to accept more difference (as long as it comes with respect).

I'm pretty firm on the qualities I desire in a relationship too. I don't need my husband to prioritize *exactly* the same qualities as me, but I do need there to be some overlap and general compatibility. I mentioned before that my top five list of qualities I desire in a partner is: loving, honest, open, adventurous, and intelligent. Nick's personal list is made up of: soulful, nurturing, open, loving, and authentic. As you can see, though we've used different words, we're painting similar pictures. This is important to me, and makes me feel like we're on the same page and shooting for the same star.

When it comes to interests, as I've mentioned, I'm quite fluid. I love that Nick and I share a deep passion for meditation and we meditate together daily, but it wouldn't be a dealbreaker if he wasn't into it. I love that we're both keen cooks, but again — it wouldn't be a huge deal if he didn't share my interest. We're also both very big on giving each other space to pursue our own interests. For example, Nick is passionate about rock climbing and surfing, and although I've tried both, they're not my jam. Similarly, I'm into pottery and dance classes, and that's 100 percent not Nick's cup of tea. **But we always respect each other's interests, even when we don't share them, and we consciously create space for the other to pursue them.**

WHEN YOU'RE LOOKING FOR ALIGNMENT, BE SURE TO DIVE DEEP

Sometimes, the way things appear on the surface isn't a reflection of how they truly are. One of my friends, Rosie, started dating a guy who worked at the local organic cafe she visited daily. "I was so excited when I met him," she told me. "I'd been wanting to meet someone who was as passionate about health and wellness as I was, and here he was!" After a few chai-fuelled conversations, it seemed like they had loads in common. But when they finally went on a date, it became apparent that his definition of living a healthy life was very different from Rosie's. For him, living a healthy life was a "weekday" thing, while on the weekends, it was drinking, partying and pulling all-nighters with his friends. When

Rosie realized this, it felt like a big area of difference. "We had so many interests in common — yoga, surfing, traveling ... He even loved visiting the farmers' markets, which made me think he was my dream guy! But he was still partying his pants off on the weekends and drinking himself under the table. My gut just kept telling me he wasn't the one for me, and I couldn't look past it."

For Rosie, not being aligned on drinking and partying was enough to make her walk away. That was *her* Truth. Of course, for others in exactly the same scenario, that might *not* have been a dealbreaker. None of this is about judging anyone, or figuring out what you "should" do according to some external standard or rulebook. This is simply about staying true to *you*. (And remember, every time you ignore your Truth, there is always a price to pay and the Universe will give you a metaphorical kick in the butt.)

Appearances can also be deceiving in the other direction too — it can seem, at first glance, as if you *don't* have many areas of alignment with someone, when in fact you do. My friend Jacinta experienced this. When she first met her partner, Simon, it seemed that they were complete opposites. She was a nerdy, academically minded lawyer whose favorite pastimes were reading and writing. He was a tradesman who (by his own account) had barely made it through high school and hadn't picked up a book in ten years. "I always thought it was important to me to have a partner who was college educated. That was one of the things I looked for when I was dating," Jacinta told me. "After all, education is so important to me. I wanted a partner who was intellectual, and who valued education as much as me. And Simon did NOT fit that mold." The two had an undeniable bond, however, and just seemed to "click." "The more I got to know him, the more I realized how aligned we were on the stuff that *actually* mattered to me — family, friendship, loyalty, generosity, being a good person ... I quickly came to realize that even though the surface layers of our lives looked to be polar opposites, our hearts were beating to the same drum, and we cared deeply about the same stuff." Jacinta also came to realize that her desire for a partner who was college educated wasn't actually what she wanted at all. "When I dug beneath my own preconceived ideas, I discovered that whether or not someone had sat through four years of lectures and received a scroll of paper meant nothing to me. What *did* matter was that they were open minded, curious about the world, and that they valued learning — in whatever form. Because I'm so academic, I'd limited myself to thinking that those things only come in the form of someone who's 'book-smart' and been to university. I couldn't have been more wrong. It scares me to think that if I'd clutched onto that idea, I would have walked away from the love of my life: the man who became my husband."

Jacinta's story is a potent reminder to **Open Wide to ALL possibilities**. It's easy to get caught up in creating a "wishlist" of what you want in a future partner — "I want someone who's blond, six foot tall, who's a doctor or lawyer, and who earns loads of money." But getting this fixated in detail about jobs and looks might be shutting you off from being with a truly amazing person. The thing is, if you look beneath all of these desires — if you Open Wide and dig deeper — you can often find the *real* quality or value you're craving. For example, if you think you want a partner who's a doctor or lawyer, it might be you actually desire to be with someone who values *hard work* as much as you do, or you might actually be craving the quality of *security* in a partner. With this newly expanded definition of your true desire, you might be pleasantly surprised to find that this value or quality exists in an array of people, not just a tiny pool of professions.

"BUT WHAT IF WE'RE NOT ALIGNED?"

It's also super important to note that if you don't have alignment with someone, it doesn't mean you can't get together, or that you must break up immediately. Not at all! This is where conscious awareness, letting go of expectations, and embracing acceptance are key.

So if you're on a first date, and you're not seeing a heap of alignment, you don't have to slam down your clipboard, get up, and walk away. Consider staying put and Opening Wide — like Jacinta, you could be surprised by what unfolds. (Of course, if your intuition is telling you to get the hell outta there, follow that advice, sister — it always knows best.)

Likewise, if you're with someone, and you've just realized you're each swimming in water that's a little — or a lot — different, this could be an amazing opportunity for growth. Or it could be a sign that you're both ready for new horizons and separate paths ... only you can make that decision.

Here are some strategies that may help you when it comes to a lack of alignment.

OPEN WIDE WITH EACH OTHER

Now is the time to get vulnerable, stay open, and practice Crystal Clear Communication, or CCC (see Chapter Five). Let your partner know you'd like to talk openly and lovingly about this topic. Consider setting some ground rules before your discussion, for example: "We don't judge each other for our values. We choose to speak to each other lovingly at all times. If we can't, it's okay if we need to take a break and regroup later."

DIG DEEP TO FIND THE ALIGNMENT UNDERNEATH
Often, it's easy to get hung up on our differences, even when there are acres of alignment between us.

A funny example from the health and wellness world: people who identify as "Paleo" and people who identify as "vegan" often have vigorous debates about which philosophy is better. When I see these arguments online — and they can get super heated — a part of me always wants to blow a referee's whistle and shout at them, "Guys! You've got far more in common than you do in opposition: you both think vegetables are the bomb, you both believe food is medicine, and you both believe in eating intentionally and responsibly. Let's keep that in mind, shall we? Then we might have a constructive conversation!"

If you and your partner both value education dearly, but one of you wants to send Little Mikey to a Montessori school and one wants to send him to a Steiner school, consider trying to identify all the areas of education you both agree on, and starting the conversation from there. In these moments, it always helps me to remind myself that my husband and I are on the same team. This simple reminder shifts my perspective so I can more easily see the areas we agree on, rather than automatically jumping straight to conflict or defensiveness.

LOOK FOR WAYS YOU CAN BOTH BE FLUID
Constructive compromise — where both of you feel like you're "winning" — can be a powerful way to deal with a lack of

alignment.

So, for example, if you can see that the two of you are not aligned with regard to money, maybe together you can come up with a strategy for how you're going to work through this issue when it comes up. Maybe he loves buying things while you want to save for your dream home. If that's the case, together you could come to an agreement to fulfil both your desires. For example, you both agree that he has X amount to spend per month on whatever he likes, but you both also commit to saving Y amount per month toward your dream home. That way, you both get to have what you want, while allowing the other person to have what they desire too. It's a win–win for all.

DO NOT BANK ON THE OTHER PERSON CHANGING

When it comes to values, qualities, and interests, people *can* change. They *can* evolve. They *can* expand … I've seen it happen, and I've done it myself.

But to *bank* on someone changing, or to try to change them yourself, can be an exercise in frustration and futility.

So if you decide to stay with someone even though you disagree on something significant, it's important that you're okay with the possibility that they might never change. Let go of your expectations and accept this with your whole heart, and you'll be able to sidestep a lot of suffering, arguing, and pain down the road.

IT'S OKAY TO TAKE TIME TO FIGURE THINGS OUT

You don't need to rush anything here, sister. You don't need to figure things out in your next conversation, or in the next week … heck, you don't even need to "figure things out" at all! Plenty of couples live in wonderful, fulfilling relationships, despite having a lack of alignment in certain areas. Remember, there is no right and wrong. **YOU are in charge of your life, YOU know your own self best, and YOU get to decide what's true for you.**

IF YOU'VE ENCOUNTERED A TRUE DEALBREAKER, YOU DON'T NEED TO EXPLAIN YOURSELF

If you're on an initial date, and the person does something that's highly antithetical to your beliefs — like, say, they use a racist slur, or they speak to the waiter like they're an idiot, or they call their ex-girlfriend a derogatory name — you're allowed to excuse yourself immediately, or turn down a second date. **You don't owe anyone anything** — including an explanation, if you choose not to. In these instances, one of my favorite sayings is "No is a complete sentence." So feel free to just say no, sister — no justification or reason required.

STAY OPEN TO DOING THE WORK

As I said earlier, a lack of alignment does NOT mean the relationship won't work or that you need to end it immediately. What it does mean is that you need to open up to each other, fully listen with both ears, sit in a space of non-judgment, and treat each other with love and respect as you figure out the path forward. This is called **working on your relationship**. It takes bravery and guts to do, but when you're both committed, it can be one of the most incredibly rewarding experiences of your life, and can bring you more joy and fulfilment than you ever thought possible.

KEY TAKEAWAYS FROM CHAPTER FOUR

- **JUST LIKE THE FISH THAT DOESN'T REALIZE IT'S SWIMMING IN AN OCEAN FULL OF WATER, OFTEN WE DON'T REALIZE WE'RE LIVING OUR LIVES BY A UNIQUE SET OF VALUES, BELIEFS, AND PRINCIPLES.**

  Even if we're not aware of them, they still govern how we think, feel, and navigate through life … which means they also have a huge impact on how we show up in our relationships.

- **YOUR 'OCEAN' IS MADE UP OF YOUR UNIQUE VALUES, QUALITIES, AND INTERESTS.**

  These may change over time, so it's important to check in with yourself regularly to make sure you know where you're at.

- **YOUR JOB IS TO FIGURE OUT WHAT PARTS OF YOUR OCEAN YOU'RE FIRM ON (I.E. WHERE YOU REQUIRE ALIGNMENT) AND WHICH YOU'RE FLUID ON (I.E. WHERE YOU DON'T REQUIRE STRICT ALIGNMENT).**

  There are no right and wrong answers here, and no one can make this determination other than you. Figuring it out requires you to Open Wide, get incredibly honest with yourself (and your partner, if you have one), and be accepting of whatever comes up.

- **WHEN YOU'RE LOOKING FOR ALIGNMENT WITH YOUR PARTNER, OR A PROSPECTIVE PARTNER, BE SURE TO DIVE DEEP.**

  Sometimes, the way things appear on the surface isn't a reflection of how they truly are.

- **THAT SAID, YOU'RE ALLOWED TO CUT YOUR LOSSES AND RUN, SISTER.**

  YOU get to decide what's right for you, YOU are in charge of your life, and YOU get to decide what counts as a dealbreaker. If you've encountered something you're not willing to accept, you're allowed to walk away.

- **A LACK OF ALIGNMENT DOESN'T MEAN YOUR RELATIONSHIP IS DOOMED. FAR FROM IT.**

  It can be an exciting opportunity for growth. As always, the key to moving forward is to Open Wide, practice Crystal Clear Communication, and commit to doing the work.

CHAPTER FIVE

How to Have Rocking Relationships

As I touched on in Chapter One, relationships are the highest stake "games" you'll ever play, and yet most of us don't know the rules. Despite the fact that we're "in relationship" with everyone and everything that surrounds us, we've never been taught how to navigate these dynamic energy exchanges successfully, or with ease and grace. Relationships can affect every area of our life, our health, wealth, and capacity to love. The result? Way too many of us have been "flying blind" our whole lives, not realizing that we could be experiencing so much more fulfilment and happiness in our relationships … if only we knew the first flipping thing about them!

For most of us, our idea of what constitutes a romantic relationship was formed by watching our parents. Your beliefs are mainly formed up until the age of seven, while you're a sponge, and what happens in those formative years shapes our mindsets and belief systems for the rest of our lives. So your cute little two-year-old self, without even realizing it, was soaking up your parents' every word and action. *Oh, so THAT'S how you speak to someone, and THAT'S what happens when you have an argument, and THAT'S how you make up afterward.* Essentially, your parents' relationship was your interpersonal training ground and where you formed your meaning and definition of love. This means that most of us are acting out close replicas of our parents' relationships ... which may or may not be ideal! But don't worry, though our relationship blueprint is strongly conditioned from childhood, it's not permanent (nothing is) and your reality doesn't *have* to play out that way. (So if your parents had a less-than-stellar marriage, relax — you're not doomed!) You have the power, if you employ it, to choose an entirely new relationship paradigm for yourself. Are you ready to find out how?

You can experience relationships overflowing with love. It *is* possible! And it's your birthright!

For most of my life, I entered all my relationships — not just with men, but friends too — with an unconscious intention: *What can I get out of this?* This was something I learned growing up watching my parents. Both my parents are divine human beings and I love them dearly, but they people pleased (still do), because that's just what you "should" do, right?! They gave a lot to others — money, time, energy, food, a bed to sleep in, clothes — but there was always an underlying expectation that they would get something in return, even if it was simply a "thank you" or some sort of acknowledgment (which is all they ever really wanted). Then one day, I read this quote from Tony Robbins: *The only way a relationship will last is if you see your relationships as a place that you go to give from that place of love, and not a place that you go to take.* His words hit me like a ton of bricks and changed everything.

Cultivating rocking relationships starts with YOU!

Once you deeply understand and embody that, you're then ready to learn how to have rocking relationships with those around you.

Jim Rohn famously said, "You are the average of the five people you spend the most time with." In saying that, of course we are our own being and can make our own choices, but research has shown we're more affected by our environment — and the people in it — than we think.

Whip out your pen and paper and write down the five most prominent people in your life. This may be your partner, bestie, a colleague, your mom or sister. For me it's Nick and four of my besties. (FYI, this doesn't include your kids; I'm talking about adult relationships here.)

When you look at your list of five people, how do you feel? Are you excited, jumping for joy and feeling inspired? Or did you just have to pick up your jaw from the floor? If it was the latter, it doesn't mean you have to go and dump your friends, ditch your mom and break up with your boyfriend over text right now. This is about awareness! When you are aware of something — and are in the present moment — you can make inspired choices that are going to serve you and the good of all beings.

If you were fist pumping when you looked at your top five, then great! I'm going to teach you how you can be of even more service to those relationships and how you can take them to the next level so that ALL your relationships are rocking.

But first, if your jaw is still on the floor, I want to talk to you about creating space in your life for some other divine souls to enter.

Creating Space

Quantum physics has shown that everything is energy. Everything in the Universe — all matter, including ourselves — is energy. From the book or device you are holding in your hands, to the chair you're sitting on, it's all energy.

And the matter you choose to fill your space with matters!

When you fill your space with something negative, "toxic," or uninspiring, there is no room for anything else. For example, think of your stomach. If you fill up on white bread before you eat your veggies and protein, you're not going to have any space left for the nourishing main meal. But when you leave the bread out, you have plenty of room for what is going to truly nourish you — the veggies and protein. Same applies for the relationships in your life. If you fill your space with Negative Nancys and Debbie Downers, then you have no room left for Inspiring Inger and Happy Holly. The people and things we choose to fill our space with matter, because they affect our life, health, and happiness. And if you're ready to call in rocking relationships, it's time to create some space so more amazing people can enter your life.

As I mentioned before, this isn't about dumping friends right now over text; it's about bringing your awareness to how you *feel* when you're in their presence. Do you generally feel inspired, uplifted, and expansive in their presence? Or do you walk away feeling down, contracted, drained, and depressed? It's also important to note that of course Inspiring Inger may not always be inspiring (heck, who is?), but what I'm talking about here is an overall general feeling when you're in that person's company. Tune into that! And if you walk away from an interaction feeling like the life has been sucked out of you, there are two things you can do ...

1. You can fully accept those relationships — and the other party themselves — wholeheartedly and unconditionally. Full stop, end of story, and no more whining or complaining about it/them ever again.

2. Or you can decide to create some space within that relationship, not dump them, but hand it over to the Universe. Ask the Universe for some support and guidance on how to best handle this situation. Become aware of where you're placing your time and energy. And you can stop putting so much time and energy into those relationships that make you contract. Open yourself up for new, inspiring, and soulful relationships to enter instead.

So my invitation to you is to be mindful of how you feel when you're with your five most prominent people. Do create some space if you need to, and Open Wide to the possibility that rocking relationships are coming your way.

Drop Your Expectations

Expectations are the fastest way to ruin relationships, and if you want to experience rocking relationships you have got to drop your expectations ... right ... now.

As I've said, growing up in a very strict Catholic Italian family, expectations were par for the course. This attitude then carried over into my other relationships. When I first started dating, I thought the guy "should" text me all day, he "should" say yes to me, and he "should" make me feel a certain way ... Sound familiar? Many of us "should" all over the place, and as you can see, I was a champion "should-er" myself.

But running around with a mental spreadsheet of expectations is not fun. Expectations set you up for disappointment and arguments with your loved ones.

Instead, you could choose to have *preferences* that you hold loosely and don't get attached to. For example, you may have a preference that your partner takes care of dinner while you're working, that it's sunny tomorrow, or that your friend returns your call. If you expect all those things to happen, you'll inevitably wind up disappointed when someone (or something) fails to meet your exacting specifications. But if, instead, you hold on to them gently — *Sure, that's what I'd prefer, but either way is fine!* — then you can save yourself a whole lot of stress, heartache, and disappointment.

When I find myself feeling disappointed, it's usually because I have placed unrealistic expectations on someone ... of which they often had no idea! In that way, expectations are like setting yourself up for a lose–lose situation, when it's so easy to reframe it as a win–win.

The other thing is, when you're hell bent on your expectations, you close yourself off to things unfolding in other (and maybe even better) ways. It's like walking into a dark forest with one torch: if you only point your torch forward, that's the only path you'll see. But if you shine the light to the left and to the right you may see another, quicker, more beautiful path you wouldn't know existed had you never looked.

Let go of your expectations and Open Wide to the possibility of things unfolding in other — maybe even more magical — ways. Stay Open Wide!

When we have unrealistic expectations of how we think things "should" look, we close ourselves off to the miracles around us.

For example, how many times have you heard someone say something like, "I'll only date someone who's taller than me." Meanwhile, you can see they're completely missing the gorgeous, caring, five-foot-eight guy standing right in front of them.

The same sort of thing often plays out in friendships too. When you expect Tamara to call you back immediately after you call her, or to let you borrow her clothes, or to send you flowers on your birthday, you're closing yourself off to possibilities that are potentially way better, and setting yourself up for some serious disappointment in the process.

Expectations and Soulful Sex

The bedroom is another place where expectations can be rife.

There have been times when I've been on my back, a man between my legs, and thought to myself, *What the heck is he doing down there?! This feels like crap! I'm so not enjoying this — why is he doing it like that? Ouch, he's hurting me! Grrr, I really wanted to orgasm, but he's so bad at this. I'm bored ... what should I make for dinner — again, ouch, dude! I should just get myself off, it's quicker that way.*

I would place a bucketload of expectations on how I wanted our lovemaking to unfold. For example, he will swoop me up in his arms, kiss my neck, throw me on the bed, touch my whole body, and we would have the most beautiful lovemaking session of our life. When it didn't go that way, I would roll over disappointed, annoyed, and unsatisfied. The guy would turn to me and say, "Everything okay?" To which I would reply, "Yep, fine!" which was a big fat lie. He had no idea and was completely unaware of the laundry list of expectations I'd placed on him and our lovemaking sesh. And every time we tell a lie or don't speak our Truth, a seed of resentment is planted, which, if suppressed for long enough, will grow bigger and bigger over time.

Instead, what I could have done in those situations was release my expectations, put my Mean Girl on mute, and gotten fully present. I would have then opened myself up to the magic of the present moment — and practiced Crystal Clear Communication so my partner had a chance to tune in with me. But because I had a long list of expectations, I closed myself off to it being any way other than what I had made up and planned in my mind. Who missed out? Me! Opportunity gone. Moment lost forever! And I will never, ever get it back.

Giving and Receiving Love

When I was growing up, my mom would buy me clothes and little gifts to express her love. She is one of eight children and didn't have a lot growing up, so she loved being able to buy me treats and trinkets to express her love. But to me, those gifts weren't what I truly desired. What I desired was quality soul time with her, and physical connection like cuddle, and kisses. I craved those moments when we would sit on the couch and drink tea together. To be clear, it's not like I was *ungrateful* for the gifts she gave me; they just didn't have the same impact as her sitting with me for ten minutes and doing my hair. The way she expressed her love was different from how I like to receive love. Neither was right or wrong — just different! I then discovered the work of Gary Chapman and his five love languages, and what I then realized was that we all have a different way of communicating our love and a different way we love to receive love.

So I asked five people how they love to express and receive love and here's the results. Tash loves when her partner (or anyone for that matter) does thoughtful gestures for her. Things like making dinner so she can take a bath, picking up the kids from school so she can have some time for herself. She even loves it when she receives a "Just thinking of you" text from her sister.

Poppy loves verbal love. Phrases like: "You're amazing, I love you, thank you so much for helping me out, I'm so grateful for you" really light her up.

Tanya loves meaningful presents no matter how big or small, a thank-you note from a friend, or a flower picked on the way home from work from her lover excites her.

Amanda very much loves soul time. She gets so excited when her partner says, "Honey, I'm leaving work early so I can take you out to dinner," or, "Baby, I've cleared our Saturday afternoon so we can go on a picnic"; or when her bestie wants to go out to lunch just the two of them.

I personally love physical, emotional, and spiritual connection. Growing up, I remember my mum tickling my back and stroking my hair before I fell asleep. I remember sitting on my dad's lap while we watched TV, and my parents hugging and kissing me a lot. And maybe I got it from them or maybe it's innate, who knows, but my besties will tell you I'm a very touchy-feely person. So all those years my mom was buying me gifts to express her love to me weren't as powerful and meaningful to me as those precious moments of quality soul time and physical, emotional, and spiritual connection that we shared. When you understand how someone loves to express and receive love, you open yourself wide to deeper, more soulful connections, which is what we all desire.

It's very handy that Nick and I both love physical, emotional, and spiritual connection, so we make sure we do that every day. But if you and your sweet have different ways of giving and receiving love, don't worry: Open Wide and ask them how they love to receive love and express to them how you love to receive it.

It's important to note that you may love all the different ways to give and receive love, and that's cool too. Remember, there is no one right way.

You can apply this to all the other relationships in your life too. When you're thinking about each of your friends or family members, try to work out or simply ask them how they love to receive love. Maybe your bestie loves little hand-made cards from you, and your mom loves to hear you tell her how much she means to you. Understanding this will allow you to experience deep love.

Leo loves soul time with Nick and me. Once I recognized that, I made some massive shifts in our home, which has deepened mine and Leo's and Nick and Leo's relationships. I now make it a priority that we both get some soul time with him each day. That may look like ten minutes of kicking the ball before school with Nick, or playing a game after dinner with me. To be honest, what we do and how long we do it for is irrelevant; what matters is that he gets that soulful time with each of us. What Nick and I realized is that when we make it a priority and we take ten minutes out of our day to really play, be present, and adhere to how Leo loves to receive love, it not only makes his day, but he's a much happier kid.

INSPO-ACTION

- Write down how you desire to receive love, and make time to express that to your lover, family, and friends. Bring it up at your next dinner party or ask your girlfriends how they love to receive love when you're next out to lunch. Not only is it an amazing conversation to be had, but it will deepen all your relationships.
- Write down how you love to express your love, find people who love to receive love in that way, and go out there and give it. The world needs your love!

GIVING AND RECEIVING IN THE BEDROOM

Knowing how your partner loves to give and receive love is a key ingredient for soulful sex. For example, because Nick and I both love physical, emotional, and spiritual connection, we know that's our starting point and a great way for us to seduce each other. We will mostly begin with physical connection like a grounding massage or full-body tickle. But someone like Tash will get turned on when her partner runs her a bath, lights some candles, or gives her a foot rub. Poppy on the other hand would totally get off on hearing "I love you, you look so sexy, you're so beautiful." Tanya may love when her partner buys her some sexy lingerie. And Amanda loves it when her partner takes her away for a weekend sex-cation — a weekend dedicated to soul time for soulful sex.

Understanding how your lover desires to give and receive love is fun, and will help you experience soulful sex because it allows you to be of service to them even more.

Quit Judging

Every single person you have in your life, or who you meet for the first time, is there to teach you something about yourself. **There are NO mistakes and nothing is by accident!** Everyone is your teacher and is there to take you deeper into yourself, and to help you evolve to your full potential and to understand yourself better. But in order for that to happen, you need to have awareness — otherwise you will continue to point, judge, and blame everyone around you, hindering *your* growth.

Every time you judge, you're stagnating your growth and blocking yourself from Opening Wide to deep love.

Here are the three major reasons we judge others.

1. YOU'RE DISOWNING PARTS OF YOURSELF THAT YOU'VE YET TO FULLY EMBRACE AND OWN

A few years back, one of my then-partner's friends – let's call him Ben – triggered the crap out of me. I couldn't stand to be in Ben's presence. I thought he was arrogant, loud, obnoxious, and annoying. For years I judged him, putting him in the "seriously annoying person" box and avoiding him at all costs. Until one day it hit me like a semitrailer: I realized that all the things I disliked so much in Ben were actually present within me too. They were things that I had yet to fully own and accept within myself, that's why it triggered me so much. There were parts of *me* that were arrogant, loud, obnoxious, and annoying, and I was not fully owning them.

Whenever anyone triggers us, there is a lesson in it for us.

There are a bajillion different human traits, and we have ALL OF THEM inside each of us! So it's time to quit judging and own them all.

It wasn't until I fully owned those parts of myself that I stopped judging Ben and no longer felt triggered by his presence.

2. YOU WOULDN'T TOLERATE THAT BEHAVIOR WITHIN YOURSELF, SO YOU JUDGE OTHERS

I once had a client, Michelle, who was very shy and introverted, so extroverted people triggered her. She came to me with so much anger and resentment toward her sister. She said her sister was annoying, loud, and obnoxious (much like I felt with Ben). She shared a story with me that happened many years before that she was still holding onto. At her mom's fiftieth birthday, her sister got up and took over the limelight, right in the middle of her mom's own birthday speech. Michelle was shocked and couldn't believe that her sister had acted that way. She was disgusted and said she would *never* act like that herself.

If you can relate to this situation, this type of judgment might reveal a lot to you. It may be that you are not fully expressing your true self, and are therefore easily irritated by people who are. And even though that person may express their Truth clumsily, it triggers you because you're not expressing yourself fully.

A few years ago, I was sitting in my local organic cafe when this tall, handsome man came and sat down next to me. I could see he was quite distressed so I turned to him, smiled, and said hello. He then opened up to me and told me that his wife had recently kicked him out. He'd found out she was having multiple affairs – and was conducting them inside their family home while he was at work. He also shared that they had two daughters he was scared he would never get to live with again. He was devastated – a hard-working, forty-year-old man who now believed he had nothing and was living back at home with his parents. He went on to explain how he'd tried to give her everything she had said she ever wanted – the dream home, beautiful children, the hard-working husband – yet it wasn't enough for her. She took him to the cleaners and now he was broke in every sense. Immediately upon hearing this story, I went on a judging frenzy: *What a cow! How could someone do that?! Seriously, this guy is a great catch – what the hell is wrong with that woman? How could someone be so horrible? I would never do that. I want to slap her across the face – what a bitch!* As soon as I became aware of these thoughts, I stopped myself. Why was I feeling so triggered by this? Two reasons swam to the surface: firstly, because I would never tolerate that type of behavior within myself; and secondly, because there were obviously parts of myself I wasn't owning. Where was I "cheating" on myself or not fully loving myself?

There is a great lesson in every interaction with everyone, if you choose to see it.

3. YOU'RE ENVIOUS OF WHAT SOMEONE ELSE HAS BECAUSE YOU'RE DISOWNING THAT WITHIN YOURSELF

When Nick and I got engaged after two weeks, it triggered some people ... but not us. While others were reacting around us, we were (and still are) madly in love – so grateful that we found each other again in this lifetime, and so excited to just be in each other's presence. Some friends and family members were over the moon, stoked, and couldn't be happier for us. They were the people who were happy and overflowing with love within themselves and their relationships. Meanwhile, some others said we were rushing and that it was irresponsible of us to get married so quickly. But all those words just bounced right off us – we were so happy and in the present moment together. Those who felt envious of what we were experiencing, and resented the feelings that were being triggered within them, tried to come up with reasons why it was a bad idea. But when it came down to it, what we were experiencing was what they innately desired ... so they projected their stuff onto us.

If we learn to open our hearts, anyone, including the people who drive us crazy, can be our teachers.

PEMA CHÖDRÖN

Remember, everyone is your teacher, and your judgments on others can teach you a lot about yourself.

If you want to experience rocking, mind-blowing relationships, it's time to quit judging once and for all. When you judge, the only person you're hurting is yourself. So let's give it up already and judge no more.

JUDGING YOUR LOVER

My nonna once told me that when my nonno passed away, it was all those little things that used to drive her crazy when he was alive that she missed most. Things like him leaving his dirty socks on the floor, not hanging up his towel, the dirt trail he walked through the house after a day at work. They had also been the things that she'd judged the most when he was earthside: *Why is he doing that again? He is such a mess. I can't stand how he leaves his towel on the floor every single morning!*

Once he was gone, she realized how much time she'd spent stressing, getting angry, and judging him over those little things. She couldn't believe how silly they suddenly seemed, and how pointless it had been to judge him over them.

We enter a partnership (and friendships) knowing that the other person is human — they have dirty socks, stinky farts, bad moods, down days, the whole shebang. Yet I see so many relationships where one or both parties metaphorically bang their head against the wall for years (even decades) trying to fix, change, and improve their partner, their friends, or family members to get rid of these "flaws." But in this situation, you really only have two options ...

1. Accept it — and them — wholeheartedly and quit judging.
2. Change it, by leaving the relationship or creating space between you and the other person.

If you can't accept it and them wholeheartedly, then leave or create space. Though if you choose to leave, do know that what you don't own within yourself you will most likely create in your next relationship. Even if you get a new partner, a new job — heck, even if you move to a new country — it won't matter: whatever you don't own within yourself will follow you.

Quick side note: Please note that I am NOT talking about abusive relationships here — whether that be physical abuse, emotional abuse, *whatever* abuse. That kind of behavior is completely unacceptable, and you do NOT need to sit around working on yourself or pondering your triggers while your partner is harming you. In those circumstances, please do whatever it takes to get yourself out of harm's way and keep you (and your children) safe. We will talk more about toxic relationships later, but I just wanted to make a quick mention of it here too.

CRAZY 8

Have you ever found yourself whining or stressing over something that you know will never change? For example, during the day Nick likes to leave all his supplements spread out on the kitchen counter. It bugs me because I love things ordered, neat, and tidy, so this gives me the shits. But it's important to him, so he kept doing it ... and every day, I kept getting annoyed by it. For years I let this annoy me. For a while I would put them away. Then I would say nothing and quietly steam on the inside. Then there were days I would just snap: "CAN YOU PLEASE JUST PUT YOUR STUFF AWAY?!" This is what my friend and business coach Bruce Campbell calls "Crazy 8" — going round and round, getting upset, frustrated, and annoyed about something you cannot change. You are basically stuck in an infinite crazy loop. Then one day, Nick said, "Honey, I know you like everything neat and tidy, but I need to leave these out as it helps me remember what to take and when. So please just let me do this and stop putting them away. You're going to stress yourself out every day if you don't just accept this." It then hit me! I can stop going round and round on the one issue and Crazy 8-ing myself into a stress spiral, or I can feel grateful that I have him in my life in the first place. Nowadays, whenever one of us can see the other is Crazy 8-ing over something, we gently remind them by simply saying, "Crazy 8, honey!" Leo even joins in too.

In fact, the Crazy 8 principle is great to teach to kids. For example, making sure the whole family is eating loads of vegetables (especially green ones) is super important to me. So every night, you will most likely find something green on our plate, much to Leo's disgust. Leo hates broccoli and most green veggies, but he has to eat them. They're very nutrient dense, and so essential for his growing body, that this is something I won't budge on. But most nights, we were having the same discussion about it:

Me: Leo, please eat your broccoli.

Leo: But I don't like broccoli.

Me: This is not up for discussion, darling.

Leo: But I don't want to!

We'd go round and round for hours, until one night Nick explained the concept of Crazy 8 to Leo, which he fully understood. Now, when Leo makes mention of how much he hates broccoli, Nick simply says, "Crazy 8, buddy!" Not only does Leo immediately stop whining, but we all crack up laughing … Hallelujah! Praise the green veggie gods, no more broccoli hating!

I use this technique in my friendships too. For example, I personally don't like talking on the phone; I'm much more of a "Let's catch up in person and have a heart-to-heart over a cup of tea" type of person. But in the past, my phone aversion has driven some of my friends insane. I'd try to explain myself, but they'd still ring and ring, and then send loving (but exasperated!) text messages saying, "WILL YOU PLEASE PICK UP YOUR PHONE, WOMAN?!" Finally, I told them about the Crazy 8 concept, which they totally got. (Some of them even loved the idea so much, they now use it in their own lives!) They realized it was pointless getting frustrated over this one tiny thing that was unlikely to change. So these days, most of them fully accept that phone calls aren't my preference and have stopped their Crazy 8-ing cycle, and we *all* feel better for it.

INSPO-ACTION

What are you currently Crazy 8-ing over with your partner, family, or friends? Where do you find yourself constantly going round and round and getting upset over and over about the same thing? Now ask yourself if you're willing to let this go? Yes or no? If no, enjoy Crazy 8-ing. If yes, it's time to sign the Crazy 8 contract, which will save you a lot of time and stress in the future.

I, _____, commit to no longer Crazy 8-ing over

[INSERT WHAT YOU CRAZY 8 ABOUT].

I promise that the next time this issue comes up, I'll do my

very best to let it go and to hold myself accountable. If I do

find myself Crazy 8-ing, I will gently let it go and remind

myself to come back to love.

This I promise.

[Sign name]

Quit Fixing, Changing, and Improving

One of the keys to open and fulfilling relationships is letting go of the need to fix, change, and improve the other person. For many years, I wanted to fix people. Like my mom, whom I desperately wanted to see eating more healthily, meditating, and moving her body every day. I wanted my dad to do the same. I wanted former partners to be excited about personal development, when all they were really interested in was sports. I wanted my friends to stop swearing, my brother to read my favorite spiritual books (which I was *convinced* would solve all his problems), and my bestie to date the guy I "knew" was right for her. But what I eventually realized was that wanting to fix, change, or improve anyone else is a quick route to Unhappy Land. Not only is it detrimental to your relationship with the other person, but it can cause a whole lot of unnecessary stress.

Instead, the easier and more pleasant route is to fully accept others just as they are. That's unconditional love. I know it can feel hard, especially when you can see someone not acting in their own best interest. But you know what? That's your opinion — or your judgment — and it doesn't mean it's their Truth.

You are the guru on you and they are the guru on them. We must honor each person's inner guru!

Even if you think you're "right," let's face it: you can only lead a horse to water, you can't make it drink. You can, however, inspire them another way: by being the living, breathing, walking, talking example of whatever it is you believe ... In the end, this truly is the only thing you can do.

What does this look like in action? Well, for years I agonized over what my parents ate, until I realized that I can't fix, change, or improve them. All I can do is be the example. So instead of trying to shove fermented veggies down their throats, I decided to walk my talk. I ate as healthfully as I could around them, I provided a bunch of super nutritious (and super tasty) options at every meal we shared (without making it a "thing"), and I continued striving to get fitter, stronger, and glowier in my own life. And guess what happened? All of a sudden, Mom was baking her own kale chips and boiling her own broth (bless!). But I know that none of that would have happened if had continued to pressure her into eating and living a certain way. Don't get me wrong, she still has a long way to go, but I will continue to lead by example. That's all I can do.

One could say I live in a little bit of a bubble. Most of my friends eat kale, do yoga, meditate, practice self-love, play with angel cards, charge their crystals under the moonlight, call on deities, and worship nature. But one of my oldest friends doesn't! Naomi and I have been besties since our first year of high school, and I love her to bits, but I swear she thinks I'm a little cray-cray with all my "self-helpy" stuff. But she has never judged me or tried to fix, change or improve me, and I've never tried to do that to her. Instead, there has always been a deep respect and unconditional love for each other and our unique differences. So unlike my "bubble besties," Naomi and I don't talk about crystal healing, the latest self-help book, or what came up in our meditation that morning. We have our own go-to topics of conversation, and we're both happy to hear about each other's "world," knowing that there's only ever love in the eyes of the other.

The Universe is funny though: a real hoot. Because so often, it's when you allow other people that judgment-free space — where you're not trying to fix them, you're just modeling your own choices with no strings attached — that they suddenly become curious and interested in what you have to teach them. And the fact that it's arisen entirely of their own volition makes it that much more powerful. Like one day, when I got a phone call from my beautiful Naomi. She and her husband had been trying for a baby for almost two years, with no luck. Suddenly, with no prompting, I get a very distressed phone call from her … "All right, Mel, what's this meditation and self-love stuff you teach about? I am desperate and will try anything — can you help?" *YESSSS. Welcome home!* I thought to myself — and without ever pushing, fixing, or trying to change and improve her, but by simply being the example. She went on to learn meditation and within one month of practicing daily, she became pregnant. Maybe it was a coincidence or maybe the process of letting go of all that stress allowed her body to actually do what it's innately designed to do.

There is such power and grace when you can firmly and confidently stand in your Truth and be the living, breathing, walking, talking example of what you believe. It's so inspiring! And maybe people will inquire (like Naomi did) and maybe they won't. All you can do is stay true to you, quit trying to fix, change, or improve anyone else (even your kids), and simply be the example yourself. This is one of the quickest ways to fulfilling relationships.

Get Generous

For most of my life, I was a pretty selfish human being … I'm not gonna lie, I was! I felt separate from others and I did my own thing. I never went out of my way to help other people or perform random acts of kindness. It's odd, because my parents are two of the most generous and giving people I know. I watched my mom get up at four a.m. to make lasagne from scratch for people she hardly knew who had just had a death in the family. My dad would pay for friends, family members, and random strangers at dinner. They would take in teenagers, exchange students, and children of family friends who were going through a hard time. They would look after pets for friends, even though they weren't "animal people." They would drive two hours just to drop something off to someone. They would sit in the car for fours hours and wait for me to finish dance practice, because we lived too far away for them to drive home and then back again to pick me up. They both worked extremely hard and long hours to provide my brother, sister, and me a different experience from what they had growing up. My mom worked the night shift as a nurse, just so she would be home at six a.m. to make our lunches and drop us all off to three different schools. They would bend over backwards for anyone and still do. That's just the type of people they are — so incredibly generous with their time, money, possessions, and energy. But for some reason, it was only when I hit rock bottom that I really saw and appreciated how generous they were/are and the lessons it taught me. I also realized and witnessed firsthand that the more generous my parents were, the richer — in all senses — they became.

The more you give from that full, overflowing place of self-love the more you get.

From then on, as an experiment, I decided to get seriously generous with my time, energy, money, and things. And you know what? I've never felt more deeply satisfied and fulfilled in my entire life. It has also exposed me to some of the most soulful people and opened me wide to rocking relationships I didn't know existed.

Give without expectations.

It's super important that you give without desiring anything in return. Give because you want to. Give from a place of love and give like your life depends on it, because it does! The more you give the more you get.

The getting is in the giving.

Giving doesn't have to be grandiose. It can be as simple as a smile or making some chicken soup for a friend who isn't feeling well. The size of the gesture doesn't matter; it's the thought that counts.

HERE ARE SOME WAYS YOU CAN GIVE TO OTHERS

- Give your time to a friend who's going through something. Just listen to them talk without interrupting.
- Help out at your kid's school.
- Smile at a stranger.
- Help a friend with something.
- Mentor someone younger than you.
- Give your time to your child to sit and help them with their homework.
- Make a dish and drop it off to a friend.
- Pay for the next person's juice at the cafe.
- Be nice and friendly to the person serving you at the cafe or shops. They are real human beings and have real feelings too. Don't speak down to them.
- Ask your taxi driver how his day is going.
- Volunteer at a charity or the local community center. According to sociologists Christian Smith and Hilary Davidson, people who volunteer on average 5.8 hours per week describe themselves as "very happy." Those who are "unhappy"? Just 0.6 hours.
- Help someone who is sick or in pain. People suffering from chronic pain report decreased intensity of pain, and less disability and depression, when they reach out to others in similar pain. In a 2002 Boston College study, pain was reduced by thirteen percent through social interaction. Scientists believe the release of endorphins explains this phenomenon.
- Pass on things you don't need or want anymore.
- Practice patience.
- Ask a friend what's new and exciting in their life at the moment. Most people love to talk.

- Redirect gifts. At your next birthday, ask everyone to donate to your favorite charity instead of buying you a gift.
- Create a "Love Box" full of raw chocolate, a book you've finished reading, some herbal tea, angel cards, etc. and drop it over to a friend or family member.
- Help someone cross the road, carry their shopping bags, or fix their flat tire.
- Teach someone something you're skilled at.
- Give a massage to your lover or a friend. A study that recruited retirees to give massages to other people showed that their cortisol levels – as well as their levels of anxiety and depression – dropped significantly afterward.
- Ask your partner, 'If there's one thing I can do for you today that will make your life easier, what would it be?' Then go do it!
- Send your besties an "I love you" or "You're AMAZING!" text message.
- Send a lovely email to a friend with an inspiring YouTube video or song in it to pump them up for the day.
- Send a thank-you card (snail mail style) to someone you love.
- Praise someone publicly on your social media or blog to show you appreciate them.
- Babysit your friend's kids – at their house – so they can have a date night.
- Love and be love. Find ways to be love and express your love to all. A hug, a smile, being kind and friendly ... it all matters and makes a huge difference.

These are only some examples of ways you can give. You are only limited by your imagination, so get creative and think outside the box.

Love only grows by sharing. You can only have more for yourself by giving it away to others.

BRIAN TRACY

INSPO-ACTION

How can you give to someone else today? What are you going to do? Come up with three things you're going to do today and then go and do them right away. Don't put it off until later (if you do, it won't happen). Do it now! And most importantly — as always — have fun with it.

Notice how you feel before, during, and after you have given. Your heart will feel warm and wide open, you may get tingles in your body or "God bumps" (as I like to call them). You may feel a rush of the "love hormone" oxytocin and get a boost in your immunity. When Harvard students watched a film about Mother Teresa with orphans, the number of protective antibodies in their saliva increased. The same thing happened when the students were asked to think of times in their life when they'd felt love/d, and their antibody levels stayed elevated for an hour. And when they ticked a list of organizations they wanted to donate to, their brains' pleasure centers lit up.

We make a living by what we get.
We make a life by what we give.
WINSTON CHURCHILL

Value Vulnerability

In the wise words of Brené Brown, **vulnerability makes people lean in**. The glorified world of social media can make people feel superior, but vulnerability makes you more human and real. It deepens your connection with others and opens you up to greater depths of love within yourself and with others. But I know it can feel scary. Sharing your Truth can make you want to puke! I get it. After I handed in my manuscript for *Mastering Your Mean Girl*, I wanted to hurl. I didn't sleep for a week because I had a massive "vulnerability hangover." I felt like I had been too open. Mean Girl thoughts were running rampant through my brain: *Had*

I overshared? Was it too much? Would people judge me? But when I tuned in, I knew it was my Truth to share those stories, and once I mastered my Mean Girl, I realized that what I had shared was perfect. I'm sure I will feel the same when I hand in this book too.

Vulnerability is key for deep love.

When you are vulnerable and true to yourself, it allows others into your heart and increases their trust in you.

For most of my life, my relationship with my parents has been very surface level. I yearned for a deeper connection with them — especially my mom — but I'd accepted that it wasn't my reality. Until one day, I was on the phone with one of my besties, Emma, chatting about step-parenting. I was expressing how I felt like I was failing as a parent, because I had yelled at Leo that morning. She told me to talk to my mom about it. To Open Wide and ask her for advice. My immediate reaction was, "Oh no, I don't talk about that sort of thing with Mom! And I don't really go to my parents for advice!" Emma encouraged me to do it and I'm so glad she did. The next day, I had the most open, loving, and vulnerable conversation with my mom about parenting, my childhood, and what it was like for both of us. This deepened our connection and since then (when it feels right) I have gone to her, Opened Wide, been vulnerable, and expressed my Truth. Each time it feels scary (although this has lessened with time), but I now have a relationship with my mom that I didn't know was possible, all because I found the courage to be vulnerable. Someone has to go first — to lean in, Open Wide, and be vulnerable. Will you be that first person?

In 2015, after my best friend Jess put on her angel wings and flew away, I closed myself off. From then on, there was a little bit of fear that all my girlfriends were eventually going to leave (which they will, of course, because we're all going to pass on one day). But

I really held onto this fear and told myself I couldn't let anyone get too close or let anyone fully in. Until one day, another friend and I were sitting in her car overlooking the ocean. We were talking about Jess and I openly shared with her how scared I was that she was going to leave too, whether it was that she would pass away or that we wouldn't be friends at some point. This was scary for me to vocalize. I felt very vulnerable, like I was standing naked on a stage in front of thousands of people. My palms were sweaty, my heart was racing, and my gut was in a knot. But you know what? Expressing this has only made us stronger. From that moment, our friendship deepened, all because I was vulnerable and spoke my Truth.

VULNERABILITY WITH YOUR LOVER

Of all the places to practice being vulnerable, this is it! If you can do it here, you can do it anywhere. Expressing your Truth can feel scary, but the ramifications are magnificent. When we suppress our Truth it only causes us pain. It eats away at our soul. It builds resentment deep within, which grows and grows and grows. And if you want to experience deep love and soulful sex, Opening Wide and being vulnerable are key.

In my early twenties, I remember feeling very scared to be vulnerable with my boyfriends. I didn't want them to fully "see" me, either physically or metaphorically. I wore a tank top while making love, even though the lights were always off. I was so scared to be "seen." I would put up with feeling like my vagina was being attacked and my boobs bitten off, all because I was too scared to speak up. This is ludicrous, not to mention detrimental to your health, happiness, and soul. When we put our beautiful temple (and especially our most sacred passage, our vagina) through something that is not our Truth, there are repercussions.

During my twenties, while I was having sex with men and not speaking my Truth, my period was irregular, and my hormones were out of whack. When I started loving, honoring and treasuring my beautiful temple and speaking up, my period balanced out, and my skin started to glow.

If you're having trouble speaking up for yourself in the boudoir, it can be as simple as saying: "Hey, honey, I really like it when you do X. Can you try Y? What about doing this instead? Can you move more like this? I'd really like to try this with you. What do you think?"

Being vulnerable and speaking your Truth in the bedroom, and lovingly encouraging your lover to do the same, will open you wide to deep love and mind-blowing sex. It will also have flow-on effects through all the other areas of your relationship and life. Expressing your Truth in other situations becomes easier because you're practicing being vulnerable in the most intimate of settings with your most intimate relationship.

INSPO-ACTION

On a scale of one to ten, how vulnerable are you currently with your lover? How vulnerable are they? Do you speak your Truths openly and honestly, or are you always holding your tongues because you're afraid of hurting each other, or being rejected?

On a scale of one to ten, how vulnerable are you with your family? Are you speaking your Truth or suppressing how you truly feel?

On a scale of one to ten, how vulnerable are you with your friends? Do you share how you truly feel in each moment or do you shut off that part of you?

Whatever your score, make a promise to yourself that you're going to be more vulnerable and speak your Truth. This doesn't make you weak or a "pushover," but rather a powerful, confident goddess who knows who she truly is and what she wants.

It's powerful to look at the flipside of this too: do you hold space for the people in your life to express *their* vulnerability? Sometimes, especially if we're used to a person in our lives being "strong" and "powerful," we can subconsciously try to avoid or shut down their vulnerability — perhaps because it makes us uncomfortable, or because we don't know how to react to it, or because we want them to keep on playing the role we've subconsciously allocated to them. I've definitely been guilty of this. Growing up, I always thought my dad was pretty much invincible. He was like my own personal Superman — he looked after us, he fixed everything, and I always knew he'd be there to protect us. So when I was a teenager, and saw for the first time that he had his own worries and vulnerabilities, it was quite confronting. I had to consciously expand my image of my father from being somewhat one dimensional (Strong! Manly! A wonderful provider!) to being delightfully, wholly three dimensional — in other words, human — as we all are. Once I realized this, and stopped blocking our relationship from evolving, we experienced a whole new level of love and understanding. It's not like we have deep and meaningful conversations every single time we chat. But when he does open up to me about things, you can bet your sweet patootie that I listen and hold space for him with the fullest heart I can muster.

When someone you love (whether it's your partner, your sister, your dad, whoever) makes that first brave move to speak their Truth, do you allow them to share freely? Or do you shut them down — whether subtly or overtly? How can you hold space for them to express their vulnerability?

Different Operating Systems

Everyone has an opinion on pretty much everything, and that's okay. What we have to realize and fully accept is that everyone is entitled to their own opinion and it's not our role to judge. What I believe is "right" is just that — a belief, not a fact. Someone believing differently is not "wrong." And what is "wrong" in my book may be okay to someone else. Our job is to simply stay true to our soul and to live that Truth. That's all we can ever do. This will save you a lot of stress in all your relationships.

When I first started on this journey of self-exploration and was experiencing such profound results through stillness and meditation, I wanted to shout it from my medi-pillow. I tried to get everyone I knew (especially my family, besties, and partner at the time) on board, but they weren't having any of it. They simply weren't interested! This peeved me. I could see that they were dealing with stress and feeling overwhelmed, and I had "the" answer. I wanted to help them. But although my intention was coming from a good place, at the end of the day, I had to realize that meditation may not be their path. And I had to accept and respect that they — and everyone else, for that matter — have the right to choose and follow their own path. This was a tough pill to swallow — *I* wanted to fix them, *I* wanted to help them, so why wouldn't they just listen to me? But in the long run, this was one of the most valuable lessons I've ever learned.

The truth is, we're all on different "operating systems." Think of it like your iPhone — I'm on iOS Green and you're on iOS Blue. Neither's better than the other ... just different! Let's celebrate diversity. And just like your smartphone gets upgraded, by doing *your* "spiritual squats" and "self-love sit-ups" you're upgrading your own operating system. (In fact, simply by reading this book you're upgrading your operating system — how awesome is that?!)

You may notice that you and your lover are on different operating systems too, with some features similar but some not. And that's okay! You have two options in this case ...

1. You wholeheartedly accept them and don't try to upgrade their operating system to yours (because you can't anyway).
2. You choose to leave the relationship.

You will cause yourself a lot of pain, stress, and heartache if you try to change someone else's operating system to yours, especially if they don't want theirs changed. That is not your role! Sure you can inspire and teach them things, but as we've seen, the best way to do that is by being the living, breathing, walking, talking example of your Truth. I know this can feel challenging — especially if you can see a loved one struggling (and describing it in those terms is still a judgment, by the way) or going through a really hard time. Let them know that you love them dearly and that you're there for them one hundred percent if they need. That's all you can do.

Trust that the Universe has a plan for them. Trust that they are on their own unique journey. Trust that they need to experience whatever is unfolding for them. Trust that if they don't get the lessons now, they will have to repeat the same thing later in life. Trust that their operating system is strong enough.

SEE THE OTHER SIDE

Left and right, up and down, front and back, love and fear, light and dark, on and off … There are two sides to everything, and when there is confrontation in any relationship, you've failed to see the other side. When you feel stuck, frustrated, angry, upset, or mad, ask yourself, *What am I not seeing here?* The answers will come flooding in, if you Open Wide to them.

Nick and I wrote SEE THE OTHER SIDE in massive letters on our glass doors to remind us that we need to consciously look and make sure we're always seeing the other person's perspective. We're all simply looking at things from a different viewpoint (or with different glasses), so take a peek through their glasses before dismissing the other person's feelings, opinions, or ideas.

To be clear, seeing the other side isn't about condoning what that other person has done or said. All you're doing is remaining detached, looking through their glasses, and opening up to a different possibility — an essential strategy for fulfilling relationships.

INSPO-ACTION

Are there any relationships where you're currently not seeing the other side? Why is that? What's blocking you from seeing the other side and letting that story go?

Know that whatever is blocking you will keep you from experiencing deep love. It's time to see the other side in all your relationships and to open yourself up to a deeper level of love.

To remind yourself to see the other side, try writing yourself a message on your bathroom mirror or on a sticky note and putting it somewhere obvious. You can also share this concept with your partner, family, and friends, so you can all hold each other accountable.

Even Leo understands this concept and will pull me up when I've failed to see his side on something. (Such a cutie!) It's a great concept to teach your children, as it reminds them to stay open to both sides of everything and to see other possibilities in all situations.

TAKE OFF YOUR CONTROL CAP

As I've confessed, I used to be a world-class control freak. I loved — and still love — things to go my way. It makes my Mean Girl feel safe and secure ... but this is actually a sure-fire way to ruin any relationship.

As I mentioned before, there have been many times when I've called one of my besties — Emma — in tears, proclaiming that I'd failed as a parent. "I'm the worst person on the planet! I'm such a bad stepmom! Leo hates me!" And on and on I would go. You see, Leo and I sometimes butt heads, and for years I couldn't work out why. *Was I parenting wrong? Should I read more conscious parenting books? Does he not like me? Am I a stepmonster?* But after a few deep chats with Emma, I realized that the reason there was friction was that I had my "control cap" on. I wanted things to go *my* way. I wanted Leo to do things in a certain way. I wanted him to say things a certain way. I would get angry if he didn't clean up after himself and put away his toys, *my* way.

I wanted to control the way he brushed his teeth, the way he did his homework, the way he sat, the way he tied his shoelaces, the way he held his knife and fork, the way he ate, and how he spoke. *Hello, control freak!* When I realized this, I saw how much of a Controlling Cathy I was being and what this was doing to him and our relationship. It was metaphorically squishing him and stunting his growth. This (in my book) was not okay! And not the type of person I wanted to be. So I had to pivot and pivot fast. In that moment, I made a conscious decision to take off my control cap. **I surrendered to the unknown and trusted that everything was unfolding exactly the way it was meant to.** It definitely wasn't a walk in the park for a gold medalist control freak like me, but I wasn't willing to let the discomfort ruin my relationship with him. I wanted to experience deep love, so this was my only option.

After I hung up my control cap, Leo had the space to really flourish and grow into a beautiful young man. This may not have happened if I'd continued to "squash" him with my controlling ways.

INSPO-ACTION

In which relationship/s do you have your control cap on? Are you willing to take off your control cap and surrender to deeper love, once and for all? If yes, great! If no, why not? What's blocking you?

There have also been times when I've caught myself with my control cap on in the bedroom. I had mapped out exactly how

I wanted Nick to seduce me, and I wanted it to go *my* way. So when it didn't, I was upset and disappointed. (Oh, hey there, expectations — I thought I'd said goodbye to you guys?!) Poor Nick, of course, was totally oblivious to the fact that I even had expectations in the first place (and was very confused as to why his wife was suddenly so distant and upset with him). By wearing my control cap in the bedroom, I had blocked my experience with my love. I could have surrendered to the moment, melted into his arms, let him take the lead, and had the most mind-blowing experience of my life. But because I had my control cap on, I didn't ... so our lovemaking was *uncomfortable*. It hurt because I was contracted. My vagina, my chakras were not wide open because I was trying to control how the night was going to play out, and pain was the result. Definitely not conducive to deep love and soulful sex, that's for sure.

Nothing good comes from wearing your control cap, so let's hang it up once and for all and surrender to the magic of the present moment.

Understanding Unity

It's part of the human condition to want to feel connected and united, and that overall feeling of true oneness. This desire is strong, to the point where we will go to great lengths and do whatever it takes to experience unity. We may join in on a bitch sesh or say something nasty about someone, just to feel united and "at one" with the person standing opposite us. You may find yourself getting sucked into a gossip huddle with your work colleagues, even when you actually *like* the person they're talking about. Despite thinking nothing negative about them, you join in the gossiping, which leaves you feeling gross and icky. So why do we do it? The reason is we're all seeking *unity*. And for those two minutes, when you're chatting conspiratorially with your friends or colleagues — all professing to be on the same side, all affirming each other's point of view — you feel a hint of unity. It's a cheap replica of true unity, to be sure. But it gives us *just* enough of a taste that we get fooled and sucked in.

I used to get so upset and annoyed every time I would see one of my cousins, Eva, because she would constantly bitch and say nasty things about other family members I dearly loved. Sometimes I found myself getting sucked into the bitching vortex, but mostly it just got me really down and made me not want to ever be in her presence, to the point where I would avoid situations so that I didn't have to be around her. The whole thing felt totally lose–lose. If I contributed to the bitch session, I walked away feeling guilty; if I didn't join in I *still* walked away feeling guilty, because then I'd turn into a Judge Julie and start thinking mean thoughts about Eva herself: *What a bitch, how could she say that?* Either way, I felt like crapola.

Then, after many years, I realized that Eva was simply trying to seek unity with me. All she wanted was to feel united, and the only way she knew how to do that was by bitching about people we both knew. This was a revelation for me. My judgment and anger immediately dissolved when I realized this. She is on a different operating system and was simply doing *her* very best to seek unity with me. Understanding this made me soften toward her.

We're all doing the very best we can given the knowledge and understanding we have at that time.

It's not our role to be Judge Julie and to think someone else's "best" is not as good as your "best."

But what if someone hurts your feelings or is rude to you — do we simply remind ourselves that they are seeking unity and let it go? Well, yes, kind of. But it doesn't mean you have to put up with it. If you know the iron is hot, don't go back and touch it. You see, **hurt people** *hurt* **people**. And when you remind yourself that they're doing the very best they can in that moment, it allows you to not take it too personally, knowing that they may be dealing with their own inner turmoil. Let's face it: you have no idea what's going on inside for anyone else. We have no idea if they're going through severe pain. Their mother may have just passed away, their cat could have just died, they could have just been told they were fired, they could be feeling depressed or suicidal, or they could have just come from the doctor's office where they received news that they have a life-threatening disease. The point is, you just don't know what is truly going on for anyone else. But what we *do* know is that they're doing the very best they can in that moment and it's not our role to judge them. What they — and everyone — need most is love! This doesn't mean you need to suppress how you feel, sweep it under the carpet, and just whack a big ol' love sandwich on them (but if that's your Truth, go for it!). What I am saying is to meet them with softness, show up with an open mind and heart, and remind yourself that they're seeking unity and doing the best they can. It takes courage to be the first one to show up with love. It can make you feel very vulnerable, but all we can do is show up fully with love in each moment and remember that they're seeking unity and doing their best.

Crystal Clear Communication (CCC)

The only time Nick and I argue is when one of us has failed to practice Crystal Clear Communication (CCC). I may have expected (there's that word again!) him to do something or know I wanted help with X. But if I didn't communicate that clearly with him, how the heck was he supposed to know?! You see, we often think our dearest loves can read our minds, BUT THEY CAN'T, SISTER! And the sooner we realize that the better. In fact, this goes for all our relationships — we can't read each other's minds! It's a straight-up fact many of us need to be reminded of (me included). That's why practicing CCC is imperative and the best tool you can have in your relationship tool kit.

WHAT IS CRYSTAL CLEAR COMMUNICATION?

Most people don't practice CCC. Instead, their communication can be vague, fear based, unclear, and wishy-washy. They're not fully present, not speaking from their heart, and not fully listening with both ears, resulting in unclear outcomes. CCC, on the other hand, is about creating a heart connection while communicating. It's about speaking only from your heart (not your head), being fully present with the person in front of you, and listening with both ears (not just one ear, while you wait impatiently to give your two cents' worth on the topic at hand). It's about speaking your Truth openly, honestly, authentically and crystal clearly.

When you practice CCC, you reach the other person's heart; when you speak from your head you reach their head.

There have been many times when I've caught myself mid-conversation with Nick, not practicing CCC. In those instances, I will say to him, "Honey, we're not practicing CCC right now. I'm going to go for a walk and when we can both practice CCC let's come back together and talk." And he does the same with me.

Like everything else, **awareness is KEY for any internal shift**, because once you're aware of something you can pivot.

Think back to a recent disagreement you had with someone. Can you see that one (or maybe both) of you weren't practicing CCC? How could you have practiced CCC in that moment?

Practicing CCC will save you a lot of time and stress, and open you up to deeper levels of love with those around you. It's a beautiful thing, and like anything, the more you practice it the easier it becomes.

I had a client, Suzie, who really struggled with CCC. She grew up in a home where not only did they not practice CCC, they rarely communicated at all. She kept everything bottled up, and when she began dating, she didn't know how to express herself. This resulted in men always leaving her, a pattern that repeated itself for years. She also didn't have many close girlfriends because she was so scared to speak up and be her true self. But after reading *Mastering Your Mean Girl*, she realized what was unfolding and decided she wanted to rewrite her love story and start practicing CCC. Since implementing and making CCC a priority in her life, she has been in a loving relationship for two years and has surrounded herself with beautiful soul sisters she feels she can be her true self with.

Another client, Rosie, came to me devastated after falling out with her parents. She had just finished high school and they wanted her to go on to study law like the rest of the family. But her heart and soul were in nutrition and personal training. She had a burning desire to help people feel healthy and strong, and she lit up like a disco ball when she spoke about anything to do with health and fitness. She felt obliged to carry on the family tradition, but knew deep in her bones that it wasn't for her. I told her to practice CCC. At first she was scared and thought she couldn't do it, so we did some role-playing. We pretended I was her mom and she practiced on me first. This gave her the confidence to speak her Truth. A few days later she told me they'd ended up having a beautiful, open, and honest conversation. She'd consciously practiced CCC, and, although she felt scared at the time, it had worked! Her parents agreed to let her study what she desired, and she was thrilled to have their heartfelt support.

When you practice CCC, anything is possible.

When you're in the heat of an argument, CCC can sometimes feel way out of reach. If that's the case, the best thing you can do is break the cycle by removing yourself from the situation. Now, this may take some practice, as we can become so consumed by the emotion that we forget to walk away. But when you *do* remember, take the opportunity to remove yourself — that's all you can do. Recently, I could feel myself about to lose it at the fact that Leo had again taken forty-five minutes to drink a smoothie and we were going to be late for school. But instead of losing my cool, I decided to break the cycle. I left the kitchen, washed my face, and then re-entered the room when I felt like I could practice CCC with him.

Another time, Nick and I were going around and around in circles over who said what to whom about something that was no longer even relevant. He was the first one to become aware of the fact that we'd lost touch with our CCC goals, so he deliberately started dancing mid-argument to break the cycle. Not only did this work, but it made us both crack up laughing.

Here are some other ways you can break the cycle next time you feel yourself in the heat of an argument:

- Move your body. Shake, dance, do jumping jacks or burpees, or jump up and down on the spot. Do whatever you need to do to shift the energy in your body and change your state.
- Go for a walk in nature to create some space between the two of you.
- Leave the room immediately, take a shower, splash your face with water, or dive in the ocean.
- Go meditate.
- Use your voice. Scream, shout, laugh, or say something silly, like "Elephants like to eat poo!" Not only will you get a giggle, but you will definitely shift the energy and break the cycle.

- Place your hands on the other person's heart and stare into each other's eyes. Don't say anything, just hold this position for a few seconds.
- Hug, even if you don't want to.

It doesn't really matter what you do to break the cycle, just as long as you do. Find things that work for you, your lover, and your kids. There have been times when I've sat in a negative spiral not just for weeks or months, but years. It's boring, not fun, and not worth it! Quickly break the cycle and come back home to your Truth … you know what that is by now, right? LOVE!

I know sometimes it can make you feel vulnerable, and it can be scary and hard to be the first one to lean in and break the cycle, but just do it. Go first. Take responsibility and lean in, because you will open yourself up to depths of love you didn't even know existed. You'll also be setting a great example for the people around you.

INSPO-ACTION

Is there anyone you need to currently break the cycle with? If so, how are you going to do that? What creative things are you going to do to break the cycle?

_____

_____

_____

_____

_____

Healthy Boundaries

A lot of spiritual folk struggle with setting boundaries. Some even struggle just saying the word "boundary." They worry that having boundaries isn't spiritual, or that it will make them feel closed off from the world, as though they're surrounded by a fifty-foot-high barrier. But you know what? The opposite is actually true. **Setting healthy boundaries allows you to Open Wide.** Know why? Let me paint you a picture ...

Imagine you own an empty block of land in the middle of a busy street — there's no house, no fence, nothing but lush green grass butting up to the sidewalk. With no boundary like a brick wall in place, random people walking by might start trespassing on your property, maybe using it as a shortcut, or dropping their garbage there ... They might even let their dog poop on your beautiful freshly mowed grass! How would that make you feel? You'd probably find yourself getting angry or defensive that these people weren't respecting your property. You might even become one of those cranky people who yell at passers-by before they've even done anything wrong. (*Get off my lawn, kids!*) Of course, though people should know not to drop garbage in your yard, there *is* something you could have done in the first place to make everything a lot easier on yourself ...

Imagine now, that as the owner of that lovely block of land, you instead choose to erect a wooden fence with a gate for people to come in and out. This fence — all painted and pretty — lets people know that the land is owned and cared for. Suddenly, people *respect* that boundary — they don't randomly trek across your block as a shortcut anymore, or toss their litter, and they definitely don't let little Fido poop there any more. Why this change in behavior? **Because you've proactively set the guidelines for them**, they know how to interact with your property. You're not leaving things to chance: you're setting your boundaries upfront. You're not totally rigid about it, of course — there's a gate in your fence, so that people who you know or who you *want* to be there (like the postman or the gardener) can enter and exit without hassle. But any unwelcome visitors? They know to steer clear and stay on the right side of your fence.

This fence analogy is exactly how personal boundaries work too. Having your own personal "fences" with a gate in place allows you to relax and feel safe, because you've proactively laid the guidelines for how people should interact with and treat you. These boundaries also mean you don't have to get prickly and defensive with people — worrying that they'll disrespect you — because the line in the sand (so to speak) is clear and obvious. And just like a real fence, you can have your "gates" in place too, so you can allow energy in and out, and you can let whomever you like through your entryway.

That's the power of boundaries — and because they have a gate that you choose who and what you let come through, you've proactively asserted that something is okay and something else is not. With your fence in place, the world knows where you stand, energy can come and go, and you feel safe and relaxed.

Boundaries tell others what is acceptable for your body, mind, and spirit.

When it comes to boundaries, you have to set the benchmark for everyone else by honoring and respecting your own boundaries first, then others will do the same. *Honor* your boundaries and honor and respect other people's boundaries too. And remember, we're all on different operating systems, which means we will each have unique boundaries that support and protect what's most important to us.

It's important to remember that we teach others how to treat us.

Once you've set and clearly established your boundaries, try to be consistent. Don't move the goalposts just because someone pushes against them (unless, of course, YOU have chosen to make a conscious boundary shift). You have the right to firmly — but politely, of course — enforce them.

BOUNDARIES 101

The reason many people don't like the idea of setting boundaries is that it can seem like you're restricting yourself by setting up a bunch of annoying rules. But this couldn't be further from the truth. While boundaries may seem like rules on the surface, it's important to understand that they're not rigid. They're actually far more subtle, and are as unique as the individual. And they're not set in stone — you're in charge of them. Meaning if you don't like them or they no longer feel true for you, you can change them! I change my boundaries as I grow and expand. I adjust them consciously to serve my highest self and that of others, when and if the need arises. The flexible, nuanced nature of boundaries requires plenty of ongoing "fine-tuning," and I believe that this is one reason so many people find boundaries challenging — you can't just "set and forget" them; they're constantly evolving as you decide and wish.

Boundaries are also not just about you... they're about other people too. Not being clear about your own boundaries and not being able to communicate about them clearly with others can often result in blame and resentment (and, consequently, a closed heart and breakdown of your relationship).

WHY IT'S IMPORTANT TO IDENTIFY AND ESTABLISH CLEAR AND CONCISE BOUNDARIES

We all know what it feels like to have the energy sucked out of us by someone else, but setting healthy boundaries can protect you from that. We can all also relate that there are people who no matter how many times you've clearly told them what your boundaries are, continue to overstep the "line." While this could be a lack of respect, perhaps they simply need help in understanding why it's important to have boundaries and to respect those of others.

To put it simply, having strong, clear boundaries allows you to be the best version of yourself possible. It allows you to share your unique gifts with the world with love (because you've taken care of yourself first). **Having strong clear boundaries is an act of self-love.** When you truly care for yourself and your loved ones (and your belongings, which are extensions of the "self") you will naturally want to create a healthy set of boundaries that will not only support you, but those you love and the world at large.

WHY IT'S IMPORTANT TO RESPECT THE BOUNDARIES OF OTHERS

Most of us have experienced that moment when someone oversteps your "personal space" boundary with little or no regard for how we feel about the intrusion. (You know the types I'm talking about!) Sometimes you can practically see up their nostrils, they're so close! You can smell their breath, they may touch you, they may even cough on you or spill their drink on you. What do you do in these circumstances? Are you too nice to say anything, so you just sit there feeling uncomfortable? Or is your worthy-o-meter so high that you *know* your boundaries are worthy of respect, so you politely but firmly ask them to step back?

What about if someone has borrowed something from you and not returned it? Or returned it broken (without offering to replace it)? Do you speak up?

Or the person who continues to try to make you eat or drink something you don't want, even though you've already said "No, thank you" five times?

These are all boundary issues. We all know how annoying and irritating these experiences can be. We feel the intrusion, but we sometimes don't have the courage and confidence to speak up and say anything. So we "settle." We brush it under the carpet but continue to feel resentful towards the other person for invading our space ... We also end up feeling disappointed in ourselves for not speaking up. This level of low-grade annoyance and irritation is totally unnecessary, and we can choose to live without it.

If you're not great at asserting your boundaries yet, don't worry. You may have had very few boundaries in your life — perhaps because that's what you had modeled for you as a child, or because you've mistakenly believed you don't deserve to have boundaries, or maybe because you've simply never understood how empowering they can be. Take heed though: this is a skill that's simple to master (though not always *easy*), and daily life presents us with plenty of opportunities to practice!

Some people, when they realize they've had no boundaries in place, can suddenly swing in the opposite direction: creating a bunch of overly rigid emotional fences for themselves that can actually end up restricting their progress or growth. This is why it's so important to consciously choose your boundaries with love — and to adjust them when you feel the need — so that they serve you and others. Find the middle ground that makes YOU feel best.

I have consciously implemented healthy boundaries in all areas of my life. I've listed some of them below, broken down into different areas. Let them inspire you to create your own boundaries, or to adjust any you've already got that may no longer be serving you. (Remember, the boundaries *you* need to make you feel safe, supported, and like your best possible self *will* be different from mine. The following lists are to get your creative juices flowing, not to dictate what you "should" be doing.)

HEALTH BOUNDARIES

- I honor my temple and treat it with love and respect.
- I don't eat when I'm feeling emotional, sad, stressed, or overwhelmed, as this affects the way I absorb and digest my nutrients. I wait until I'm calm and then I sit, give thanks for my food, take three deep breaths, and enjoy it with a relaxed tummy and calm nervous system.
- I consume the highest quality produce I can find that is going to nourish my temple, not hinder it.
- I listen to my body and give it rest and relaxation when it needs it.

What are your health boundaries?

(Pssst! If you're interested in the full story on my health boundaries, I go into them in detail in *Mastering Your Mean Girl* in the "Fabulously Healthy" chapter, and also share them in my ebook *The Glow Kitchen*.)

FINANCIAL BOUNDARIES

- I believe we vote with our dollar, and every time I hand over money, I'm saying "I believe in X." That is why, before I spend, I check in with myself and make sure it's aligned to my Truth.
- Over-consumption makes me feel contracted, so I try to limit what I purchase by asking myself, *Do I really need this?* before I buy anything.
- I spend with love. Money (like everything) is energy, so I make sure that every time I buy something I do it with love and not guilt.
- I give generously.
- I employ the "Joy Factor." Before I purchase anything, I ask myself, *Will this bring me joy?* If the answer is no then I don't buy it.

What are your financial boundaries?

WORK BOUNDARIES

- I only do work that I love, that lights me up, and that brings me joy.
- I choose when and where I want to work.
- I only check and respond to social media once or twice a day. We're so much more contactable these days, but we don't have to reply to every message we receive at

that exact moment, and it's okay to turn your devices off. I choose when I'm available to others and when I use social media.

- I only check email twice a day and I only respond when I'm ready. Your inbox can be a massive energy sucker. How many emails come into your inbox each day? WAYYY too many? This is a boundary issue. Unsubscribe to everything that doesn't bring you joy, then delete or deal with the rest.

What are your work boundaries?

ENERGETIC/SPIRITUAL BOUNDARIES WITH OTHERS

These subtle energies can sometimes be hard to see and feel, but when you're still and quiet enough you will feel them more. And by the way, YES! You can still be connected to All That Is (God, the Universe, love, etc.) while having loving boundaries in place!

- I do energy clearings when I feel the need. (For example, yesterday at the post office the woman in front of me was yelling at the man behind the counter because he couldn't find her package. It was intense and, as I left, I felt quite shaken up because my body had absorbed her energy. So when I got home I had to clear out that energy to release the experience. I did this by jumping up and down on the spot, shaking my body – especially my arms and legs – vigorously. I also find taking a shower, diving into the ocean, bouncing on the trampoline, and dancing around the room helps clear and release stored energy in my body.)
- Energetically, if I'm not feeling up for something I honor that.

- I choose what feels good on *all* levels. For example, say at the end of the day I'm feeling tired, and don't want to go home and cook, so I decide to order in. Before I follow through on an urge like this, I listen to my body, mind, and soul, to see if they're in complete alignment with the idea. More often than not, a small part of me realizes that it would be just as easy – and a hell of a lot more aligned – to quickly steam some greens and crack an egg. So that's what I do. The lesson? If one part of you is questioning the decisions made by other parts of you, then you're not in complete alignment with that decision and you're crossing your own boundaries if you go ahead regardless.

What are your energetic/spiritual boundaries?

MIND BOUNDARIES

- I fuel my mind with the best "mind food." I don't listen to depressing or hardcore music, I only listen to music that makes me feel good in my body. Same for TV, films, and the media (including social media) – it's all programming our subconscious mind, so I consciously choose what I let in.
- I refuse to allow the aspects of the "group consciousness" that are not for my highest and best good to seep into my own set of beliefs. When we look at what's in the group consciousness regarding food and sexuality for example, what's perceived as being "normal" isn't necessarily healthy (think: sugar, pesticides, and porn). Being aware that what's common isn't necessarily for your highest good, and making conscious choices about what you choose to believe in is imperative for your expansion.

- I master my Mean Girl. I don't settle for limiting, negative Mean Girl thoughts and I consciously choose thoughts that serve and support me instead.
- I speak to myself with love and respect. I do the same to others too.

What are your mind boundaries?

RELATIONSHIP BOUNDARIES

- I consciously choose to not engage in low-grade bitching and gossiping with others.
- I only spend time with people who love, nourish, support, and inspire me. (Remember, you become like the people you spend the most time with.)
- I don't engage with people who drain my energy. (Who's got time for energy vampires? Not me!)
- I choose to not hang out with Negative Nancys or highly critical, rude, or mean people.
- I choose to not engage in other people's drama. Of course, I'll freely offer support, love, and guidance – but I won't participate in any game-playing or drama. I aim to live drama free.

What are your relationship boundaries?

HOME BOUNDARIES

- I create a clean, clear, mold-free, toxin-free, inspiring home environment for myself and my family.
- I use Feng Shui and essential oils to energetically support our home environment.
- I open all the windows daily to allow fresh air to flow in.

- I use plants to help detox the air we breathe.
- I only use one-hundred-percent-toxin-free cleaning and beauty products, so as to limit my exposure to synthetic chemicals.

What are your home boundaries?

CLOTHING BOUNDARIES

- I only wear clothes that make me feel good and that represent me.
- I choose comfort first.

What are your clothing boundaries?

TIME BOUNDARIES

- I choose when and where I dedicate my time.
- I politely say "No, thank you" to people and events that don't feel good in my body and aren't aligned to my Truth.

What are your time boundaries?

I have sex boundaries too, but I'll share them with you when we get to the sexy stuff.

KEY TAKEAWAYS FROM CHAPTER FIVE

- **WE ARE "IN RELATIONSHIP" WITH ALL THINGS, ALL WAYS.**

  Our beliefs about relationships are formed when we're young, but *you* get to choose how your relationships play out, *you* get to rewrite your relationship story.

- **DROP YOUR EXPECTATIONS FOR ROCKING RELATIONSHIPS.**

  When we have unrealistic expectations of how we think things "should" look, we close ourselves off to the miracles around us. Let go of your expectations and Open Wide to things unfolding in other — maybe even more magical — ways.

- **EVERYONE HAS DIFFERENT WAYS THEY LIKE TO GIVE AND RECEIVE LOVE.**

  Understanding that some people love thoughtful gestures, verbal love, meaningful presents, soul time, and physical, emotional, and spiritual connection will open you up to deeper, more soulful connection.

- **STOP JUDGING, ONCE AND FOR ALL!**

  Every time you judge, you're stagnating *your* growth and blocking yourself from Opening Wide to deep love.

- **QUIT TRYING TO FIX, CHANGE, OR IMPROVE ANYONE ELSE, AND BE THE EXAMPLE YOURSELF.**

  'Nuff said, really!

- **GET GENEROUS!**

  Give from a place of love and give like your life depends on it, because it does. The more you give, the more you get — but give without expectations.

- **VULNERABILITY IS A KEY TO DEEP LOVE.**

  When you're vulnerable, true to yourself, and speak your Truth, it allows others into your heart and increases their trust in you, ultimately deepening your relationship and connection with each other.

- **WE'RE ALL ON DIFFERENT OPERATING SYSTEMS ... AND THAT'S OKAY!**

  You will cause yourself a lot of pain and heartache if you try to change someone else's operating system, especially if they don't want it changed. The best way to inspire someone is by being the living, breathing, walking, talking example of *your* Truth.

- **CCC IS ESSENTIAL FOR NEXT-LEVEL LOVE AND CONNECTION.**

  When you practice CCC you reach the other person's heart; when you speak from your head you reach their head. And like everything else in life, you'll get better at this oh-so-important skill with practice.

- **HAVING STRONG, CLEAR BOUNDARIES IS AN ACT OF SELF-LOVE. THEY'RE ESSENTIAL, SISTER!**

  Clear boundaries allow you to be the best version of yourself. They allow you to share your unique gifts with the world because you've taken care of yourself first. Stay true to your boundaries and respect others in return.

CHAPTER SIX

Soulmate City

As I've said, I never used to believe in "soulmates" or "the one." I thought it was a load of B.S. I mean, with over seven billion people on the planet, how can there be only one? Besides, all the evidence I'd seen on the history of human sexual evolution led me to believe that we're not hardwired for monogamy. And also, I liked the idea of having total sexual freedom — did I really want to just have sex with one person forever anyway? Isn't that the textbook definition of boring?

Then, on top of the unlikely mathematics of soulmates, if I *did* happen to run into my magical person, how in the name of hairy Zeus was I supposed to know that it was him? People say stuff like, "When you meet the one, you'll know." But to me, that seemed like such a cop-out answer, and I didn't buy it.

Basically, to me, the whole concept of soulmates seemed like a trumped-up trope from a Hallmark movie that had no actual anchor in reality ...

… That is, until I Opened Wide to the possibility and I experienced what I experienced with Nick.

I now have a whole new perspective on soulmates and believe your soulmate, "the one," your twin flame — whatever you want to call it — is whoever *you* declare it to be. And if that's one person or twenty-one, it's totally up to you.

SOCIAL CONDITIONING AROUND SOULMATES

Your soulmate should be no more than X years older than you.

You should only have one soulmate, per person, per lifetime.

You need to be on exactly the same page as your partner on EVERY SINGLE THING for them to be your true soulmate.

You have to be with a person for X number of years before you get engaged.

Then you should spend X amount of time engaged before you get married.

And if you're not married, and don't plan on it, then they're not your soulmate, full stop.

Heard any of these before? Or other "rules" like them? Pffft. Who made up this stuff? It's crazy! Yet that doesn't stop loads of people having deeply ingrained beliefs about what it means to be someone's soulmate. Many peeps even have a full set of criteria in their heads, which they use to mentally "assess" a relationship, whether it's their own or someone else's. ("Oh, you've only known your partner for a year? And you guys don't want to get married? Sorry, your relationship is only at C+ level. He can't *possibly* be your soulmate — you need to wait at least five more years, and preferably get hitched. Then maybe you'll make the grade. *Maybe*.")

As someone who's been on the receiving end of many of these rules and judgments, I can say firsthand how hurtful and disconcerting they can be, not to mention totally absurd. So before we delve into the methods and magic of calling in your true love, let's come up with a new, more empowering definition of what a soulmate is, shall we?!

Your soulmate is whoever *you* declare it to be.

It's as simple as that.

When it comes to your soulmate, *you* make the rules. You get to decide who you want to give that title to, no one else. There are no criteria that need to be met, no benchmarks that need to be reached, no checklist that needs to be ticked off ... The only person who can determine if someone is your soulmate is you!

So if in this present moment (the only moment we truly have) you know deep in your heart that you want to declare a person your soulmate, then what the heck are you waiting for? Do what feels right for you! Don't conform to what society prescribes as the "right thing to do" or "the right time to settle down" or "the right type of person." Only *you* know your Truth, so get out of your head and flow with it, beautiful!

WHAT DO OUR GENES HAVE TO SAY ABOUT SOULMATES?

Both Nick and I, in those early days, had a block with the concept of monogamy. We knew we were experiencing something otherworldly and magical with each other, but both of us had been cheated on, and had had our hearts blasted apart. Both of us, too, had done extensive research on the evolutionary history of relationships, and had come to the conclusion that humans were closer to being "promiscuous primates" than "committed cave people." We both firmly believed that, as individuals and as a species, we simply weren't wired for a single "soulmate."

This belief was so prominent that on our very first date, one of the very first things we bonded over was our mutual questioning of monogamy — as I mentioned at the start of this book, we even toyed with the idea of having an open relationship and went on dates with other people.

But (to our great surprise) this was a belief that we both shed very quickly, as we soon realized it did not jibe with the intense feelings and sacred bond we had suddenly stepped into.

But it took Opening Wide and *meeting* Nick for my ideas to change. It was then I realized that the experience of love, surrender, and companionship could be far more compelling than the liberation of sleeping around. And it was only once I'd met him that my innate desire for a committed relationship naturally surfaced ... So then I was thinking perhaps it wasn't human evolution and we *are* in fact hardwired for lifelong monogamy?

We'll never truly know what the Creator/Mother Nature/ the Big Bang intended for us, but from my perspective, that's actually far less important than what we consciously decide for ourselves.

So if you're someone who's found — or is keen to call in — the delicious, sacred experience of a soulmate, let's delve deeper into what that actually means ...

What Is a Soulmate?

Imagine you are the most delicious, gluten-free, double-chocolate cupcake you have ever tasted in your entire life. You ooze warm, chocolatey goodness from your center and could make anyone's heart melt. You are so delicious and full of goodness, everyone wants a piece of you. You don't need marshmallows or crushed activated nuts on top: you are perfect just as you are. Now imagine your soulmate is the sugar-free sprinkles on top of your already delectable and perfect chocolate cupcake. You don't necessarily *need* the sprinkles (you're already ridiculously delicious as you are), but the sprinkles are nice. This metaphor applies to your soulmate too. **Your soulmate is there to add color to your life. To be the embellishment and your complement, but not to complete you.** You are not two halves of one whole, but two whole people who come together to make each other's lives even better. You both come from individual places of awesomeness and you enhance each other's lives. It's about interdependence, not co-dependence. This is where I went wrong for many years. I was looking for a guy to complete me. To fill those voids I didn't feel I could fill myself. I wanted a man to save and rescue me and to be my knight in shining armor. But the truth is, your partner is not there to save, fix, or improve you, nor to fill your voids …

Your partner exists to complement, not complete you. To teach you, to help you grow and evolve to your fullest potential, and to offer an equal balance of support and challenge.

With your soulmate, there is nowhere to hide. They are your biggest teacher. There has to be that balance of support and challenge for the relationship to last. If it's too easy and boring, you will leave; if it's too hard, you will think the grass is greener and also leave. This balance must exist.

The Great Delusion

Before I did my soul work and was still a tad cynical about soulmates I used to think that when I was finally with my soulmate, it would be all rainbows, unicorns, and butterflies. That it would be a piece of (gluten-free) cake and total smooth sailing from the moment I said "I do." This is the greatest delusion about relationships, and if you've subscribed to it, you need to toss it to the curb right now. The intimacy level is high with your complement, which means there is nowhere left to hide from each other and yourself. You may trigger, teach, and show each other all the areas you have yet to fully embrace and love within yourselves. That's why your soulmate can be a great teacher, and can take you to depths of love you didn't know existed ... if you are willing. It truly can be the most magical, heart-opening, expansive relationship if you wish, but you have to be willing to open your heart extremely wide.

Are you willing?

A Ritual to Call in Your Soulmate

By now, you're aware that you can't even *think* about calling in your soulmate until you're bursting with love within yourself. This is paramount! Once you feel overflowing with love within yourself, then you're ready to call them in. This doesn't mean you will always feel a hundred percent bursting with love (heck, there are definitely days I don't) but you will have the awareness to take the steps to fill yourself back up.

Follow these "Soulmate Steps" to call in your love.

- Make sure you've done the work on yourself first. Make sure you're overflowing with love and you're not carrying around any old, limiting Mean Girl baggage that's no longer serving you. Make sure your energy is clear and strong.

- Write down a list of how you want to *feel* when you're in the presence of your love. For example, on my list before I met Nick, I wrote that I wanted to feel deeply connected, heard, safe, light, joyful, present, overflowing with love, and like a queen.

- Write down the core values you desire in your love (head back to Chapter Four if you need a refresher). Be specific: for example, "I desire him to value the importance of health and wellness, and I would like him to have a keen interest in movement, cooking, and healthy living. I also desire him to have an interest in meditation and wanting to be the best version of himself. I desire him to believe X about money and Y about parenting. I would love him to be in a job that lights him up and inspires him and that has him jumping out of bed each morning." (Revisit these desires as you grow and adjust them as necessary. And remember, it's okay to change your mind.)

- Ask for your most compatible soulmate. Things won't always be romance and roses, so ask the Universe for someone who is keen and willing to go on the ride with you, so you can both support each other to unlock your full potential.

- Meditate on it. Once you have your list in front of you, actually cultivate the feeling state of already having that person in your life right now. Act "as if." Really *feel*, in your bones, what it's like to already have them in your life.

- Now let's take it to the next level. While you're still in your meditative state, start to feel deeply grateful for already having that person in your life. Keep feeling it. Don't stop. Keep going. Gratitude for the win, baby!
- Then surrender it to the Universe, get out of the way, and trust that everything will unfold in divine time.

Perform this ritual daily for thirty days and make a note each day of how you feel. It will help you get crystal clear on what you truly desire so when it manifests you will know.

Remember, there are no rules here. The relationship you call in doesn't have to look a certain way. If you decide to have one soulmate and be with that person your whole life then great. If you want ten partners, go for it. Likewise, if you decide you desire someone who wants a gaggle of children, that's totally cool. If you'd rather call in someone who's happy to stay footloose and child free, that's awesome too. It's *your* choice!

You can also use this process to call in your soul sisters. When I first started on my journey, I didn't have girlfriends who shared my newfound passions and values, or who were open to a new way of living and thinking. I did a visioning process like the one I just described to call in some aligned sisters, and would you believe it? *Whoosh!* Divine women started appearing in my life, as if by magic. (Who am I kidding: of course it was magic!) These divine souls were as curious, committed, and enthusiastic as I was, and I felt more supported and "seen" than I ever had before. They are still in my life today, and I could not be more grateful for their presence.

Take Action for Soulmate Success

Ask yourself: if you had a soulmate right now, what would you be most excited about doing with them? Trying out new restaurants? Joining a mixed basketball team? Spending your weekends at film festivals, farmers' markets, or antique fairs? You know what I'm going to ask you to do with your answers, right?! Yep — go do these activities by yourself! With joy, enthusiasm, and a heart full of love! The benefits of taking action like this are many and magnificent:

- You'll be filling your own love-tank, right to the brim.
- You'll be surrounding yourself with an abundant pool of likeminded people (a.k.a. potential soulmates and soul sisters) who are *also* filling their love-tanks to the brim.
- You'll be raising your vibrations to peak happiness levels (meaning that when a compatible person crosses your path, you'll be absolutely magnetic to them).
- And you'll be building up an epic library of experiences and stories that enrich your life and give it meaning (rather than passively waiting around for someone else to fulfil you).

One of my besties, Leisa, has a beautiful example of this technique in action. She wanted to travel and explore the wonders of the world, but had always imagined she'd do it with a soulmate. But once she'd saved up enough money (and had truly been bitten by the travel bug) she wasn't going to let the fact she was single hold her back. So, with a heart full of love (and a suitcase full of cute outfits!), she jetted off to the other side of the world, ready for her solo adventure. She did all the things she'd always dreamed about — hiking, trekking, wandering, exploring — and loved every minute of it. Her brave actions showed the Universe that she was *serious* about living her dream life — she wasn't just daydreaming about it, she was taking inspired action, which the Universe LOVES to see. So the Universe sent someone very special her way: a soulmate. *Her* soulmate. And he showed up smack-bang in the middle of her trip — in the Amazon Jungle, of all places! That's the power of acting "as if." (And they've been together ever since!)

Acting "as if" works really well if you want to call in divine friendships too. Go through the same thought exercise, but substitute "friend" for "soulmate." What would you be doing right now if you had a true soul sister? Or a big, beautiful group of friends? How can you start doing those activities now, without waiting? If you've always wanted a bookish friend to start a book club with, then go out and find an existing club you can join. If you've always wanted a friend to do yoga teacher training with, go sign up solo with an open heart and see who shows up. Yes, these actions can feel uncomfortable at first (believe me, I know!), but remember: (1) The benefits are hu-fricking-mungous, and (2) the Universe rewards those who put themselves out there and take inspired action. And I *know* you can do it, beautiful.

How to Be an Epic Lover

If you want a plant to grow, you have to water it. You have to tend to it, pull out any weeds that you've allowed to grow, nourish the soil, give it the right amount of sunlight, protect it from the harsh winds, and give it love and energy every single day. Otherwise it will die.

Similarly, if you want to master the piano or learn how to speak French, the more time and energy you invest into practice, the better you will get.

Both these principles apply for your relationships too. The more love, time, and energy you invest in them, and the more consistent your efforts, the more your relationships will grow, Open Wider and go deeper.

The grass is greener where you water it.

Nick and I are both aware we can never rest on our laurels (so to speak) when it comes to our relationship. Just because things are good now, doesn't mean we can ignore our relationship and coast along in complacency. Instead, we work on it *now*, while the sun is shining — nourishing it, strengthening it, and cherishing it. Both of us want to continue to grow, support each other's evolution, and be of service to the relationship and each other. And we both fully believe that **when we serve the other, we serve ourselves**.

If you want to serve your partner — and be an epic, wholehearted lover — here are my top "lessons learned" to evolve and strengthen your relationship ...

BE A TEAM PLAYER

The two of you are a team. And you're on the same side, not opposing sides. (I think sometimes we forget this.) That means there's no point keeping score (i.e. "I took the rubbish out, so I get to put my feet up." Or, "I picked up the kids, so I get to go to yoga.") Bitter tally-keeping will not do either of you any good. You're on the same team, so help each other out! If Nick is full with work, I will do school drop-off and pick-up, and vice versa. You are there to help and support each other, not tear each other down.

SUPPORT THEM

Take interest in their passions and work. Ask how you can help and if there's anything you can do to support them furthering their dreams – and engage them in supporting yours. This doesn't mean you have to pretend to like football, wear the jersey, of his favorite team, down beers, and scoff Doritos. Simply listening (with both ears) to your partner talk about how much he loves football and how his favorite team just won the Super Bowl can really make his day. Just as trusting them to care about your passions gives them room to return the favor.

LISTEN

We humans want to be heard all the time. So it's imperative that we practice consciously listening to our partners – without interrupting and without simply waiting until it's our turn to talk. It's challenging because we all have opinions and we want to give them, but when your partner walks in the door, open your arms and just listen and let them express themselves. Once you can feel they're finished, then you share.

PRAY FOR THEIR HEALTH AND HAPPINESS

At the end of my meditations, I pray for Nick's health and happiness. I pray he feels inner joy, peace, happiness, and contentment, and I send him love.

BE THE PARTNER YOU DESIRE

It's very easy to sit back and demand our partner to show up a certain way, pleasure us a certain way, and make us feel like a queen. But why can't *we* be the ones who show up first? Be the partner YOU desire instead of waiting for them to take the lead. YOU show up first!

DECIDE TO RISE

I'll be the first to admit that there are times when I act like a three-year-old and throw an Oscar-worthy temper tantrum. But really, is that serving anyone?! The answer is a big fat NO! Make the choice to rise above the moods and pettiness that affect us all sometimes.

REMEMBER YOUR LOVER IS YOUR LOVER

Your lover is not primarily your consoler, coach, hairdresser, personal trainer, bestie, spiritual healer, fashion stylist, yoga buddy, accountant, business advisor or (metaphorically speaking) your punching bag. Sure, he might actually *be* a personal trainer and train you three times a week, but first and foremost he is your lover, so treat him that way. Let him sit in his zone of genius and be your lover. Your relationship will be way better for it.

GET YOUR FIX ELSEWHERE

Perhaps you LOVE a long conversation but your partner isn't a massive talker. And that's okay! Don't try to fix, change, or improve him. Your man may not want to sip herbal tea and chat for hours with you. If that's the case, go get your fix somewhere else. Chat with your girlfriends on the phone, meet them for a walk, or catch up for a tea, whatever you need to do to get your fix. The same applies if he loves a chat and you're more of a thinker – he will always have other friends who can answer that need. Don't see your differences as fatal incompatibilities – simply give each other permission to satisfy those areas with siblings, friends, or colleagues.

TREAT THEM LIKE ROYALTY

I call Nick my "king," because I realize that if I want him to treat me like a goddess queen, I must first treat him like my king. If you started treating your lover like your king, how would you speak to him when he walked into the room? How would you act around him? Treat your lover the way you want to be treated.

LET GO OF "WHITE KNIGHT" SYNDROME

Are you always waiting for your partner to rescue or save you? Take responsibility for your own life. Look after yourself in the relationship and don't make your happiness the other person's job. Say to yourself, *I am responsible for my own happiness and inner joy.* Then ask yourself, *What will bring me the most happiness and joy today?* Then go do it! So often we sit back waiting for our partner to make us feel joy and happiness, but YOU are responsible for your own happiness and joy each day.

BE THEIR LOVER, NOT THEIR MOM

Neither you nor your partner wants to be bossed around and told what to do. So not sexy! Of course, if they're not pulling their weight around the house, an open conversation may need to be had and vice versa – but remember, there's nothing sexy about being yelled at and ordered around.

PRACTICE CCC

To be an epic lover we must always do our best to practice Crystal Clear Communication at all times. (Dip back into Chapter Five whenever you need a refresher.)

PERFORM RANDOM ACTS OF KINDNESS

There are so many things you can do to keep the magic alive each day. For example, leave love notes around the house or slip them into his bag before you leave for work, book in a "date night" once a week, send some cute (or sexy) text messages to him throughout the day, give him a full-body massage, run him an Epsom salts bath after a long day at work, make him his favorite meal, or pop a pair of your sexy underwear in his work bag or lunch box ... that'll be sure to get him smiling!

MAKE TIME

We're all full and we all have to-do lists and inboxes that seem to never end, but if you don't make the time to "water" your relationship, it will not grow. You have to make it a priority, just like you would with exercise or a work deadline. Schedule your "lovers time" in your calendar and stick to it. Otherwise you're just roommates who occasionally have sex or "rub genitals," as author David Deida would say. A strong relationship requires time and nurturing.

Get Your Gratitude On

Gratitude is the healthiest of all human emotions. The more you express gratitude for what you have, the more likely you will have even more to express gratitude for.

ZIG ZIGLAR

I am massive fan of gratitude work in relationships because it *works*. It's impossible to feel angry and grateful at the same time, and no matter what's going on in your life, there's always something to be grateful for. Plus it really helps balance out your perception of who's doing what! If you're being grateful for the beautiful meal you've been served, you realize that complaining about having had to do more vacuuming isn't that bad.

I have a few different gratitude practices I perform daily.

GRATITUDE PRACTICE ONE

Every morning I roll over to Nick and the first thing I say to him is, "Good morning, honey, what are three things you're grateful for?" He says his, then I say mine.

GRATITUDE PRACTICE TWO

Every day, a reminder flashes up on my phone: *What are you grateful for?* I then type as many things as I can think of into my phone.

GRATITUDE PRACTICE THREE

Over the dinner table, after we've blessed and given thanks for our food, we each say three things we're grateful for. Getting the kids involved is not only seriously cute, but great for their growth and expansion too.

GRATITUDE PRACTICE FOUR

Once we're in bed and about to doze off, I ask Nick again which three things he's grateful for, then I share mine as well. That way, we both drift off to la la land with full and grateful hearts.

GRATITUDE PRACTICE FIVE

While I'm driving or out walking I repeat to myself, *Thank you, thank you, thank you, I'm so grateful for XYZ.*

You can also write down everything you're grateful for in your journal or get yourself a cute gratitude notepad. There are no rules here, no right or wrong. The only suggestion I have is to implement some form of gratitude practice into your day *today,* then commit to doing it daily.

Whether you've been with your lover for ten years or ten days, don't get complacent — express your gratitude every single day.

Empowering Your Partner to Be Their Best

Before Nick and I got together, I was hell bent on buying my own apartment to set myself up for the future. *I don't need a man,* I thought. *I can do this thing called "life" all on my own. I'm a powerful, successful woman and I don't need anyone.* So every weekend was spent zipping around from one viewing to another, going to auctions and battling the competitive crowds, just to try to get in the door. I was also focused on working my tushie off to earn as much money as possible. All of this go-go-go energy sharpened my edges. *You have to hustle,* I told myself, *You have to go harder and faster.*

Then, of course, Nick came along. But as a strong, very capable, independent woman who didn't "need" a man, I struggled to give him space to do his share of caring for me — even though I was loving caring for him.

Luckily, I realized in time that the true nature of community is shared responsibility, so why should I deny my partner that? Instead of resisting it, I decided to embrace it. And holy moly, dear readers, did that mutual surrender lead to the most mind-blowing lovemaking of my life! When you fully allow your partner that close, watch out! It will unlock a primal part of him — *and* you. You'd better be ready for multiple, mind-blowing cervical orgasms! (More on those bliss-bursts later!)

This took me a little while to get used to, but I now allow Nick to perform all sorts of thoughtful gestures (remember, this is one way to give and receive love). I let him open the car door for me. Do I need him to? No. Can I do it myself? Of course! But does it make him feel empowered? Absolutely! So I let him.

If you're anything like I was, you might need to break through the Mean Girl fear around allowing your man to "take care of things." I used to think, *Will he think I'm lazy or greedy for accepting his support? AM I lazy or greedy? Does this make me weak? Am I betraying the sisterhood by letting him serve me? And does this mean we're not equals?* This is when I really had to master my Mean Girl. I wrote out all my limiting Mean Girl blocks and got to work mastering them.

INSPO-ACTION

What limiting Mean Girl beliefs do you have around letting your partner serve you? Do you think any of the following thoughts?

All men are bastards and untrustworthy.
You can only count on yourself.
I've been stung before and I won't give my power away ever again.

Once you've written down all your limiting beliefs, next to each one write down where that limiting Mean Girl belief came from.

For example ...

After watching my father cheat on my mother and leave.

After going through my own bitter divorce.

After being cheated on by X.

I now invite you to rewrite your love story with your true desires about other people. What would you LOVE to replace those current beliefs with?

For example ...

I surround myself with people of high integrity and honor.

People are trustworthy, respectful, open, and honest.

People treat me the way I desire to be treated.

People are love.

Nothing changes if nothing changes, so if you want to change your beliefs about others, and especially about men, *you* are the only one who can change your mind within.

From now on, any time your Mean Girl tries to pop up and plant those old limiting beliefs in your head, it's your job to catch her and take yourself through my three-step Mastering Your Mean Girl process. (See Chapter Three for a refresher!) Remember, the more you practice this process, the better and stronger you'll get. So keep at it!

A SIDE NOTE ON SOULMATES

If you read this chapter with a sinking feeling in your stomach, because you suspect that the person you're with is *not* your true soulmate, that's okay, angel.

For starters, please know that we *all* go through bumpy patches where we're on different pages from our partner. In those instances, a gentle heart, patience, and a willingness to Open Wide can be absolute game-changers.

But sometimes, of course, it truly can be that the person you're with is not your "one" any more, and your partner isn't complementing you (or treating you) in the way you desire and deserve. That's okay too, because as Neale Donald Walsch says, *you can choose again.* If that's the case — and only you can know the difference deep in your heart — don't beat yourself up, my darling. Everything is perfect and no, you're *not* a failure. It's likely you've both been teaching each other some incredibly important soul lessons, but perhaps you're now ready to move on to the next chapter in your life.

This realization — that a relationship has run its course — can lead some people to experience epic shame. But that's not serving you, beautiful. When I first met Nick, in one of our many deep conversations, I remember asking him if he felt like a failure for being a divorcee. He said, "Absolutely not. Even though that was the hardest thing I've ever been through and the stress from it put me in the hospital, it was one of the best things and greatest lessons I've ever had, because it led me to the true me, and then to you."

So please don't let your Mean Girl beat you up or tell you that you've failed, because you haven't. You've just discovered something truly empowering for your soul. And these are all lessons for our growth. To begin this new phase in your life, I'd encourage you to revisit Chapter Four in detail to get laser sharp on what you desire in a partner. And if you decide that it's time for a change, revisit the section in Chapter Five on "Creating Space."

How to Move Through a Breakup

Breakups can feel hard. Notice how I didn't say "Breakups *are* hard"? That's because not all breakups are hard, though some can feel like your heart is being ripped out of your chest. Like when my then-boyfriend cheated on me in my early twenties then dumped me like a hot potato. That one felt like it tore me apart. But breakups can be done with ease and grace, if you choose. Like when I broke up with Dom after three years of being together. I recently saw him walking along the beach and we stopped and had a beautiful long chat. It was so lovely catching up with him and hearing how he was. I walked away feeling so much love and gratitude for him and our time together. When I got home, I shared with Nick how nice it had been to see him and how I thought it was so odd that we can spend so much time with one person, get deeply intimate with them, love them, Open Wide to them, and share everything with that person … and then one day we break up, and never see or speak to them ever again. That's not the paradigm I want to subscribe to. I believe that every relationship serves a purpose, and when that relationship is done we don't need or have to hate that person.

By now you know that *you* get to choose your reality and *you* are creating your life moment by moment, so *you* get to choose your breakup experience, and whether your intention is to do it with as much ease and grace as you can muster or not. Ideally, both parties would be on the bandwagon, but if the other person isn't interested in ease and grace, that's okay — that can still be your intent without the other person being on board.

If you believe everything is unfolding exactly the way it's supposed to, and that YOU are responsible for your life, then there truly is no need to hate your ex. Ask yourself what you learned from the relationship — that's where growth occurs. Was there an area where you were acting out of fear instead of love? Is there something you'd do or embody differently next time? If you don't stop and ask these questions, you will most likely play out the same relationship with your next partner (and the one after that) until you finally *get* the lessons you need to learn in order to evolve.

Of course, every situation is different, and I'm not going to promise this will work for everyone. However, what I *can* promise is that you will only know if you Open Wide and give it a go.

Here's one way to do it ...

STEP ONE: FEEL IT ALL

When you first make the decision to end the relationship (or when your partner first tells you that's what they want) it can bring up all sorts of feelings and emotions. My advice is to feel them all. Don't suppress anything – the anger, sadness, frustration, hurt ... allow it ALL to wash over you while reminding yourself that this too shall pass and nothing is permanent. You may need to spend some time processing and "feeling all the feels" before you can have these conversations, and that's okay. Always do what feels right for you.

STEP TWO: PRACTICE CCC

If you haven't yet told your partner, you then need to sit down and have an open conversation with them. You must use CCC and be committed to Opening Wide. If you feel like you can't, maybe wait until you can get yourself into a mental space where you can, or you could write things down instead. Depending on the situation, you could say something like, "As I'm sure you are aware, I think our time together has come to a beautiful end. I have loved our experience and have grown and learned a lot, and I honor the space we held together. We shared so many great times and I respect you, which is why I'd love to depart with as much ease and grace as possible. Do you think this is something you would be open to? If so, I'd like to sit with you and chat about the next steps so we can move forward." Now, this may not be the script for everyone, but use it as a template. Then, before you say or write anything, Open Wide and connect into your heart space. (Remember the golden rule of CCC: if you speak or write from your head you will reach their head; if you speak or write from your heart you will reach their heart.)

STEP THREE: DON'T TUNE IN TO THE NEGATIVE CHATTER

When Dom and I broke up, I couldn't believe how much people wanted to bitch about him and say negative things about him. Instead of joining in the sledging, try to remember that at one point you loved this person. You shared so much with them and they were a huge part of your life. Maybe you lived together. Maybe you share kids with him. Maybe a pet. Maybe you were married. Whatever your situation, try not to listen to or engage in any Negative Nancy talk – that energy will NOT serve you or anyone.

STEP FOUR: DON'T TUNE IN TO ANY OTHER CHATTER EITHER!

I've also experienced the opposite – where I've broken up with someone, then had a bunch of people say, "Oh! Why did you let him go? You won't find another one like him!" It can be easy to start doubting yourself when people make statements like this, but do your best to tune them out and tune into your heart instead. You made your decision for a reason, beautiful. Back yourself wholeheartedly.

STEP FIVE: REMEMBER WHAT YOU SHARED

Write down three things you loved about that person. For example, "I loved how generous, kind-hearted, and funny he was." Or you could write down three amazing times you shared together, such as your wedding day, the trip to Greece, or your weekly Sunday movie sessions. While you're going through this process, keep your list somewhere you can see it – maybe on a sticky note or in your phone. Then, whenever you feel the need, read over it to remind yourself that you used to love this person deeply, although you may not feel that way any more. This will help you stay connected to your heart and not get too caught up with your Mean Girl in your head.

STEP SIX: WORK OUT THE LESSONS YOU'VE LEARNED

Every relationship is here to serve our growth. So grab your journal, Open Wide, and reflect on what you learned from the relationship. What did you discover about yourself, your values, and your desires? What did you learn about loving another human, living with them, and sharing with them? What did you uncover about your relationship with intimacy and vulnerability, and how you cope with conflict? There's a lot of gold here, and digging for it can help you slide into a space of perspective and gratitude for what's unfolded.

STEP SEVEN: AIM FOR EASE

There's a mantra I like to adopt during trying times: I learn life's lessons with ease and grace. This affirmation acknowledges that though there can be challenging lessons in life, we get to *choose* how we experience them. Ideally, we choose love and joy. But when it's extra hard – like, *My heart is in a million pieces right now, and if you tell me to "think positive" I might just scream* hard – it can be a struggle to shoot for joy. So aiming for ease and grace can feel more aligned, and help you bridge that gap (and maintain your sanity!) until you're ready to reach for joy again.

STEP EIGHT: THANK THEM

After you've mined your soul, healed your heart, and written down all your lessons, it's time to thank your former partner. In your next meditation session, visualize the person standing in front of you. Thank them for the lessons and your time together (you might find yourself getting quite emotional during this process, or you might not – either is fine, just stick with it). I did this when Dom and I broke up, and even now, on the occasions when I see him, I still thank him in my mind.

STEP NINE: LET IT GO AND MOVE FORWARD

It's super important to feel whatever comes up for you – whether that's anger, sadness, fear, whatever. Feel everything and let it wash over you. Then, when the time feels right for you, you can make a conscious choice to let it go and move forward. No more holding onto the past, that will only hold you back and hinder your growth. Give yourself a time frame. Say to yourself, *Okay, I'm going to allow myself to feel really peeved, sad, or angry for X days and then I am going to let it go.* Tell your bestie or your mom to help hold you accountable. You can do this with anything. Practice it daily if something comes up. Allow yourself to feel really angry over something for ten minutes, and then let it go.

On the flipside, of course, you don't want to beat yourself up if you're not where you thought you'd be by your allocated time. Just reflect (maybe in your journal) and continue to move forward and let go simultaneously. A client once said to me, "I thought I'd be fully over my divorce in six months ... Ha! I had no idea. Little things kept popping up for me for *years* afterward." If that's the case – and remember, it's all perfect – try not to wallow in every little detail, or choose to stay stuck. Just allow the feelings and grief to happen naturally, and fall away like the layers of an onion when the time is right.

STEP TEN: REMEMBER THAT YOU ARE LOVE

At the end of the day, you are Love. And *they* are Love. And we are here on earth to grow and evolve. And breaking up with ease and grace *is* possible if you so wish. You can do it, sister.

How to Be an Amazing Friend

Earlier in this chapter, I mentioned how your relationship with your soulmate requires regular love and attention, just like a plant. The same is true of ALL your relationships. So I wanted to briefly touch on some specific pointers that will help you be an epically amazing friend and soul sister ...

HOLD SPACE FOR EACH OTHER

When your sister speaks, hold space for her to express whatever she needs to. It's not your job to "fix" her, or "diagnose" her problems ... just be there, and make sure she feels seen, held, and heard.

BE IMPECCABLE WITH KEEPING YOUR WORD

If you say you'll do something, do it. If you say you'll be somewhere, be there. The simple act of following through on your words is so powerful, and helps build a strong foundation of trust and loyalty in any relationship.

REMEMBER THE SMALL THINGS

The littlest things can make the biggest impact! Take note of the things that mean a lot to your friends but that are easy to overlook or forget when life gets full. Has she got an important performance review coming up at work? Maybe she finds the month of August tough because it's the anniversary of her mom's passing? Perhaps she's been dealing with an ongoing health issue that's been getting her down? Make a point of asking her how she's feeling about it, and genuinely listen to her answer – with both ears. If there's a specific date that's important to her, I like to pop a note in my calendar so I don't forget. That way, I'm reminded to send her a supportive text or a bunch of flowers when it matters most.

CELEBRATE HER WINS

When we, as women, lift each other up, the whole world is strengthened and filled with love! So don't hold back in handing out meaningful compliments. Love the meal she just cooked you? Tell her. Proud of her latest blog post? Sing it, sister. Inspired by her current fitness efforts? Shout her praises from the freaking rooftop! (By the way, if you feel awkward getting all gushy, don't let that stop you – you can always send your thoughts via text!)

DON'T TAKE THINGS PERSONALLY

We're all "full" at times. We all have stressors in our life. We all get tired, frazzled, overwhelmed, premenstrual, and just plain cranky. So if your friend does something that upsets you, before you react, ask yourself: is this *actually* personal? Could it, perhaps, be explained by a bad day? So often, the slights we perceive – a harsh word, a forgotten phone call, a late arrival – aren't personal at all. Give your friend the benefit of the doubt, release your hurt, and let it go.

IT'S OKAY TO STEP BACK AND CREATE SPACE
This tip is the flipside to the previous one. If your friend has stopped acting like a "friend" – say, if there are a few too many instances where she doesn't seem to respect you and your boundaries – it's okay to create some space while you ponder how you feel. Sometimes, a little space can help you see things all the more clearly. And ultimately, YOU have to take care of YOU, beautiful.

KEY TAKEAWAYS FROM CHAPTER SIX

- **WHEN IT COMES TO YOUR SOULMATE, YOU MAKE THE RULES. YOU GET TO DECIDE WHO GETS THAT TITLE.**
  There are no criteria that need to be met, no benchmarks that need to be reached, no checklist that needs to be ticked off. The only person who can determine if someone is your soulmate is *you!*

- **YOUR PARTNER EXISTS TO COMPLEMENT, NOT COMPLETE YOU.**
  With your soulmate there's nowhere to hide. They're a great teacher. There has to be that balance of support and challenge for the relationship to last. If it's "too easy" and boring, you will leave; if it's "too hard," you will think the grass is greener and leave. This balance is essential.

- **BE AN EPIC LOVER.**

  Be a team player, support your partner, listen (really listen), pray for their health and happiness, be the partner *you* desire, rise up, treat your lover as your lover, treat them like a king/queen, let go of "white knight" syndrome, be their lover (not their mom), practice CCC, perform random acts of kindness, make time for each other, and, finally, get your gratitude on!

- **EMPOWER YOUR PARTNER.**

  We want to serve each other … so let your partner serve you.

- **IF YOU'RE NOT WITH YOUR LOVER YET, DON'T WORRY.**

  Don't let your Mean Girl beat you up, and don't fall into the trap of thinking there's something wrong with you that needs "fixing," changing, or improving. You are perfect just as you are. Use your time wisely and channel your energy into as much self-love and self-care as possible. Open Wide and create space for a new phase in your life to begin.

- **IT *IS* POSSIBLE TO BREAK UP IN A HEART-CENTRED, CONSCIOUS WAY.**

  You get to choose your breakup experience. Ideally, both parties would be on the bandwagon, but if the other person isn't interested, that's okay — you can still turn your separation into a constructive experience without them being on board.

- **YOUR FRIENDSHIPS REQUIRE LOVE AND ATTENTION TOO.**

  Hold space for your sisters, be there for them, and celebrate their wins. Be the kind of friend you'd like to be friends with.

PART THREE

SOULFUL SEX (THE GLUE THAT BINDS US)

CHAPTER SEVEN

Sex, Shame, Taboo, and Guilt

Considering what a significant part of life sex can be, and how much of it there is all around us, with explicit scenes in TV shows and movies, and women's bodies posed in sexual ways in music and advertising, it's weird how hard it is for most of us to talk about it in meaningful ways. A lot of us accept the bare minimum of sexual satisfaction rather than really thinking about what we want (and deserve), let alone asking for it. We don't question our own old assumptions about sex nearly as often as we should. So let's do that! It's been an amazing journey for me, beautiful, and I know it will be for you too.

A few weeks ago, my parents were in town for Leo's birthday. As they were leaving for the airport to head home, my dad came up to give me one of his signature awkward hugs — where he sticks his butt out at a weird angle (so there's no chance of torso-on-torso contact), and his arms (which hardly make it around the other person's body) give an awkward little pat on the back. You know the type of hug I'm talking about, right? It's awkward and a little uncomfortable for everybody involved (even for those just watching!). As you know, one of the ways I love to receive love is with physical connection, so it's no surprise I'm a *massive* hugger. So when my dad tried to drop one of these on me again, I decided to speak up. "Dad, what was that?" I said.

"What, love?" he asked.

"You hugged me like I have leprosy, why is that?"

He went bright red and I could feel he was uncomfortable. "Oh, because I don't want to touch your boobies."

Boobies?! I'm in my thirties; I'm not twelve!

The word "boobies" took me straight back to my childhood. I remember when I started going through puberty, my dad shifted. I guess he felt uncomfortable (I don't blame him), and I was no longer allowed to sit on his lap and get cuddles and kisses on the lips. (Yep, before that we kissed on the lips.) I loved that time with my dad, where we would be on the couch watching TV totally wrapped up in each other's embrace. I grieve for that time, but he had to do what he knew was best.

It's also not all that surprising, looking back. I grew up in a house where your vulva was called your "rosetta" — meaning "rose" in Italian. The words "vagina" and "penis" were never uttered. That area "down there" was considered "dirty," "disgusting," "rude," and "naughty," and we were never allowed to see each other naked. I remember occasionally walking in on my parents in the bathroom, to which they would scream in shock, "Get out, that's rude!"

When two painful little bumps started to appear on my chest, my mom didn't explain to me how my body was changing or what was going on. It was swept under the carpet and everyone pretended it wasn't happening.

The first time I bled, I thought I was dying. I was so scared that I hid it. I threw out my undies, started using toilet paper inside my underwear, and was scared to tell my mom (or anyone) because I had never been educated on what was happening to my body.

I distinctly remember asking one of the older girls at dance how to use a tampon, including which hole it went in and how far you push it up. I was terrified I was going to stick it in the wrong hole or too far up, never to be found again. (And remember, this was all before we had Dr. Google at our fingertips!)

Another time I walked in on my mom in the bathroom inserting a tampon, and I asked in my innocent voice, "Mom ... what are you doing?"

"Nothing, get out!" she said, quickly closing the door.

In P.D. (Personal Development) class in high school, we were given a condom and a banana and in between bursts of laughter we were taught how to put it on and told not to get pregnant ... that's it! (Great, thanks for the tip!) We weren't educated on STDs, how to tune into our bodies, chart our cycles, or even the different ways we could avoid getting pregnant.

On the night of my first kiss, hormones started racing through my cells, my body buzzed, and I had no freaking clue what was going on. For the rest of my teenage years, I explored with my then-boyfriend on the movie theater floor during movie marathons, in the back of cars, down at the local park, in the bushes at parties, and in the bathroom at school dances (sorry, Mom!). Because of what I'd been taught about sex, this type of normal teenage exploration felt "naughty, dirty, and wrong," and I thought it was something I had to hide. My parents never sat me down to have "the birds and the bees" talk. I missed that lesson. Instead I was thrust into the world thinking sex was unsavory and unmentionable, and that I had to hide and shame my body, especially my "private parts."

Of course, it's not just my parents who are uncomfortable with sex, or who forgot to give their children the sex-ed lesson …

Front butt, flower, hoo-ha, yoni, vajayjay, lady garden, mossy patch, meat curtains, tuna canoe, bag, box, muff, gash, fanny, pussy, snatch, kitty, foo-foo, hooch, hoo-hoo, mini, downstairs, girlie parts, pink bits … You've heard names like these before, right? This is how *so many of us* talk about one of the most sacred parts of our body. (And I haven't even included the highly derogatory terms out there too, which are becoming distressingly commonplace.) I mean, come on, people! Literally half the world has a vulva and much of the population entered the world through one … and yet most people don't even know what to call it! Are you kidding me?!

The media and pornography have portrayed sex and our bodies in a certain way, but this is *not* the whole truth. As is always the case, however, you don't know what you don't know, and if you were like me, you only knew what you saw growing up and you didn't know there was any other way. But, my sweet friend, the good news is, there *is* another, more fulfilling, soulful, heart-expanding way to talk and think about these subjects. And if we can change our beliefs about sex and our bodies, we will inspire our children, our children's children, and maybe — just maybe — break the long lineage of sexual shame (and the hideous abuse it helps to facilitate) once and for all. **But it all starts with us breaking the cycle in our own homes.**

Different cultures around the world haven't always been so prudish. Take the Mosuo culture in China, for example, where, from age twelve to fourteen, one of the most important and celebrated ceremonies is the "Coming of Age." This is where the females have the "skirt ceremony" and are given their skirt to wear, and boys have their "pant ceremony" and are given their pants to wear. Before this they all live within communal quarters, without their own bedrooms. Then once past puberty the females are allowed their own rooms and are able to start inviting men in.

You know what I love about this? There was nothing shameful about it and certainly nothing to hide. Sacred rites of passage were performed, which allowed young people to learn more about themselves and their sexuality. It was not taboo like today. They didn't have to sneak off into the bushes at parties, or lie on the floor at the movie theater to explore; they were provided a safe environment to explore themselves and their partner.

This is one of the reasons we need to educate and talk openly with our children, so they feel safe. Otherwise they may just "bang one out" in the bush at the next blue light disco. It's our job as parents to let go of the taboo and create a safe, open, loving environment where they not only feel they can come to you with their problems or questions, but they can explore within themselves and with their partner if they wish. Let's face it, wouldn't you rather your children explore in the safety of your home than the backseat of a crusty car in some dark, sketchy alleyway?! **Our sexuality is something to be celebrated not suppressed**, and it's time to get over this culture of shame and taboo.

Nick and I choose to model very body-positive and sex-positive practices in our home. We let Leo see us naked, we don't slam the door in his face when he walks in, and we don't scream at him to "Get out!" Sure, there will most likely come a time when being naked in front of him might not feel right any more, and I trust that my intuition will guide me on that. When it happens, I won't make a big deal about it, I'll simply close the door when I'm showering and getting dressed.

Also, we always use the words "vagina" and "penis" when they come up in conversation (the language you use is *so* important), and we tell Leo that when our bedroom door is closed, it means we would please like some privacy as we are making love. That's the truth! We are very open and honest with him about everything. We have never patronized him or dumbed things down for him.

I'm also open with him about everything that's typically thought of as "women's stuff." Recently Leo and I were both in the bathroom and he asked me what was in my silver box of goodies. So I showed him my juju cup, organic cotton Red Moon pads, and organic tampons. I explained to him how women menstruate every month and what each of these products does. To be honest, he wasn't too interested … but I planted the seed. I could have said nothing was in that box, but not only is that a lie, I didn't want to hide my period from him — he asked, so I'm going to show him and tell him the truth. So many boys are never taught about "women's stuff," so to them it's a big, scary unknown … no wonder there are so many grown men who don't understand menstruation, think it's "gross," or who are full-blown disrespectful about it. Parents, we need to educate our sons about this stuff as well as our daughters! Menstruation is a beautiful thing — it means our bodies are healthy — and if we teach them about it, they will understand how truly magical and sacred it is.

Now, I'm not saying the way Nick and I have chosen to approach these things is right — by now you know there *is* no right and wrong, as long as kids can access the information in a clear and constructive way. But what I do want to encourage you to do is Open Wide, let go of the taboo around sex and body shaming, and be mindful to educate your children. It's so important to provide them with a safe and open environment in which to express and explore themselves, so that they don't grow up hating their bodies and having warped ideas of what sex really is.

INSPO-ACTION

The words you use are powerful. They matter. And it's never too late to take back your power and upgrade your language for a higher vibing choice. Grab your journal or use the space provided to answer the questions below:

This is also an important conversation to have with your partner. It can be very interesting to find out what language they were taught as kids (for example, in Nick's family home, they used "willy" and women's genitals were never, ever spoken about in front of him).

- What words were you taught to use about bodies and sex when you were a child (whether by your parents, teachers, friends, the media, whatever)?

_____

_____

_____

- Are you happy with these words? Do they reflect your true beliefs? Do you still use them? Would you rather consciously replace them with something else? If so, what?

_____

_____

_____

- If you're a parent, what language do you use with your kids when you talk about sex and their bodies? Are you happy with the message those words are sending? Would you rather consciously replace them with something else? If so, what?

_____

_____

_____

- What language do you want to use to talk about sex with each other? And how do you want to talk about these topics with your children (or future children)?

_____

_____

_____

Personal Sex Shame

As well as our childhood conditioning, sexual guilt and shame can also come from an experience you may have had in your own explorations. Maybe you were forced into a situation you didn't desire or that didn't feel right. Maybe you felt like you had to say yes when you really meant no. Maybe a partner wanted to get intimate before you were ready, and you thought you "had" to go along with it and were ashamed of your "prudishness." Personally, there have been a few times I have been in uncomfortable situations with men that weren't my Truth. They affected me for a long time afterward, and triggered some intense feelings of shame and guilt.

For example, I remember one guy who had absolutely no interest in whether I was enjoying myself or not. We'd be busy doing the deed, he'd climax, then everything would come to an abrupt halt … even though it was blatantly obvious that I was still building. If I tried to initiate further contact or movement, he'd brush me off: "I'm tired now, babe." He would literally roll over and start snoring, while I was left confused, unfulfilled, and only halfway there. The message was clear: my pleasure was entirely secondary to his. In fact, I wasn't really worthy of pleasure. At least, that's how I understood it, and what I let my Mean Girl tell me. Though I might have the tools and self-awareness *now* to deal with this situation differently, back in my early twenties, I internalized it and it became embedded in my psyche. I came to believe that my pleasure was not as important as a man's and that my job was to please *him*. If he decided to return the favor, then I was lucky. If not … well, that's just how sex is for women.

I also remember one guy who dissected my "performance" and gave me a "rating," straight after we'd done the deed. (Such a gentleman, right?) There we were, lying in bed, me engulfed in a haze of orgasmic bliss, when he started comparing me to his previous sexual partners. He liked that I'd done such-and-such, but thought I needed more practice with other areas. He was also kind enough to point out that my boobs weren't as big as he normally liked, but that my "great ass" made up for it … Ummm, what?! Instead of enjoying the sensations running through my body, I was suddenly stricken. *See? You're NOT good enough!* my Mean Girl yelled triumphantly. *I knew it!* Obviously, this guy had some lessons left to learn. But lying there — an insecure, naked, vulnerable, twenty-something young woman — what I took away from the incident wasn't that this guy needed to grow up, but that my worst suspicions had been confirmed. I wasn't good enough — in my actions, in my sexiness, in my body. And now I had proof. My Mean Girl had a field day!

This is just a tiny sampling of stories I could regale you with. The truth is, most women don't need to think too hard to come up with instances where they've felt shame in the bedroom. I canvased some of my friends recently, and the examples flowed freely ...

My friend Tammy shared how one of her sexual partners made her feel disgusting and unworthy if she had even a hint of pubic hair. So she'd dutifully wax, even though she liked having hair and waxing wasn't her Truth. "He told me it was gross, and wouldn't touch me if I had the slightest bit of regrowth," she said. "I'd feel so ashamed. But looking back, it makes me mad — I mean, that's how our bodies are made! That's what's natural! And to be honest, I love it — it makes me feel sexy and beautiful. But it took me years and years after breaking up with him to ever let a boyfriend see me with hair down there."

Another friend felt ashamed of her sex drive. "I never used to enjoy sex that much," she said. "But my boyfriend at the time had a crazy-high sex drive. It used to start so many fights. He'd imply that there was something wrong with me because I didn't want to have sex very often. He'd say I was frigid and that I should get myself checked out by a doctor. Looking back, it's easy to see that I just didn't enjoy sex with *him*, but at the time, I thought I was abnormal and felt a lot of shame around it."

My client Amanda had been made to feel inadequate about her own pleasure preferences. "I like to have my clitoris rubbed to orgasm. But a guy I dated made me feel like I was defective or something — like my body wasn't 'right,' or I wasn't 'doing sex right' — because of that. As though a vaginal orgasm is the only kind that matters!"

At one of my Goddess Groups, some women shared stories about being forced to do things they weren't really into and that weren't their Truth. "It's not like it was abuse or anything," said one of them. "I mean, he was my boyfriend and we loved each other. But he wanted to try anal and I didn't, and I didn't know how to say no in a way that wouldn't offend him. I also didn't want to be 'that girl' — the one who's boring and unadventurous. So I did it. But I didn't want to, it wasn't my Truth and I didn't enjoy it. I felt crap about myself the whole time. We broke up soon after and I really wish I'd spoken up in that moment. But back then, I didn't have the confidence and my Mean Girl was too loud."

There were also many stories about periods. "Once, I thought my period had ended, so I had sex with my then-partner. Turns out, it was still going, and when he pulled out, he had some blood on him. He freaked out and thought it was disgusting. I was ashamed and *mortified* that my body had done that, and it made me hate my body and period for ages."

Another friend found out that her boyfriend had shown naked pictures of her to a friend. "When I found out, I was absolutely livid. But even worse than the anger was the shame. I felt like a slut, even though I'd done nothing wrong, and I was terrified of what the other guy would think of me. I broke up with him, but it still had a lasting impact on me. I held back in the bedroom for years after that, and was always paranoid about being too sexual with men, in case they thought I was slutty. It also took me ages to trust someone again sexually."

It's obviously not just women who have these stories. I was chatting with a male friend recently to ask about his experiences. Though he didn't have an immediate treasure trove of answers like my female friends, he eventually gave me an example about a one-night stand he'd had. Well, *nearly* had. When push came to shove (so to speak), he realized that he was not into the girl at all and didn't want to sleep with her, so he politely made his excuses and went to leave. At which point the girl insinuated that he wasn't a "real man," because he didn't want to have sex. He also shared that in his younger days, he'd been incredibly paranoid about the size of his penis — never sure if it was big enough, and always comparing himself to the hugely endowed men he saw in porn films and coming up short (no pun intended!).

I could go on and on here, sharing stories of personal shame. But hopefully, just through this small selection, you can see they're incredibly common. So if you've got your own story, you are absolutely not alone. Hopefully you can also see how damaging they are. These kinds of experiences may seem "trivial" — and may pale in comparison to the horrific sexual trauma that some people face — but they can still be damaging. In fact, a tiny incident or two can result in a lifetime of guilt or shame, if not properly addressed. The point here isn't to compare or rank how bad someone's experience is, just to acknowledge that no matter what you've gone through, you are not alone, you are not abnormal, you are not broken, and you can let this story go now and experience deep love, rocking relationships, and soulful sex.

The good news is, it doesn't matter what happened in the past. The past is in the past, and in this present moment (the only moment we really have) you have the power to choose how your present and future unfold. This isn't about denying or suppressing what happened to you. By all means, feel all the feels fully. You may even like to reach out and get some support if you feel the need (I cannot recommend this highly enough, if you're struggling). But what I so desperately want you to know is that **your past does**

not define you, who you are, or your future. You *can* create a new sexual future full of deep love and heart-centered intimacy. The first step is having the willingness to open up to the possibility of things being different. Simple willingness is all it takes to Open Wide to infinite possibilities.

Are you willing?

Great, angel! I am so proud of you, and don't worry — I've got your hand through all this.

Once you've got the willingness factor in place, the next step is to let go of the past so that you can be here in the present. **You can't be fully present if you're holding on to the past.**

By "letting go" you're not condoning what that person has done or said; all you're doing is freeing yourself from its grip on you. You see, when you hold on to anger, pain, or frustration it eats away at your soul. Over time, this can manifest as suffering or disease in the body.

One of my clients, Jessie, was raped when she was fourteen years old. As you can imagine, this was incredibly traumatic for her. At the time, she didn't have the tools to cope or anyone to talk to, so the only sensible route she had to deal with the trauma was to close off her heart and sexuality and vow to never let anyone get close to her again. As a way to "protect" herself and to numb the pain, she also began binge eating. When she came to see me she was obese and pre-diabetic, and her health was plummeting. After we worked together, she realized she'd been holding onto that pain for fifteen years and was finally ready to let it go and free herself. She could see it was blocking her from experiencing true love and vibrant health. (She also realized she needed expert support, and found herself an amazing holistic therapist who specialised in sexual trauma.) The change in her, since making the decision to consciously deal with her feelings, has been incredible. It was a privilege watching her come back into her body, rediscover her desires, and make positive changes to her health and life. Her bravery in facing and releasing her pain was what made it all possible.

AN IMPORTANT NOTE!

I've said it before and I'll say it again – I am not a doctor, counselor, therapist, psychologist, or practitioner. If you have feelings of sexual shame or trauma that you're struggling with or that you've been suppressing for years, I highly recommend seeking the support of an expert, or a team of holistic therapy experts.

Sexual trauma is NOT something that needs to define you, that you need to overcome alone, or that needs to stop you from experiencing intimacy, pleasure, or deep love for the rest of your life.

It's also never too late – whether you've had these feelings for a day, a decade, or half a century, it is NEVER too late to get support and choose a different reality for yourself.

I also want to issue a heartfelt note of caution here. You know how at the start of any book on diet and fitness, there's always a note in fine print, recommending that you speak to your doctor before making any lifestyle changes? The same applies here. If you've experienced sexual trauma, I recommend you seek expert advice or assistance before trying the exercises in the rest of this chapter. I'm going to be sharing some techniques that I've personally found useful in releasing and recovering from my own sexual shame. These may appeal to you, but they may not – which is totally okay. As with everything in this book – and in life in general – you are your own best guru, so please exercise your common sense and LISTEN to your intuition. You're in control here, sweetheart – it's *your* journey, *your* choices, and *your* rules.

How to Physically Release Sexual Shame

Once you've decided you no longer want a limiting past story to ruin your life, if you feel called you could perform a physical releasing ritual to let go of any sexual shame, pain, or trauma. Just as painful memories can get lodged in our minds, so too can we store them in our physical bodies and our chakras. In order to Open Wide to life (and experience soulful sex) we need to release those blockages. The technique I'll be teaching you is called *de-armoring*.

But before we dive into de-armoring, I want to give you a lesson on chakras. See illustration on next page.

CHAKRAS CLASS 101

Chakra is a Sanskrit word for wheel, also used to name the nodes of the natural energy system of the body, and the ancient practitioners of Indian religions identified that there are seven chakras within the body. When your chakras are clear and functioning well, the energy flows through these seven areas smoothly. When energy is blocked in any one area, it can lead to illness, pain, discomfort, or disease in the corresponding part of the body. This is why it's super important to understand your chakras, so that you can release the blocks and stagnant energy, and allow the energy to flow freely through your body.

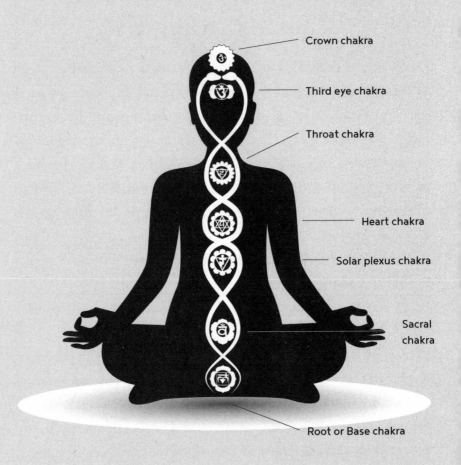

Crown chakra

Third eye chakra

Throat chakra

Heart chakra

Solar plexus chakra

Sacral chakra

Root or Base chakra

The Seven Chakras of the Human Body

CHAKRA ONE: ROOT OR BASE CHAKRA

Located at the base of your spine.

It's our foundation and represents the feeling of being centered, grounded, and supported.

When this is out of balance it can make us feel rocked off our center and create fear about basic survival issues such as financial independence, money, abundance, family, and food.

CHAKRA TWO: SACRAL CHAKRA

Located at your lower abdomen.

This represents our connection and ability to accept others and new experiences.

When this is out of balance, it can bring up abundance and well-being issues, and also blocks around pleasure, procreation, creativity, and sexuality. This is one of the main chakras where we can store a lot of pain from past sexual experiences.

CHAKRA THREE: SOLAR PLEXUS CHAKRA

Located at your upper abdomen in the stomach area.

This represents our ability to be confident and feel in control of our lives.

When this is out of balance, it affects our self-worth, self-confidence, and self-esteem. This is one place where our intuition resides. When it's out of whack, it affects our ability to trust, follow, and lead with our intuition.

CHAKRA FOUR: HEART CHAKRA

Located at the center of your chest.

This represents our ability to love and to be loved.

When this is out of balance, it affects our ability to feel and experience love, joy, inner peace, and contentment. This is another chakra that can be blocked by past sexual trauma.

CHAKRA FIVE: THROAT CHAKRA

Located at your throat.

This represents our ability to communicate our Truth clearly with ourselves and others.

When this is out of balance, it can manifest in losing our voice, throat infections, a tickle in the throat, coughs, or colds, because we feel we cannot express our Truth clearly or we're not speaking up about something that is of importance to us.

CHAKRA SIX: THIRD EYE CHAKRA

Located at the middle of your forehead.

This represents our strength and ability to see and focus on the big picture.

When it's out of balance, this chakra affects our intuition, imagination, and creativity and our ability to tap into our innate wisdom and make decisions.

CHAKRA SEVEN: CROWN CHAKRA

Located two inches above the very top of your head.

This represents our ability to be fully connected to our spirituality or higher self.

When this is out of balance it can affect our connection to our higher self, the Universe, God, the Creator.

Blockages in any of your chakras need to be addressed, as they can spill over and affect everything, not just that particular area. And while I strongly believe that **we are not this physical body**, you are still *in* this physical body for the time being and we need to support it and give it love. We need to treat it like our temple, honor it, and look after it ... after all, we only get one for this lifetime.

Take care of your body. It's the only place
you have to live.

JIM ROHN

When Nick and I first got together, I quickly discovered I was holding onto trauma in my root and sacral chakras. The reason I learned this was because there were times when intercourse was incredibly painful and I would get a shooting, stabbing pain in my vagina. I was so worried that I went and spent thousands of dollars and saw a bunch of specialists to see if anything was wrong with me, because I know many women have physiological issues with their pelvic floor and vagina. After getting ultrasounds and seeing multiple "woo-woo" and mainstream practitioners, it was an energy worker who finally helped me realize I had blockages in my chakras. Super glad I spent all that money trying to work that out … NOT! From there, I got to work on releasing those blockages, which is key if you want to Open Wide to deep love. Once I did I was able to make love pain free.

One of my clients, Bec, kept experiencing bleeding and pain during sex. There seemed to be no physical reason for her to have these symptoms (and the doctor had no answer for her), so she came to me to do some inner work. Together, we dug into her childhood. She'd been raised in a very strict religious family, where she'd basically been taught that sex was for reproductive purposes only. She realized that this belief had been playing on her mental mix-tape every time she'd gone to bed with a man, so instead of Opening Wide and relaxing into the experience, she was actually riddled with tension and anxiety in her body, which was contributing to the pain. As soon as Bec had this epiphany, she decided to swap that limiting belief — that sex was for reproduction only, not pleasure — for one that actually reflected what she believed: that sex was a beautiful, sacred act she could engage in whenever she wanted to express herself fully. It took some work (and plenty of relaxation exercises), but soon she'd let go of the shame about sex that had followed her for years, and was instead enjoying intercourse for the first time in her life.

Another one of my clients, Anaya, used to regularly get urinary tract infections (UTIs) and yeast infection after having sex with her partner of three years. She couldn't understand why this was happening. She was healthy and the doctors said she was simply "unlucky" and would give her another round of antibiotics and toxic yeast infection cream to slap on her vagina to sort it out ... until the next time she had sex and it happened all over again. But being an intuitive person, Anaya sensed the real issue went deeper than that. She came to me and we uncovered that she had a decades-old belief that sex was dirty. When she was a little girl, she would touch her vagina and her mother would say, "Stop that right now, that's dirty." This planted a seed in her mind, so every time she had sex, unconsciously she thought it was dirty and for her this seemed to be manifesting as recurring UTIs and yeast infection. Together, we worked on re-programming that belief and she is now not only UTI and yeast infection free, she also experiences deep love and soulful sex. Praise the vagina gods!

I share these stories NOT to dictate the "right" course of action — for you the best path may be a more common Western medicine approach (and it's always important to make sure there isn't anything really wrong when you feel pain or experience unexplained bleeding). My point is that **addressing the underlying spiritual, emotional, or mental imbalances is an important part of**

healing, and for many women, this kind of inner work can be the catalyst for incredible growth and transformation.

On that note, it's time for me to share one of the most powerful forms of inner work I've ever encountered. (And when I say "inner," I mean *inner*!)

Are you ready for some de-armoring?

A QUICK NOTE ON LUBRICANTS

Ideally your body produces its own moisture so you won't need any external lubrication. However if you do, please don't go slapping over-the-counter chemical-bomb lubes on your precious mucous membranes. (Have you seen the ingredients lists on those? Gross!)

I'm fastidious about what I allow on and in my body, and my vagina is no exception. For me, one of my personal care boundaries is this: if I wouldn't put it in my mouth, I don't put it on my skin. And I DEFINITELY don't put it in my vagina.

For that reason, my go-to choice of lube (if I choose to use it) is organic coconut oil.

Please be aware though, **if you're using latex condoms, oil-based lubricants are NOT a good idea, as they can seriously reduce their effectiveness**.

If condoms are your chosen form of contraception, please do your vagina a favor and find yourself a high-quality, water-based organic lubricant with no nasties. They're out there, and they're a million times better than the stock-standard supermarket ones. You can also source non-toxic latex condoms made without spermicide and from all natural ingredients. Sure, it might take a little extra effort, but your vagina deserves it.

SO WHAT EXACTLY IS DE-ARMORING?

De-armoring is an internal trigger point massage that can help your vagina become softer and far more sensitive. It helps release blockages, ease pain, and heal numbness so that you can reconnect to your natural sexual potency and experience more openness, pleasure, wetness, internal orgasms, and love. When it's performed correctly, your sexual experiences can deepen and you might start to experience new kinds of orgasms you didn't know existed — cervix, or womb orgasms (more on them later!). It's a simple yet powerful process of applying pressure to places of contraction and tightness inside the vaginal canal for the purpose of releasing physical, spiritual, and emotional blockages.

Before I started de-armoring, I only experienced clitoral orgasms — and even then, I was sometimes faking it. After de-armoring, I started having deep G-spot, cervical, vagina, womb, and other types of orgasms I'd never even heard of, let alone experienced.

De-armoring can feel painful, as you're releasing a lot of stored emotion that has been locked in there for years, maybe decades. But afterwards, you will not only feel an incredible weight lifted off your shoulders, but a fresh new perspective on life. Some women have even reported that after trying this technique, they got their natural wetness back, their menstrual cycle started to regulate, and their yeast infection issues disappeared. It's amazing what the body is capable of, given half a chance!

Please note: if you're not used to exploring your body, or if you're not one hundred percent sure you'll be able to hear your body's messages, then start with much simpler self-touch and self-pleasure, and consult a gynecologist.

If de-armoring is something you would like to explore, you have three options:

1. You can see a professional and get them to do it for you. Please shop around and choose someone you trust and feel one hundred percent comfortable with.

2. You can get your soulmate to do it for you, using their fingers. Please make sure they read this first, though, so they know what they are doing.

3. You can do it yourself, using a crystal pleasure wand (also known as a goddess or yoni wand) to help you reach your cervix. I don't believe in putting cheap plastic dildos in my sacred passageway, so please just make sure that whatever you use is something that feels right for you. Although Nick has done it for me, this is my favorite option.

Helpful tips:

- Before you start, create a sacred space. Take an Epsom salts bath, diffuse some essential oils, dim the lights, lock the door, and maybe put on some soft meditation music so you don't feel self-conscious that others will hear you. You want to be able to express yourself freely and not feel like you have to hold back out of fear of your roommate or mom hearing you.

- Trust your body. Anger, sadness, pleasure, frustration, or joy may come up. Trust what you're feeling, and know that it's all perfect.

- Listen to your body. If it's hurting too much, back off. Always listen to your body and tune in to what it's telling you.

- There's no rush, so go as slowly and gently as you like. If you're not sure, pull back.

- Let go of judgment. Your Mean Girl will most likely pop up. Put her on mute and allow yourself to stay in your body, out of your head, wide open, and in the present moment.

- Don't hold back. Whatever comes up, let it out. Let out the tears or laughter, it's time to release those blockages, once and for all.

HOW TO DE-ARMOR

STEP ONE

Make sure your body is ready and open. Do this by giving yourself a full-body coconut oil massage. Touch yourself and get yourself slightly turned on. This is super important, to ensure your body is primed and prepared for penetration.

If you're getting your soulmate to do this for you, get them to kick off this process. A massage, gentle tickling, whatever helps you relax, Open Wide, and prepare your body. Practicing CCC is key here, so tell him when you feel wide open and ready.

STEP TWO

Once you feel open and ready, put some organic coconut oil on your dildo. Insert it into your vagina. Once inside, using your dildo, you're looking for areas of pain, tension, numbness, or anywhere that feels tight, contracted or even a bit "yuck" to touch. Really *feel* and stay connected to your body. When you find a spot, add a little more pressure and bring all your awareness to that spot. Gently push into that area. Your immediate reaction may be to "pull up," or tighten your pelvic floor to protect yourself, but instead breathe and try to relax into it. Allow yourself to fully express whatever comes up through sounds. Get it out! Don't hold back. If you want to cry, cry! If you want to scream, scream! If you want to laugh, laugh! Just allow yourself to fully express, openly and honestly. You're releasing stored emotion that might have been there for years (and which can be preventing you from experiencing deep love and soulful sex) so it's time to let it go. Once you feel it naturally subside, you can either move on to another spot or, if you've had enough for that session, you can stop. Do whatever feels right for you.

If your partner is doing this for you, remember that communication (especially CCC) is paramount. Tell them to hold, stop, or to pull out if you need.

Some women can be completely de-armored after one session, while others may take a few sessions – everyone is different. Always tune in and do what feels right for you. You can also do this once a week or once a month to let go of regular stress and tension that builds up in that area from daily life.

After your session, give yourself some love. Be gentle with yourself. Maybe have a bath, journal about your experience, or do a meditation. You will intuitively know what to do. And if you need some extra support to help you process what came up, *please* seek it. Reach out to a holistic therapist or whoever you trust.

If you're with your partner, share what came up. Ask them to give you a massage or tickle your back. Get them to hold you, and breathe into each other.

Please do not do this if you are pregnant or think you might be.

Although I have yet to experience this (and I hope I do), I have heard stories that women who de-armor regularly experience less painful births and even womb orgasm during labor (um, yes please!).

My wish for you is that you choose to Open Wide to deep love and soulful sex – it's your birthright to feel and experience this sacred pleasure in this lifetime.

KEY TAKEAWAYS FROM CHAPTER SEVEN

- **LET GO OF SHAME ABOUT SEX.**

  Some media and pornography have portrayed sex and our bodies in a certain way, but this is *not* the whole truth. There *is* another, more fulfilling, soulful, heart-expansive way to talk and think about these subjects. And if we can change our beliefs about sex and our bodies, we will inspire our children, our children's children, and maybe — just maybe — we can break the long lineage of shame once and for all. But it all starts with us breaking the cycle in our own homes.

- **LET GO OF PERSONAL SHAME.**

  No matter what you've gone through, you are not alone, you are not abnormal, you are not broken, and you have the power to let this story go and experience deep love and soulful sex.

- **LET GO OF THE PAST TO BE FULLY PRESENT NOW.**

  By "letting go" you're not condoning what that person has done or said; all you're doing is freeing yourself from its grip on you. When you hold on to anger, pain, or frustration, it eats away at your soul. Over time, this can manifest as suffering or disease in the body.

- **EMBRACE THE SEVEN CHAKRAS.**

  When your chakras are humming along nicely, energy flows through these seven areas smoothly and evenly. When energy is blocked in any one area, it can lead to illness, pain, discomfort, or disease in the body.

- **OPEN WIDE TO DE-ARMORING FOR A PHYSICAL RELEASE OF SEXUAL PAIN, SHAME, AND TRAUMA.**

  This simple yet powerful process involves applying pressure to places of contraction and tightness inside the vaginal canal for the purpose of releasing physical, spiritual, and emotional blockages.

- **REJOICE. SEX NO LONGER NEEDS TO BE TABOO, AND IT'S NOT SOMETHING WE NEED TO FEEL ASHAMED, DIRTY, OR NAUGHTY ABOUT.**

  It's your birthright to feel and experience this sacred pleasure and healing energy in this lifetime. That is my wish for you.

CHAPTER EIGHT

Getting Up Close and Personal with YOU

I truly believe that sex — and I'm talking about deep, expansive, mind-blowing, earth-shattering, spine-tingling, head-spinning (yes, this has happened to me), soulful sex — is a gift. It's a heart-opening experience of pure love, oneness, and bliss. And when it's anything less than that, we feel it in our soul. This is why you can sometimes feel empty or hollow after a meaningless and unsatisfying exchange. So then why do we "settle" (there's that word again) for anything less?

You're here, reading this. So I *know* you're ready for more. Perhaps you've been feeling called to explore more deeply within yourself; to experience more oneness, unity, and connection with your partner; or to harness your divine Goddessence and channel it sexually. Heck, maybe you just want to experience more pleasure in the bedroom! Whatever is driving you, it's all perfect, it's all possible, and it all starts with *you*.

SAY HELLO ... TO YOU

How can you tell your lover what you enjoy, or figure out what you yourself enjoy, if you don't *know* yourself intimately, on all levels? When you're acutely in tune with yourself and your body, you know what feels truly right for you (physically, emotionally, and spiritually) and, by extension, what doesn't. This is incredibly empowering, and can completely transform your experience of lovemaking. It's also amazing for your confidence, so that if you're ever in a situation that makes you feel out of alignment or uncomfortable in any way, you know it in your bones and will have the confidence and courage to speak up. This is my wish for you! It's especially important that every one of us has the capacity, courage, and self-knowledge to firmly state (with unwavering conviction) "NO!" If this all sounds like your cup of tea, becoming intimate with yourself is the first step in learning how to do it.

LET'S GET CLEAR ON YOUR STARTING POINT

When it comes to the physical act of sex, it's important to know where your beliefs are at.

For example, some women think they need to dress and act like porn stars in the bedroom, even though it's not their Truth and it's not satisfying for them. They may act this way because they think that's what sex or "being sexy" is all about, and they haven't been taught anything else. They didn't have role models so they had to scramble for titbits of guidance, wherever they could find them.

(And what do you think popular culture wants to teach our young women about sex and sexiness?!)

INSPO-ACTION

Do you have any programmed beliefs about what sex "should" look like, be like, and feel like for you? For example, do you think sex can only ever be rough? Or perhaps it's about a man "getting off" as quickly as possible?

Next to each belief, write down where that idea came from — maybe it was from your parents, a sibling, a former partner, a teacher, pornography, a magazine, the internet, or a friend.

_____

_____

_____

_____

_____

_____

_____

The actual source of your beliefs doesn't really matter. The reason I'm getting you to identify where it came from is so you can see that **it didn't innately come from you**. It wasn't *your* Truth, but more an idea planted in your mind that took root and grew. If that's the case, we can now pull out those weeds and replant a new belief that will flourish and serve you.

Close your eyes for a moment and think about deep, soulful, heart-opening lovemaking. Feel what that would be like in your body. (If you haven't yet experienced it physically, imagine what it might feel like.) Sit for two minutes and really feel this.

Now write down your new Truths about sex. This might be ... *I believe sex is a heartfelt exchange between two bodies and souls that come together to experience oneness.* Much nicer, right?! Now that you have a new belief about sex, it's your job to master your Mean Girl whenever the old belief pops up. You show her who's boss!

_____

_____

_____

_____

_____

_____

_____

_____

_____

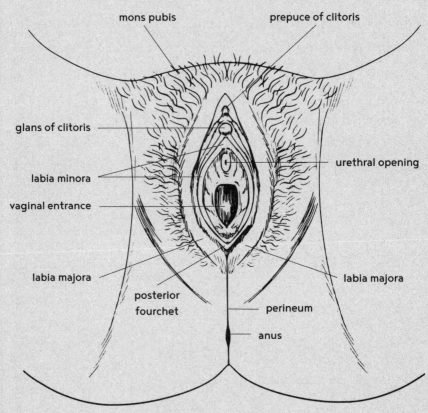

mons pubis

prepuce of clitoris

glans of clitoris

urethral opening

labia minora

vaginal entrance

labia majora

labia majora

posterior
fourchet

perineum

anus

The Female Anatomy

Now that you've re-programmed your beliefs around sex, it's time to Open Wide to *you*. It amazes me how many women don't know their own body intimately. Society has deemed it taboo, but let's put on our big girl pants — or more to the point, let's take them off — and get over it, shall we? Let's get to know our beautiful bodies.

Notice your immediate reaction when you saw that picture. Did your body tense up? Did you think it was gross? Disgusting? Rude? Dirty? How did you respond? How did your body respond? How did your Mean Girl respond?

In order to love yourself unconditionally, you must love *all* parts of yourself — even (in fact, *especially*) your labia, your clitoris, your vagina, your perineum, and your anus. And just like you learned to love and accept yourself in Chapter Three, it's now time to learn how to fully love and accept your vulva.

NAMING CEREMONY

There are tons of words people use when they talk about vaginas, but I want you to name your vagina something that feels right for you. I've felt very detached and disconnected from my vagina — almost like it was a separate entity — for most of my life. Many women have had a similar experience. But it is part of us, and in order for you to experience deep love and soulful sex and to get your juices flowing freely, you need to love it fully.

I personally interchange between "vagina" and "yoni." Yoni is a Sanskrit word meaning "sacred passage or place." I love the word yoni because it feels soft, beautiful, and feminine, and it reminds me how special and sacred that area is. After all, this is the entrance through which we bring life into the world ... What could be more miraculous than that?

I also love "vagina," because it feels strong, powerful and dignified, so I mix it up depending on my mood.

When you think about your yoni, what do you want to call her? What feels right for *you*? Vagina, yoni, pussy, flower, rose, lily, treasure, Amanda … There is no right or wrong, just feel what's true for you. Sit with it for a while; be patient and let it come to you when it's ready.

Once you have your name, write it down. Your homework is to only use that name when you speak of her and not to shy away from it. Own it!

Naming your vagina opens you up to deeper connection with it and your beautiful body. That feeling of separateness will dissolve and you will become more in tune and connected with yourself.

YONI LOVE

Many women have shame around their vulvas. They think it's ugly — too big, too small, too lopsided, too dark, too pink, too hairy, not hairy enough, too wide, too skinny, not the same as it used to be, [insert any other negative Mean Girl belief you can think of here!]. And as you know by now, **beliefs can both create and destroy, and what you think about you will bring about**. Not only that, those Mean Girl beliefs directly impact the way we celebrate and express our femininity and sexuality. They also deeply affect your self-worth, your capacity to orgasm, your presence, your ability to heal, and will rob you of the love, joy, and happiness you feel, both in and out of the bedroom.

Just like all Mean Girl beliefs, they can manifest in your body — in this case, as pain, numbness, and tightness in your vagina. And they can also block you from letting go and being fully present in the moment (which is key to soulful lovemaking), because you feel so self-conscious when your partner is close to your vulva or when the lights are on. (That's why some women slam down fifteen cocktails before heading to the boudoir — it's the only way they know how to "let go.")

So if you're feeling less than groovy about your vulva, it's time to put those limiting beliefs to bed once and for all.

You have two options here ...

OPTION ONE

Grab yourself a small mirror, lock yourself in your room, lie on your bed, and look at your vulva. Notice what comes up. How do you feel? Is it triggering any emotions? What is your Mean Girl saying to you? Stay with this for three minutes and repeat this daily for two weeks, journaling about your experience after each session.

OPTION TWO

Take a photo of your vulva on your digital camera (not your phone – God knows where that could end up!) and look at it daily for two minutes. Again, notice what comes up. How does it make you feel? Do you feel triggered? What is your Mean Girl saying to you? Repeat this daily for two weeks, journaling about your experience after each session.

Just as our souls are all unique, so are our vulvas. No two are the same and there is no "perfect" one. Let go of your idea of what it "should" look like and embrace the gift you have. Get over it and accept it, because you only get one.

(If you really want proof that vulvas come in all shapes and sizes, jump online and visit the "Labia Library" — labialibrary. org — to see a collection of photos of everyday women's yonis. What a beautiful and inspiring sight!)

No matter which practice you choose, the intention is to truly appreciate your precious yoni. To feel love, gratitude, and deep reverence for it. If you do the work, you will become deeply connected with it, and fundamentally change the way you speak, think, and treat it and your body. If you don't feel that way after these practices, keep going until you do.

Just like everything, we have to bring light to the areas we have pushed into the darkness in order to grow and evolve to our fullest potential. That's why this practice is so powerful, on multiple levels. I'm excited for you to try it!

Diving Deeper Into You

There are loads of ways to really explore your body and get to know yourself on a more intimate level, which will allow you to Open Wide to depths of love you didn't know existed.

Here are some of my all-time favorites …

SELF-LOVE MASSAGE

One of the best ways to bust body-image blocks is through regular self-love massages. Grab some organic coconut oil, lock the door, dim the lights, pop your Mean Girl on mute, put on some soft meditation music, diffuse some essential oils, and lie on your bed. Start at your feet and work your way up, touching every single part of your body. Repeat affirmations such as …

I love you.

You are perfect.

You are beautiful.

Thank you.

I am so grateful for my X.

Your Mean Girl may pop up, but gently put her back on mute and return to the present moment.

For the best results do this for five to fifteen minutes each night before bed.

THE JADE EGG

Jade what?!

Known as the "stone of heaven and abundance," the Jade Egg was invented in China and has been used for five thousand years. Fans of this ancient tool believe that it helps women fully step into their sensual selves, experience orgasmic bliss, heal negative thoughts, and strengthen their sexual organs. They advocate that regular use can stir and awaken sexual energy, creating lots of physical, mental, emotional, and energetic benefits.

So what do you do with a Jade Egg? I'm glad you asked! It's super simple:

- Attach a piece of dental floss or string to the Jade Egg. This is so you can insert and remove the egg with ease. If you don't naturally get wet (which can change once you start using the egg) rub some organic coconut oil on the tip before inserting, though I highly recommend starting with a self-love massage — this will help you Open Wide and prime your body so well that the oil isn't needed. Allow your vagina to "suck" the egg in — never force or push it. This is a great reminder to always wait until your body and soul are fully ready for the egg (or person) to enter you.

- As my friend Tara O says, do your egg-cersises! Egg-cersises are like pelvic floor exercises, only you use the egg as a form of resistance. Once you've inserted it inside you, tighten or lift your pelvic floor to hold the egg in place (imagine you're trying to hold in a pee), and feel your muscles contract around the egg.

Some experts say you can leave the egg in all day and even sleep with it in. Others say this is pointless, because if you're not consciously doing your egg-cersises (and actively squeezing your pelvic floor muscles) it's redundant — you may as well strap it to your arm and leave it there. Sure, energetically you may be benefiting from the healing powers of the egg (devotees believe that jade is super powerful), but if toning and strengthening is your motivation, many teachers suggest you need to be deliberate about doing your egg-cersises.

You might be thinking, why jade? What makes it so special? Crystal-lovers have long held jade to be a powerful gemstone, believing that …

- It's calming for the nervous system.
- It's non-porous (making it super hygienic).
- It's known for blessing everything it touches.
- It's very healing.
- It's a protection crystal.
- It recharges your energy.
- It will activate all the hundreds of thousands of nerve endings in your vagina, making you more sensitive to pleasure.
- It helps you manifest your dreams and visions in life.

As well as strengthening, toning, and tightening your pelvic floor, fans of the Jade Egg also point to other benefits, such as it …

- increases vaginal wetness
- heightens sexual pleasure

- tones and restores your reproductive organs
- connects the heart and vagina and allows you to Open Wide in both
- strengthens your intuition and amplifies your creativity
- activates and turns on your vagina and life-force energy, which affects every area of your life.

So if you feel called, give this beautiful self-love practice a whirl. Personally, I use my egg as a form of self-pleasure, then sometimes leave it in for an hour or so while I'm at home to do my egg-cersises. I walk around consciously squeezing my pelvic floor muscles around the egg for as long as I can, then I release. Squeeze release, squeeze release. If you struggle to stay contracted for long, start with just a few seconds and build up from there, with plenty of rest in between your "reps."

While there's been some recent controversy online about the health claims of the Jade Egg, my experience with them has been only positive. So you should do your own research, have fun experimenting, and see what works best for you. As always, tune into your body and only do what feels right and truthful for you. Just like everything in this book, this is simply a suggestion that you can take and try, or not — it's totally up to you.

EGG CARE

If you do decide to experiment, caring for your Jade Egg is super important. When you've finished using your egg, make sure to clean it thoroughly. Because of the sensitive nature of jade, advocates suggest that you should NOT boil it or use soap. Instead, warm running water is usually enough to clean it (making sure to run the water through the hole too). You could also try using a few drops of tea tree oil or grapefruit seed extract (again, rinsing thoroughly afterward). If you're concerned about a buildup of residue, try giving your egg a cleansing salt bath every few weeks or so. So if you want to get extra goddess-y, you can place your egg in its salt bath out under the light of a full moon — there's no better way to recharge its energy, which will then be transferred straight to you when you use the egg.

Get Naked

Society has conditioned us to think that being naked is solely connected to sex, forcing us to button up and get our prude on. But if you look at our distant ancestors and the world's indigenous tribes, they got their nudie on all the time.

Personally, I used to *hate* being naked. I would get dressed as soon as I got out of the shower, have sex with a top on, and scoff at the sight of my body whenever I caught a glimpse of my reflection. I loathed what I saw, and I judged, pinched, poked, and prodded every ounce of my flesh. My Mean Girl would run riot any chance she could get. This behavior started quite young and led to an eating disorder, which I battled for years. During that period, I put my beautiful temple through a lot. I took highly toxic fat-burning pills, I starved myself, I binged, and then made myself sick. It all took a serious toll on my health, and I'm still reversing the damage.

It wasn't until I ended up in the hospital in 2010 that I realized I needed to learn to love myself and the skin I was in — a foreign concept I'd never been exposed to before. Full unconditional love for my body has been one of the hardest lessons for me to embrace and learn, and it's a journey I'm still undertaking to this day. Shocking, right? I mean, I teach people about self-love and how to master their Mean Girl … You'd think I'd have all this stuff sorted out by now! But there's a lot of truth to that saying, **we teach what we most need to learn**.

After many years of mastering my Mean Girl and practicing all the self-love exercises we spoke about in Chapter Three, my self-loathing has substantially diminished. But I won't pretend I'm enlightened — there are still moments when I catch my Mean Girl planting nasty seeds in my mind. The difference now is that I'm able to master her quickly, Open Wide, and return to unconditional love for myself and my body with relative speed, and ease, and grace. One of the most powerful ways I've been able to do that is by spending more time naked. This one simple act has forced me to rethink my entire relationship with my body.

These days, I sleep naked, walk around the house naked, sunbathe naked, cook naked, and even sometimes work naked. (I am actually naked right now … just kidding.) I now LOVE being nude (I think my neighbors love it too). And if I went from not being able to stand the sight of my body to truly loving my temple, so can you.

Getting over your body shame is a massive step on the path to deep love and soulful sex. Each of our bodies is so beautifully unique — and, just as with everything else, we mustn't compare ourselves to anyone else, or listen to any criticism that comes our way. Treat your body like a masterpiece. Love it and stop shaming it, once and for all. And know that if you want a partner to love your body, YOU must be head over heels in love with it first!

Here's how you get started ...

I began with baby steps. I would get out of the shower and instead of putting clothes on right away, I would give myself a full-body coconut oil massage and do my hair and makeup nude, then I would get dressed.

At night I started sleeping in underwear, then slowly with no top and then no undies.

But the most powerful exercise I did was mirror work. I got naked, stood in front of the mirror, and looked at myself. Sounds weird, but it's super powerful. At the start, I could only stand there for five seconds before the tears started to stream. But even though this was hard, I made a commitment to myself to do it every day until I could stand there for five minutes without letting my Mean Girl say one nasty thing about me. Every time my Mean Girl went to say something nasty, I would reset my timer until I got all the way through five minutes with no negative Mean Girl thoughts.

It took me weeks to get past one minute. But I persisted and every day I showed up, looked in the mirror, and did the work.

After a few months, I decided to up the ante. While in front of the mirror, I would give myself a full-body self-love massage and repeat affirmations such as ...

I love you.

Thank you.

You are amazing.

I love you, legs. I love you, toes. I love you, thighs.

This is something I still practice daily. And although there are times when it feels more challenging than others, being naked to me now represents being content in my own skin. It's a declaration that I'm wide open, and willing to be my true full self and to allow others in.

Get Over It and Get Into It

Initially, when it comes to sex, what you *think* you might like and what you *actually* like may be two very different things. This is why it's important to explore and experiment, starting with yourself. This is about non-judgmental, gentle exploration with love, honor, openness, and respect for yourself and your body.

It took me years to build up the courage to try sexual self-exploration. My Mean Girl told me it was wrong, naughty, and dirty. But once I opened up to the idea and began to explore, I was blown away. I uncovered so much about myself, and it unlocked a new level of confidence I hadn't known existed.

Becoming Orgasmic

You know now that everything is energy, and an orgasm is no different. An orgasm is simply an explosion of creative life-force energy, which — when intentionally cultivated — can unlock parts of you that you didn't know existed. It doesn't matter whether you're experiencing soulful sex with your lover or yourself, you can become orgasmic. When you do, every area of your life will start to flow even more effortlessly. You will glow and vibrate at a higher frequency. You can unlock creativity, increase your happiness, experience vibrant health, kick butt in business, boost your income, and become a much nicer human to be around. **Orgasm is the lubrication of life.** It can help you soften and make everything flow more fluidly. Basically, when you're orgasmic, *everything* is better.

For that reason, your desire and ability to orgasm may have some connection to other aspects of your life.

For example, are you as dry as the Sahara Desert? That might be a sign that you have a hard time "going with the flow" in life.

Can you not reach orgasm? Maybe you're afraid to surrender.

Does your man ejaculate too quickly? Maybe he's scared to go deep and backs away from challenging situations.

Is his erection weak? Where else could "weakness" be seeping out into other areas of his life?

Can he not get it up at all? Where else is he not showing up in life?

Your body's capacity to let go, Open Wide, and orgasm may reflect what's manifesting in your own life. Pay attention and act accordingly. This is the quickest route to growth and evolution.

Later on, I'm also going to teach you how to circulate your sexual energy to make your orgasms last longer (yep, this is possible) so that you can have whole-body orgasms and so that you can carry that orgasmic life-force energy with you into your day. (Sounds amazing, right?!)

But first, it's time for ...

Orgasm School

In my early twenties, I had no idea there were different types of orgasm. I had only ever experienced what some people call a "superficial clitoral orgasm," so I presumed that was the only one ... Boy, was I wrong (and seriously missing out).

THE MANY KINDS OF FEMALE ORGASMS

There are many different types of orgasms, including.

- clitoral orgasm
- G-spot orgasm (or vaginal orgasm)
- breast/nipple orgasm
- kissing/oral orgasm
- anal orgasm
- U-spot orgasm (directly above and to either side of the urethral opening)
- A-spot orgasm (the anterior fornix)

- cervical orgasm
- blended orgasm (both clitoral and vaginal orgasm)
- fantasy/mental orgasm
- multiple orgasms
- spiritual orgasm
- skin orgasm

Just the other day my friend told me about a seriously orgasmic girlfriend he once had who could orgasm almost instantly when her lover simply sucked her finger ... huh? Come again?! Yep, sister, the possibilities are infinite!

The most amazing thing is that when you Open Wide your heart, your mind, and your yoni, you can experience any of these — it's almost impossible to experience them if you're closed, tense, or holding onto resentment, anger, or frustration. In order to experience them, we must let go and Open Wide.

Sexpert Kim Anami says, "If your sex life isn't rejuvenating, energizing, immensely pleasurable, and life-changing, you're doing it wrong." And I agree! Here are some tips to help you become more orgasmic ...

MAGICAL MORNINGS

I'm a massive fan of morning routines, so why not add an orgasm to yours? When you start your day with an orgasm, everything is better and life becomes juicier. It's a great workout as it pumps energy through your whole body. It also ignites your creative fire. **Sexual energy is creative energy.** And when you're tapping into it and using it consciously, you'll see how you approach everything in your life with more creativity, from your work to your relationships, parenting, and everything in between.

You may also notice that life flows a lot more gracefully. An orgasm sends you out into your day radiant, glowing, and buzzing with energy. You awaken your cells and you'll feel grounded and centered because you're connected to your true Goddessence. Partner or no partner, try it for a week and see how you feel. Don't have time? Get up ten minutes (or however long you want to give yourself) earlier and make *you* a priority. And if the kids are all over the house from the crack of dawn, maybe set them up at the breakfast table and then head back to bed while they are busy eating. I've found that if I leave it until night time I'm more likely to end up too tired and won't be bothered. That's why I love kicking off my day with a morning orgasm.

AT LEAST AN ORGASM A DAY

My husband and I have a saying: **an orgasm a day keeps the divorce lawyer away**. When you're connected to your sexuality, you show up to the world feeling strong, confident, and empowered, which will affect every single area of your life. Partner or no partner, try an orgasm (or two or three ...) a day to keep the doctor, lawyer – heck, even your Mean Girl – away! But don't put pressure on yourself to orgasm. Just the simple act of uniting with your lover or yourself on a daily basis can seriously alter your state. Let the good times roll, baby!

THE MORE THE MERRIER

Most women stop after one orgasm, not realizing that women are naturally voracious and multi-orgasmic beings. (I never knew I could be multi-orgasmic until I Opened Wide to the idea and I gave it a red-hot go.) The most orgasms I have had in one lovemaking session was thirteen. No joke! It was mind-blowing, and it's totally possible for you too. So don't stop after one, keep going, sister! Your orgasmic potential is infinite, and if I can go from one (or none) to thirteen, so can you.

OPENING WIDE AND GOING DEEP

It's sometimes easier to go for a quick clitoral orgasm, but for the major benefits - the life-changing, earth-shattering, healing, energizing and rejuvenating effects - open your heart and sacral chakra very wide, and experiment with G-spot and full-body orgasms.

THE HEALING POWER OF ORGASMIC ENERGY

It's scientifically proven that when the body goes into orgasm, our pituitary gland releases many hormones and neurotransmitters — including feel-good hormones, pheromones, oxytocin, adrenaline, dopamine, nitric oxide, and testosterone, to name just a few. These powerhouse chemical messengers relieve pain, ease depression, stabilize our moods, improve our sleep, enhance longevity, increase clarity of mind, prevent disease, and so much more.

I've experienced this healing effect firsthand. Back in 2013, I started experiencing pain in my right hip. After many scans, X-rays, doctors' visits, thousands of dollars, and ultrasounds galore, I discovered that I had trabecular oedema, which is basically a fancy way of saying "swelling of the bone tissue." It was excruciating. I couldn't exercise, do yoga, or even walk on it. And the only solution the doctors had was to put me on crutches indefinitely and hope it improved. Jeez, thanks! This also meant I was out of action sexually, as lovemaking was unbearable. After feeling incredibly sorry for myself, I sought solace with one of my spiritual mentors, Bhava Ram, who not only told me about the healing powers of orgasmic life-force energy, but also gave me the very sage advice to get up, stop feeling sorry for myself, and get moving. *Moving?* I thought. *How the heck am I going to move my body when I can no longer touch my toes without howling in agony?* But because Bhava had broken his back and healed it through yoga, I trusted him and thought I may as well give it a try. So each day, I sat on the floor and tried to touch my toes. The pain was intense, like someone was sticking a knife into my right hipbone and wiggling it around. Then I started to make love again ... very carefully! Me on top was torture, me on the bottom was torture, from behind ... torture. So really, that only left us with spooning style, and even that hurt, though not as much as the other positions. Each day, I showed up and kept trying. My Mean Girl told me my hip would never heal, and I believed her plenty of times. But I continued to make love and touch my toes, and slowly but surely it improved. I didn't wake up one day and the pain was miraculously gone; it was more a gradual decrease in severity. Not being able to move my body also made me feel incredibly depressed, and the orgasms helped with that too (bonus!). I truly believe that the healing power of orgasmic energy helped mend my hip and improve my depression.

For eons, different cultures around the world have used this sexual healing power to cure colds, ease headaches, help depression, relieve stress, alleviate pain, cure nervousness, ease insomnia, stop fluid retention, relieve heaviness in the abdomen, alleviate shortness of breath, dissolve irritability, remedy loss of appetite, and decrease disease in the body. One of my favorite stories on this topic comes from a friend who was studying under a great Taoist master. During one of his classes, he told his students that if they wanted to experience tremendous health, they should go on vacation for a week with their lover and never leave the room: "Get room service and keep making love. Only stop to eat, shower, use the toilet, rest, and sleep." The listening students laughed at this pronouncement, to which the master replied, "Oh, you think I'm joking? This is no joke, people. Do it! It will heal anything."

So why don't people talk about or know the healing powers of sexual, orgasmic, life-force energy? The reasons are many. Societal and cultural programming is a big one, religion another. Also, the scientific study of sex and sexuality is a much smaller and newer field than other areas of science. (For example, did you know that the full anatomy of the clitoris was only discovered in 1998?!) So it's possible that most doctors know enough to prescribe you a pill, but maybe not enough to prescribe you an orgasm.

But the lack of understanding around this healing power doesn't mean we have to forgo it ourselves. On the contrary! I say we start a revolution: fabulous health through outrageous orgasms. Are you with me, sister?!

MAKING TIME AND SPACE FOR ORGASMS

There's no doubting the positive healing impact of orgasms. (Not to mention the pure deliciousness of them for your mind, body, and soul!) Yet still, so many of us resist engaging in sex, often in the times when an orgasm would help us most. Like when you have a screaming headache — the last thing you feel like doing is dropping your pants and getting down to business, right? Yet it can actually help *relieve* your symptoms. (It's true, science has proven it!) And I know that for myself: every time I've pushed through that little bit of resistance and made love, almost immediately my headache has subsided.

I believe that regular orgasms were also part of the reason I didn't fall into a deep, dark depression after my best friend Jess passed away. I was devastated (of course), and felt grief and pain like I had never experienced before, but the regular orgasms helped lift my state. That said, I sometimes had to push through the internal resistance, and consciously choose to relax, Open Wide, and immerse in the present moment. But I always felt better with those feel-good hormones dancing through my cells after an orgasm.

Of course, there are also times when I feel "waayyy too busy and stressed" to make love, right?! After all, I run my own business, and I'm a wife, stepmama, friend, daughter, and more … so isn't my Mean Girl a little justified when she protests that I couldn't possibly orgasm when I've got so much going on?! Sometimes, she may be right — you do, after all, have to follow your Truth. But more often, those are the times when I could really use the delicious power of orgasmic energy the most — especially to decrease cortisol, the stress hormone, and alleviate some of the stress and overload I feel in my body. And I promise you that without fail, every time I *do* create the time and space, I always find myself wondering why the heck I didn't do it earlier!

It's also worth noting that there may be seasons of your life when sex and orgasms truly *don't* feel like your Truth — for example, in the months after having a baby, after trauma, the loss of someone close to you, or perhaps after a breakup. In those times, I can't emphasize enough that you need to cut yourself some slack, calm your Mean Girl down, and lean in to whatever feels true to you. Judging yourself is not going to help. Just concentrate on tuning into your body's wisdom, and lavishing yourself with as much softness, self-love, and understanding as possible. And as always, please seek expert support if you feel called.

INSPO-ACTION

The next time you're feeling down, stressed, low in energy, or anything less than Vital (with a capital V!), have an orgasm or two. Try it and see how you feel. It's free, pleasurable, healing, and available any time. You've got nothing to lose and everything to gain, and you'll only know if you try. So bring on the "Big O!"

ORGASM AND PRESENCE

Your true, natural state is presence. It's in the present moment that the magic lies. It's where miracles occur and Truth exists.

The power for creating a better future is contained in the present moment: you create a good future by creating a good present.

ECKHART TOLLE

However, one of your Mean Girl's biggest tricks is to keep you out of the present moment. She does this by keeping you stuck in the past and stressing out over the future. Most people have a very loud Mean Girl and they let her jump in the driver's seat daily, which results in constantly living in the past or future and not in the present moment. And just like the King of Presence, Eckhart Tolle, says: "You create a good future by creating a good present."

Today's society is also very good at keeping us out of the present moment. We're now exposed to more information and more "on" than ever before. So being present is more important now than ever! This is where conscious self-awareness comes in. You have to be so self-aware that you can catch yourself when you're not present and bring yourself back to the here and now as quickly as you can, otherwise you'll miss this moment and you can never, ever get it back.

There are four tools that help me immediately come back to the present moment, and they are meditation, connecting with my breath, nature, and — yep, you guessed it — orgasm. When we use any of these tools, we ascend into an ecstatic state: we shift our energy and Open Wide on every level. Our ego, our worries, our relationship to society and culture ... they all cease to be. We are at one with nature, and our self-consciousness and insecurities dissolve. There is no past or future, only the magical present. For that moment, we connect with something transcendent and much larger than ourselves. The more we let go and surrender to the sensation, the deeper we experience creation, manifestation, healing, pure consciousness, unconditional love, oneness, bliss, release, regeneration, understanding, and connection with all things. We become part of infinite possibility and we cease to be limited by what we know. Our minds empty and worry becomes impossible. *This* is the magic of the present moment. *This* is the space you want to live and create from, because when you do, life rocks!

KEY TAKEAWAYS FROM CHAPTER EIGHT

- **THERE'S NO WAY YOU CAN TELL YOUR LOVER WHAT YOU ENJOY – OR FIGURE OUT WHAT YOU ACTUALLY LIKE – IF YOU DON'T KNOW YOURSELF INTIMATELY, ON ALL LEVELS.**

  When you're acutely in tune with yourself and your body, you know what feels truly right for you (physically, emotionally, and spiritually) and, by extension, what doesn't. Which gives you the confidence to say "NO" when you need to and Open Wide when you choose.

- **HOLD A NAMING CEREMONY FOR YOUR VAGINA.**

  In order to experience deep love and soulful sex, you need to love your vagina. So choose a name for it and commit to using it. Vaginas also come in all shapes and sizes. So please take a look at yours, shower it with love, and appreciate your precious yoni!

- **INCREASE YOUR SEXUAL PLEASURE BY OPENING WIDE AND GETTING TO KNOW YOURSELF INTIMATELY.**

  Whether you choose a self-love massage, "egg-cersises" with your Jade Egg, some nudie time, or self-exploration, you'll be Opening Wide to new frontiers of pleasure and a deeper relationship with yourself.

- **ORGASMS FOR THE WIN!**

  Get your daily dose of Vitamin "O," and you can unlock your creativity, increase your happiness, experience vibrant health, kick butt in business, boost your income, and become a much nicer human to be around. When you're orgasmic, it helps *everything* flow more smoothly and easily.

- **MAKE TIME AND SPACE FOR SOULFUL SEX AND SELF-EXPLORATION.**

  It won't happen unless you make time. Switch off. Get connected. Be present. And get to know yourself more deeply.

CHAPTER NINE

Laying the Foundations for Soulful Sex

This chapter is smaller than the rest. Not because I don't have a lot to say on this topic, but because by now you surely understand that soulful sex — that is, life-changing, mind-blowing, earth-shattering sex — will only occur when you are Open Wide and bursting with love within yourself *first*. I feel like a broken record but I cannot stress this enough … the path to soulful sex starts with *you*. And even once you have done the work on yourself (or done your "self-love sit-ups") and have called in your lover, the work doesn't stop there. In fact, the next layer gets peeled back. This is because when you're with your soulmate, there's nowhere to hide; you don't *let* each other hide. You call each other out (with love, of course). You are each other's biggest mirror and you inspire each other to rise up, you hold each other accountable, and love the bejesus out of each other.

Soulful lovemaking IS life changing.

We humans can sometimes forget that we're here to love, to give and be love, and soulful sex can take us there. **Soulful sex is the best (and most fun) personal development tool ever, because you're physically and metaphorically the most naked you will ever be.** It forces you to Open Wide, surrender, face, your fears and return to love.

I cannot hide with Nick. If he sees me playing small, he calls me out on it. If he sees I haven't been flexing my own self-love muscle, he will bring it up (and vice versa). And if he sees I've been hanging out in Fear Town with my Mean Girl, he will be the first to shine light on it. It sucks sometimes, because I can't wallow in my misery, and sometimes my Mean Girl just wants to have a good old temper tantrum like a two-year-old. But it's also perfect, because really, my higher self doesn't actually *want* tantrums, and that's what being in a conscious, loving relationship is all about … calling each other to Open Wide and rise up. That polarity has to exist. Remember, you need an equal balance of support and challenge. Otherwise, if it's too easy, you'll get bored and leave. And if it's too hard, you'll get pissed off and leave … Challenge is not only healthy for relationships, it's essential.

So, my angel, do you feel bursting with unconditional love within yourself right now? If yes, keep reading … If not, remember **your Truth is love, you are love, and love is always only a breath away**. You can return to love in any moment, even right now in this instant. If there are feelings or emotions bubbling away inside you, that's okay. Never suppress them; fully feel them all. Then, when you're ready, let them go and come back to love.

In my early twenties, I had no idea that soulful sex existed or that it was actually humanly possible. I didn't learn the truth until I opened myself up to the world of Tantra and Taoism and read the work of David Deida (in particular *Dear Lover* and *The Way of the Superior Man* — essential reading for all). While soaking up his every word, I knew something was missing in my life and that there had to be more. The feeling that washed over me was hard to articulate because I had never experienced it. I thought sex was always about two people "getting their rocks off." Oh, how wrong I was! **Sex can be a sacred experience.** But I didn't know this because you don't know what you don't know. And now I know, I'm about to open *your* eyes to a whole new world of lovemaking.

But first, what is soulful sex?

Soulful sex is:

- not what you see in pornography, music videos, movies, YouTube, TV shows, magazines, or billboards
- when whole, authentic, present, unified, conscious, vulnerable beings choose to come together from a place of love not fear
- when two people Open Wide to themselves and each other and are willing to be of service to the other person
- a "holy" experience with God, love, oneness (whatever you want to call it)
- the ultimate union of love and expression of unconditional love
- where there is honestly nowhere to hide and where *all* of you must show up fully

I know what you're thinking: *Melissa, this sounds awesome, but how the heck do I make it happen?!*

Before I tell you, it's important to remember that deep, soulful, life-altering sex is only possible once you've done the work on yourself, or if you're already Open Wide. You must be bursting with unconditional love within yourself first. Showing up with your limiting Mean Girl baggage is not conducive to soulful sex. It might be easy to strip naked physically in front of someone and have sex, but to get naked metaphorically — to be vulnerable and fully real with someone — is a whole other level. So please make sure you've done everything I've mentioned in the book thus far before you move on to this section.

Keys for Soulful Sex

These keys are a synthesis of everything you've learned so far in this book, all brought together to facilitate potent lovemaking. Let the soulful sex begin!

KEY ONE: SET YOUR BOUNDARIES

We spoke a lot about boundaries in Chapter Five, but sexual boundaries are just as important. Knowing your sex boundaries will give you the inner confidence to speak your Truth.

So what are your sex boundaries? Here are mine to give you some ideas:

- I only have sex when mutual unconditional love and respect are flowing between the two of us.
- I don't allow "jackhammering." It thrashes the exquisite and delicate sensitive nature of the vagina. With past men this has numbed me, and I don't want to feel numb during lovemaking.
- No "attacking" my clitoris, either.
- I only allow Nick to enter me when I'm open and ready.

- I wait for all my chakras to open up first, especially my heart and sacral chakras, so that I can experience soulful sex. It's important never to have sex with a closed heart or when you're feeling upset or emotional about something. It's always best to express it from your heart first.
- I never fake it. I'm always true to myself, allowing any emotion to surface. (P.S. If he can't handle this, he's not the right man for you. Full stop!)
- My lover will honor and respect my temple as much as I do.

What are your sex boundaries? Take a moment to write them out now.

KEY TWO: SAFETY FIRST

Soulful sex will only occur when you feel safe with your partner. You need to feel safe in order to fully Open Wide — both your heart and your vagina. So if you don't feel safe, you don't have to proceed. You have a choice.

KEY THREE: PRACTICE CCC

Crystal Clear Communication is imperative for soulful sex. Don't be vague or wishy-washy with your requests. Remember, a lot of us (myself included) think that our partners can read our minds … BUT THEY CAN'T! We think they can magically decipher the best way to kiss, stroke, touch, and make love, but, sister, this ain't the truth! Soulful sex is a team sport and, as the owner of your beautiful temple, you need to take full responsibility for helping achieve what you desire. So speak up and practice CCC in and outside the bedroom. I know it can feel scary, but it's the best way to experience soulful sex.

KEY FOUR: BE VULNERABLE

Vulnerability connects us. Open Wide and always speak your Truth.

KEY FIVE: GET PRESENT

In order to Open Wide and go deep, presence is essential. You can't be thinking about what's for dinner, how many emails are in your inbox, what didn't get ticked off your to-do list, or what time you have to pick up the kids. Get out of your head and back into your body. Bring all your attention to your body and breath. As Tony Robbins says, "Stay in your head and you're dead!"

KEY SIX: LET GO AND SURRENDER

Let go of your expectations of how things "should" look and surrender to the present moment. Often, we ladies have mapped out how our lovemaking sesh will pan out before it's even happened. You know what I mean: *First we'll go into the bedroom, then he'll kiss my neck, then take my clothes off, then go down on me, and then we'll get to business.* Not only does future tripping like this take you out of the present moment, it stops you from having a true, real experience of soulful sex.

KEY SEVEN: GIVE AND ACCEPT PLEASURE

A giving and receiving tango under the covers is always at play. For a deeper, soulful experience ask how your lover likes to accept pleasure, and openly express how *you* like to receive it.

KEY EIGHT: GIVE UP GOALS AND THE END RESULT

Sex is not a mission to be conquered and neither are you. Sex is to be enjoyed from the moment you first think about it or the desire in your body first arises. It's about the journey, not the destination.

Enjoy every step of the process, stay present, bring lightness and joy, and have fun with it. Focusing on achieving the goal of orgasm can have you miss the whole beautiful journey along the way.

KEY NINE: JUDGE NO MORE

You can't be judging yourself (or him), be present, AND experience soulful sex, all at the same time. Sex is an expression of love. It doesn't matter whether you're in a long-term, committed relationship or not. Love and appreciation are the same vibration, so appreciate your partner, yourself, and your temple, and you'll take your lovemaking to a whole new level.

KEY TEN: MAKE TRUST A PRIORITY

Trust is the superglue of your relationship and, without it, you cannot Open Wide — either your heart or your sex chakra. Love rarely dies in one fell swoop: it's the little white lies here and there that you convince yourself won't matter but that build up over time like tartar on your teeth, eventually eroding the relationship. Trust is something that is built between two people and strengthened with time and action. To nurture trust in your relationship, you must be impeccable with your words and actions. If you act in a way that's not from a place of integrity, quickly own it, take full responsibility, let it go, then move on. If your partner does the same, choose to let it go. Do not hold on to it or add it to your mental spreadsheet of things to use against your partner in your next fight (I've seen it done). Make trust, honesty, and integrity priorities in ALL your relationships, and watch them grow. Actions speak louder than words, so show people with *your* actions that *you* are trustworthy and honest. Be honest with yourself too about whether the person you're with right now has earned the trust you're placing in them. We can't force someone else to be trustworthy, and by its very nature untrustworthiness can be hard to spot! But we do know, in our hearts, the difference between an occasional breach of trust and a genuinely problematic attitude to truth and faith-keeping.

KEY ELEVEN: TRUST YOURSELF AND YOUR BODY

In its raw, natural, innate state, our bodies know exactly what to do to experience intense pleasure. But sometimes (heck, most times), we over-complicate things in our mind. If we let our body, mind, and soul dance as one while disconnecting from everything we thought we ever knew about sex, then magical things can happen. Our body, mind, and soul take over and intuitively express themselves in ways we never knew they could. It's not about acting like a porn star. Instead, it's about being vulnerable and real, while trusting your body, opening your heart, clearing your mind, getting out of your ego state and being fully present in the moment. In other words, intuitively entwining with another on all levels.

KEY TWELVE: SLOW DOWN

It's often in moments of stillness that you can find the most pleasure in life, and sex is no exception. We need to drop out of fifth gear and back into first in order to be fully present. Soulful sex requires you to slow right down, be still, and make mindful movements. So close your eyes at times if you wish and go inward. Feel the energy vibration pulsating and circulating through your entire body and heart. Don't rush to get to the finish line; it's not a race. If you feel yourself edging closer to orgasm, bring it down a notch, pause, and breathe into it. You can even circulate that energy throughout your entire body to experience a whole-body orgasm.

KEY THIRTEEN: USE YOUR BREATH

Connecting with your breath is one of the best ways to get present and bring yourself back into your body. Try deep, long, slow inhalations and exhalations through your nose. Softly close your lips and breathe deeply and consciously down into your base chakra. Bringing the energy into your body can prolong your orgasm and also deepen your experience. I constantly use my breath to help me experience full-body prolonged orgasms. When I feel myself approaching orgasm, I deepen and extend my breath, which in turn helps extend my orgasm.

KEY FOURTEEN: BE MUTUALLY RESPECTFUL

You never, ever want to put your partner down, but most especially not when they're trusting you with the vulnerability they need to experience soulful sex. I asked my parents, my in-laws, as well as five other couples who have been married for many decades, what the key to their marriage is, and they all said respect. Do you respect your lover?

KEY FIFTEEN: CIRCULATE YOUR KUNDALINI ENERGY

The concept of "kundalini energy" is common in the worlds of yoga and Tantra. A Sanskrit word, 'kundalini' means "coiled, like a snake." I first learned about kundalini energy in 2010, when I rocked up in my whites to my first kundalini yoga class. My teacher spoke about kundalini energy lying dormant at the base of your spine and told us that we must "wake it up." In kundalini, the vehicle we use to do this is our breath. Later on, when I started studying Tantra, I was taught how to use this energy as a way to experience multiple whole-body orgasms. Sounds awesome, huh?! To circulate your kundalini energy, visualize a ball of energy spinning clockwise at the very base of your spine (I like to visualize either a white or golden ball). Then send that ball of energy up your spine, tracing over your head, then send it down in between your eyes, down your nose, inside your mouth, tracing its way from your soft palate, to your tongue, to the middle of your lower lip, down the neck, chest, navel, bisecting your vagina, and finally rejoining at the place you began — your lower spine. You can keep tracing this path (often referred to as the "Microcosmic Orbit") over and over again, intensifying the energy with every revolution. I love this practice because it also helps you be present and connect with your body and lover.

KEY SIXTEEN: PRACTICE NON-EJACULATION
Obviously this one is for the fellas! Before I dived deep into the world of soulful sex, I had no idea that orgasm and ejaculation were actually two separate processes. Confused? Stick with me. An orgasm is a rush of creative, life-force energy. This energy *can* be released as semen (i.e. an ejaculation, which according to my man can at times make you feel like you've had the life sucked out of you). This means that every time your man ejaculates (perhaps multiple times a day), they're expelling their most exquisite, potent life-force energy ... all for nothing but a patch of stickiness on the bed.

Your man can instead choose to tap into that energy and channel it into his life and creativity. Now, this concept might be completely new to you — especially as our culture has a deeply ingrained belief that male sexual pleasure is only experienced through ejaculation — but when you think about it, it makes perfect sense that all their best energy goes into the semen to create new life. In fact, ALL of your man's organs, glands, and brain power go into overdrive at that very moment to push out the most pure and vital sperm possible to make the healthiest match with the awaiting egg. It's a beautiful thing, no doubt. But too frequent releases can also leave them needlessly exhausted and depleted.

Plenty of cultures have developed practices to avoid losing this precious life-force energy. Thousands of years ago, the Chinese and Indians figured out that this energetic state could be harnessed in incredibly powerful ways. Taoists believe that if you're not making babies, then it's far better for your man to conserve that energy and circulate it throughout his body every day as a way of preserving his health ... and having full-blown, mind-rocking, whole-body orgasms in the process!

There are many different techniques (which I encourage you and your man to explore, if you're interested), but the one my husband uses is this: when he senses he is about to ejaculate, he contracts his pelvic floor muscles (the ones he uses to stop peeing) on exhalation, then breathes the energy up and then back down the front of his body (similar to the Microcosmic Orbit I mentioned before), creating a perfect circular pattern of energy. It's that simple — and my husband swears by it and can't believe how much of a difference this had made to his vitality.

This healing energy is available to our beautiful men twenty-four/seven, yet hardly any of them are aware of it. As with everything, **knowledge is power**, so together with your lover (or alone) you can educate yourself more on this (there are some epic resources at the end of the book) if you wish. It's our role to make our lovers aware of their true full power and potential.

INSPO-ACTION

If you're currently with your lover, maybe you can give him this book to read once you're done. You can invite him to explore some of the key foundations of soulful sex with you. Remember, the best way to inspire your partner (or anyone) is to be the example. And **everything should always be an invitation, not an order**, especially anything related to self-development. **Growth requires readiness, and that can only come from within.**

If he's not yet open to the idea, you can continue to explore these practices on your own. After a few days of him hearing you howling in pure ecstasy in the next room, I'm sure his interest will be piqued!

Same goes for all you gorgeous single readers. Keep practicing everything mentioned in the book thus far so that you know yourself intimately; this will only increase your pleasure when your lover enters.

It's absolutely possible for you to experience the love you truly desire. Soulful sex first requires the belief that you are worthy, then the willingness to go there. It won't always be rainbows and unicorns, but when you enter a sacred union with your soulmate, every ounce of challenge is worth it because it makes you both grow — and that's what we're here for. And when you lay the foundation at the beginning of the relationship, you set yourself up for "success," whatever that looks like for you. This is all about *you*, not living out someone else's life or living by their standards. This is about *you* and *your* journey.

In this dimension, in time and space, humans have been given the gift of six senses: taste, touch, sight, sound, smell, and intuition. We may not get these in the next realm, so use them, soak them up, embrace them, and engage in the most soulful sex possible.

We may only get one precious life here on earth (I'm not sure), but what I am sure of is that we didn't come here to suffer. God, the Universe, Buddha, whatever or whomever you believe in, did NOT put you here on earth to suffer. You are here to grow, unlock your full potential, be love, and spread love. And by experiencing soulful sex you're "making" and sprinkling more love out into the world. You're spreading love and making a difference to yourself, the people around you, and humanity. Just as you make a cake for others to enjoy, you make love for yourself and others to enjoy. Love is energy — a high vibrational frequency — and when you engage in soulful sex, you raise your vibration and spread that out into the world. Like magic!

So go forth, my sweet friend, Open Wide, and make deep, sweet, soulful, heart-expanding, mind-blowing, earth-shattering love — and loads of it — every single day.

PSSST! WANT A BEHIND-THE-SCENES PEEK INTO OUR SEX LIFE?

As part of the FREE **Open Wide Video Masterclass**, Nick and I answer some of the most commonly asked relationship questions, and share more stories about our own soulful sex journey ... including the parts that are a *liiiittle* too steamy for these pages here. (If only books came with sealed sections, right?!)

Head on over to www.MelissaAmbrosini.com/openwide to watch now.

KEY TAKEAWAYS FROM CHAPTER NINE

- **THE PATH TO SOULFUL SEX STARTS WITH *YOU*.**

  Soulful sex — that is, life-changing, mind-blowing, earth-shattering sex — will only occur when you're fully bursting with love within yourself first.

- **SOULFUL SEX IS LIFE-CHANGING.**

  It's also a great personal development tool, because you're physically and metaphorically the most naked you will ever be. It forces you to be fully present, surrender, be vulnerable, let go of your Mean Girl, and return back to love.

- **THERE ARE SIXTEEN KEYS FOR SOULFUL SEX:**
  1. Set your boundaries
  2. Safety first
  3. Practice CCC
  4. Be vulnerable
  5. Get present
  6. Let go and surrender
  7. Give and accept pleasure
  8. Give up goals and the end result
  9. Judge no more
  10. Make trust a priority
  11. Trust yourself and your body
  12. Slow down

13. Use your breath

14. Be mutually respectful

15. Circulate your kundalini energy

16. Practice non-ejaculation

- **DEEP LOVE, ROCKING RELATIONSHIPS, AND SOULFUL SEX ARE ALL POSSIBLE FOR YOU IN THIS LIFETIME.**

  It is absolutely possible for you to experience the love you truly desire. You are worthy and it *is* your birthright. So Open Wide, love yourself like crazy, and surrender to the magic of the Universe. You've got this, beautiful.

What's Next?

Keep Opening Wide

I'm a student for life and want to continue to dive deeper and crack open wider inch by inch, because there's always more to learn and uncover about ourselves and each other. The great thing about this book is that you can pick it up time and time again and different things will resonate with you at different stages in your life. So leave *Open Wide* wide open on your bedside table and refer back to her whenever you feel called.

You can also give this book to your lover and invite them to read it. It's imperative for them to understand us on a deeper level. It's powerful stuff that will only deepen your connection.

If this book has resonated with you in some way, be part of the ripple effect and buy a copy for all your besties. You're then contributing to spreading more love and light into the world. You could even start an *Open Wide* book club. Because let's face it, just reading a book isn't enough; it's about taking inspired action and implementing what you've learned into your everyday life. That's when you see real change. Creating your own soul-expanding book club is very similar to hosting your own goddess circle, which we've already covered, but there are a few differences you need to know about.

FIND YOUR TRIBE

Just like a goddess circle you want to invite people who are interested in Opening Wide and personal growth. Once you've got your crew, create a private Facebook group where you can all connect, share insights between sessions, and stay in touch. If you don't already have a soul squad, don't worry; this is the perfect way to attract your soon-to-be soul sisters. Send out an email or post about it on your social media and see who's interested, or go old school and put some flyers up in your community, maybe at your local yoga studio or juice bar. (If you build it, they *will* come, but *you* have to show up first!)

MAKE A PLAN TO MEET

The goddess circles are ideal on the full moon, so your book club could be on the new moon, which is another powerful time to bring women together. Once a month is a good time frame to read each chapter and start acting on it. Then pick a time (the same time every month is recommended so there's no confusion) and send an email with the dates of the new moon for the next six to twelve months so that everyone can add them to their calendar.

FIND OR CREATE A SACRED SPACE

Just like the goddess circle, getting together with your soul sisters to do this work is so much fun, but some deep digging is going to happen, and it's important to have a space where you feel comfortable and safe to share authentically. You can keep it simple by hosting it in your home, and even try sharing the duties by rotating the host house. You can spice up your space with flowers, rugs, pillows, crystals, and essential oils. A beautiful touch would be to diffuse a different oil each month, to emotionally align with that particular chapter. For example, for Chapter Three, which is focused on self-love you could diffuse rose oil, the oil of love.

SPEAKING OF SACRED SPACE ...

You might think it goes without saying, but it never hurts to officially declare your space one of trust, confidentiality, and zero judgment and expectations, so that everyone can feel safe to Open Wide, go deep, and share authentically. So before you begin the night, the host might like to say something like, "Bless this beautiful sacred space, know that whatever is expressed here is held in our hearts. This is an open, loving space where you can express freely and it will be received with love. There is no judgment here."

BE THE HOSTESS WITH THE MOSTEST

A book club is a collective, so while there's no official "leader," it's great to have someone nominated as host who can start the night with some guidance — maybe the blessing above, one of my guided meditations from my website, or simply a short welcome to any new members of the group. It's also great to have someone in charge of housekeeping, to organize the night and as a point of contact in case anyone can't make it or is running late.

SET DOWN THE RULES

Make your own rules. Follow whatever format feels right for you and your sisters. But if you want a little guidance to get you started, a good approach is to discuss one chapter at a time, and you can kick it off by having everyone talk about how they felt about the chapter. (What came up for them? Was it an emotional topic? A surprising one? Or maybe it's an area they've mastered with ease.) Then you can go through some of the Inspo-actions and share whatever feels comfortable. I'm sure you'll find that once you get going, the conversation will flow effortlessly.

Hostess tip: Some people are great sharers and can get really passionate (which is amazing), but this is a good place for you to ask some questions of other members of the group who don't speak up as easily — sometimes they have the juiciest nuggets to share, and you don't want to miss them.

PASS THE TALKING STICK

Just like in a goddess circle some of us could talk under wet cement (hand raised!) while others don't want to talk at all, so it's helpful if the host keeps a time frame on each person and maybe uses a talking stick. Depending on how many people are in your book club, ten to fifteen minutes per person is a good amount of time. You can use an hourglass timer and pop it in the middle of the circle, and when they're approaching the end of their time you can tap them softly on the leg.

MAKE SURE THERE'S FOOD

Soul work is hungry business! Make sure to honor and nourish your bodies as well as your souls by choosing a place with delicious healthy food and clean water, or have everyone bring a little something to share. You don't have to have a degustation. Little nibbles like veggies sticks and healthy dips, green juice, bliss balls, and herbal teas will suffice.

CAPTURE THE MEMORIES

At the start of each gathering, take some photos and videos of the group and your sacred space as a beautiful keepsake of your journey together. You can share them in your private Facebook group or on social media to inspire others to Open Wide using the hashtags #openwide and #openwidebookclub. But once you've taken photos and videos, make sure you pop your phone on silent or, even better, turn it off.

Together, let's inspire women all over the world to have the courage to Open Wide and experience deep love, rocking relationships, and soulful sex.

HELPFUL HINTS

- Tissues are great to have on hand — 'cos there may be tears! Some from the harder stuff that comes up, and some from laughing so hard your belly hurts.
- BYOB (Bring Your Own Book). Have everyone bring their own book to the party. It brings a special energy to the gathering.
- Make sure you attend … even if you didn't do the "work" that month. Sometimes life gets in the way and we fall a bit behind on our reading, but show up anyway — you'll definitely have something to give and receive no matter what.
- Two is a club! Don't worry about having a huge group; start with whoever is ready and willing to show up. Then let other people join whenever they wish. All are welcome at any point in the journey. Keep sharing it on social media to attract your tribe.
- Have a graduation party. Do something special after you've gone through all the chapters, to celebrate all the incredible

work you've done and how far you've come. And who knows, I may just unexpectedly show up to your graduation party. True story!

- Don't stop when you're finished! Opening Wide is an ongoing practice, so once you've finished, keep meeting up with your Open Wide pals or go through the book again. Opening Wide is an ongoing process, and having the support of your soul sisters is going to make it a much sweeter one.

So there you have it, sister! Now you know how to create an epic, soul-expanding book club.

My mission has always been to give you the resources to support you, and now that you have all the tools to Open Wide here are some more. But as with everything in this book, take what resonates and leave the rest. Start with one Inspo-action and implement it in your life and go from there. After all, this is your journey and you are your own best guru.

Resources

BOOKS

Dear Lover by David Deida

The Way of the Superior Man by David Deida

The Enlightened Sex Manual by David Deida

The Conscious Parent by Dr Shefali Tsabary

Buddhism for Mothers by Sarah Napthali

Buddhism Plain and Simple by Steve Hagen

The Multi-Orgasmic Couple by Mantak Chia and Maneewan Chia

The Heart of Love by Dr John F. Demartini

Orgasm Unleashed by Eyal Matsliah

Slow Sex: The Path to Fulfilling and Sustainable Sexuality by Diana Richardson

Things I Wish I'd Known Before We Got Married by Dr. Gary Chapman

For Women Only by Shaunti Feldhahn

Love and Respect by Dr. Emerson Eggerichs

Sex and God by Darrel Ray

Women Food and God by Geneen Roth

The Honeymoon Effect by Bruce H. Lipton

The 5 Love Languages by Dr. Gary Chapman

The 5 Love Languages of Children by Dr. Gary Chapman

Her Blood is Gold by Lara Owen

The Red Tent by Anita Diamant

Blood Magic edited by Thomas Buckley and Alma Gottlieb

Women Who Run with the Wolves by Dr. Clarissa Pinkola Estés

PODCASTS

UNLEASHING YOUR ORGASM FOR PLEASURE, HEALING AND POWER WITH EYAL MATSLIAH melissaambrosini.com/9

THE POWER OF SEX FOR HEALTH, WEALTH AND LOVE WITH KIM ANAMI melissaambrosini.com/22

SEX LIFE BY DESIGN WITH JAIYA www.danielvitalis.com/rewild-yourself-podcast/sex-life-by-design-jaiya-131

THE WELL F★★KED WOMAN WITH KIM ANAMI www.danielvitalis.com/rewild-yourself-podcast/the-well-fked-woman-with-kim-anami

LESSONS IN LOVE AND LIBIDO WITH KIM ANAMI www.danielvitalis.com/rewild-yourself-podcast/lessons-in-love-and-libido-kim-anami-112

NO F★CKS GIVEN: THE SEXUALLY EMPOWERED WOMAN WITH KIM ANAMI www.danielvitalis.com/rewild-yourself-podcast/no-fcks-given-the-sexually-empowered-woman-kim-anami-102

THE ARTICULATE VAGINA WITH KIM ANAMI www.danielvitalis.com/blog/the-articulate-vagina-with-kim-anami

THE MULTI-ORGASMIC SEXUALLY-EMPOWERED WOMAN WITH KIM ANAMI www.danielvitalis.com/rewild-yourself-podcast/the-multi-orgasmic-sexually-empowered-woman-kim-anami-129

CONSENT IS IMPLIED www.danielvitalis.com/rewild-yourself-podcast/consent-is-implied

KIM ANAMI ON CONSCIOUSLY CONFRONTING SEXUAL TABOOS
www.danielvitalis.com/rewild-yourself-podcast/kim-anami-
on-consciously-confronting-sexual-taboos

WEBSITES

DANIEL VITALIS – danielvitalis.com

ESTHER PEREL – estherperel.com

KIM ANAMI – kimanami.com

SUSANA FRIONI – susanafrioni.com

SAIDA DÉSILETS – saidadesilets.com

EYAL MATSLIAH – intimatepower.com

OM MEDITATION – onetaste.us

UNIVERSAL TAO – universal-tao.com

LAYLA MARTIN – layla-martin.com

MISS JAIYA – missjaiya.com

DAVID DEIDA – deida.info

DR SHEFALI – drshefali.com

CENTER FOR NONVIOLENT COMMUNICATION – cnvc.org

GARY CHAPMAN – 5lovelanguages.com

TARA O – tarao.com.au

PSALM ISADORA – psalmisadora.com

JULIE PARKER – juliesuzanneparker.com/priestess-path-the-
awakening

PRIESTESS PRESENCE – priestesspresence.com/archetypal-resonance-
quiz

KARA MARIA ANANDA – karamariaananda.com/blog/7-archetypes-
of-the-divine-feminine

TANTRA SECRETS REVEALED WITH LAYLA MARTIN – www.youtube.
com/watch?v=vVWaOPeNzw4

And a Final Invitation

I'd love to continue this journey with you, beautiful.

The **Open Wide Video Masterclass** is where we can take this conversation to the next level and *really* bring it to life. Nick and I have created this free online workshop to stir your soul, rock your world, and empower you to take action on everything you've learned within these pages.

Together Nick and I answer some of the most commonly asked relationship questions, share stories about experiencing soulful sex, and inspire you to continue this heart-expanding journey of Opening Wide.

Join us today by visiting www.melissaambrosini.com/openwide

I can't wait to meet you, connect with you, support you, and help you Open up even Wider …

Love, Melissa
xx

Heartfelt Love and Gratitude

Feeling gratitude and not expressing it is like wrapping a present and not giving it.

WILLIAM ARTHUR WARD

Writing a book takes a freaking tribe (just like raising children!) and there is no way I could have done it alone. So before the curtain comes down, there are a few people I am bursting to express my love and gratitude for …

First up … Thank you to YOU, my dear reader, for having the courage and willingness to Open Wide within yourself. I know your heart yearns for more, so thank you for saying "yes" to that feeling even though your Mean Girl may have been hesitant.

To my dream literary agent, Bill. Thank you for believing in me, my mission, and my vision for *Open Wide*. I am so grateful to have a beautiful, supportive person like you on my team.

To my amazing Australian and New Zealand publisher Catherine and the entire team at HarperCollins Australia — you guys are seriously a dream to work with again. Thank you for believing in me and my mission. I love you so much.

To my US publisher BenBella — thank you for believing in me and *Open Wide*.

To Leo, for cracking me wide open. You teach me so much every day and I am honored to be your stepmama.

To my parents for your unwavering, unconditional love and support. You inspire me to be more generous, loving, and giving.

Thank you for fully accepting me and being open to my crazy "woo-woo" ways.

To my in-laws Ros and Grazie, for opening your hearts extremely wide to me from day one. You are such an inspiration.

To my beautiful MA tribe. You wanted *more* — to go deeper, to fly higher, and to love fiercely … This book is for *you*! You inspire me daily, and I hope this cracked you wide open.

To Lorna Jane, you have been a massive inspiration to me since I was ten years old way back when we were wearing high-cut leotards. Thank you for writing such a heartfelt Foreword for this book, and for always believing in me and my mission. You have been my cheerleader, friend, and support for many years and I am so grateful.

To Jess Larsen — you, my darling, are the most epic editor on the planet. You get me, my message, my vision, and you speak my language … literally! I love working with you, angel face, and love having you on the MA team.

To Bayleigh Vedelago, for not only your love, support, and sistership, but your stunning photography. You know how to capture a moment in time so perfectly.

To my epic reading council — Di Lee, Laura Plumb, Leisa Porteous-Semple, Nina Karnikowski, Rachel MacDonald, Susana Frioni, Tara Bliss, and Nick Broadhurst — thank you for taking the time to read my words and offer honest and valued feedback. I am beyond grateful to have had your eyes over *Open Wide* before anyone else.

To Sarah Lam, thank you for holding space for Team MA and pouring so much love into the work we do. You inspire me!

To my beautiful soul sisters — Emmily Banks, Soulla Chamberlain, Hollie Azzopardi, Katie Ambrosini, Estelle Allen,

Rachel MacDonald, Susana Frioni, Emma Bridge, Ange Simson, Nicola Evans, Nicole Joy, Tara Bliss, Leisa Porteous-Semple, Nat Warner, and Sarah Holloway — you guys are the bestest friends I could ever dream of. Thank you for being so open with me.

To Jess Ainscough, my real-life guardian angel. You are always in my heart, inspiring me to Open Wide, dive deeper, and go further. Thank you for cracking me wide open, angel.

There is absolutely no way this book would have manifested without my soulmate, Nick. I am deeply grateful we found each other again in this lifetime. Walking through life holding hands with you is so freaking awesome. Opening Wide with you is freaking awesome. Practicing soulful sex with you is freaking awesome. You inspire me to be more, to show up more, and to always go inward before looking outward for answers. I can't wait to open even wider with you, my darling man. Thank you for being the cherry on top of my already delicious, gluten-free chocolate cupcake. I love you deeply!

And finally, thank YOU again for having the courage to Open Wide … you won't regret it!

NOTES

NOTES

NOTES

NOTES

NOTES

NOTES

NOTES

Mastering Your Mean Girl

You know that sneaky voice inside your head telling you that you're not good enough, smart enough, skinny enough, *whatever* enough? That's your Mean Girl. And she's doing her best to keep you stuck in Fear Town, too scared to go after the life you always imagined.

But enough's enough! Melissa Ambrosini has made a life beyond her wildest dreams, all by mastering her Mean Girl, busting through limiting beliefs, and karate-chopping through the fears that held her hostage for years. And now she wants to help you remember not only what you are capable of, but how amazing you truly are!

In this inspiring, upbeat guide, Melissa provides a practical plan for creating your own version of a kick-ass life — one that's wildly wealthy, fabulously healthy, and bursting with love. Designed to propel you out of stuck-ness and into action, it's a must-read if you are ready to stop being held back by your Mean Girl and start living the life of your dreams.